Gendered Situations, Gendered Selves

THE GENDER LENS:
A Sage Publications / Pine Forge Press Series

Series Editors

Judith A. Howard
University of Washington

Barbara Risman
North Carolina State University

Mary Romero
Arizona State University

Joey Sprague
University of Kansas

Books in the Series

Yen Le Espiritu, *Asian American Women and Men: Labor, Laws, and Love*

Judith A. Howard and Jocelyn A. Hollander, *Gendered Situations, Gendered Selves: A Gender Lens on Social Psychology*

Books Forthcoming

Francesca Cancian and Stacy Oliker, *A Gendered View of Care*

Scott Coltrane, *Gender and Families*

Patricia Yancey Martin and David Collinson, *The Gendered Organization*

Judith Lorber, *Gender, Health, and Illness*

Pepper Schwartz and Virginia Rutter, *Gender, Sex, and Society*

Gendered Situations, Gendered Selves

A Gender Lens on Social Psychology

Judith A. Howard
University of Washington

Jocelyn A. Hollander
University of Washington

SAGE   PUBLICATIONS
Thousand Oaks   ■   London   ■   New Delhi

For information address:

Sage Publications, Inc.
2455 Teller Road
Thousand Oaks, California 91320
E-mail: order@sagepub.com

SAGE Publications Ltd.
6 Bonhill Street
London EC2A 4PU
United Kingdom

SAGE Publications India Pvt. Ltd.
M-32 Market
Greater Kailash I
New Delhi 110 048 India

Printed in the United States of America

Library of Congress Cataloging-in-Publication Data

Howard, Judith A.
   Gendered situations, gendered selves: A gender lens on social
psychology / Judith A. Howard, Jocelyn A. Hollander.
      p.   cm.—(Gender lens; vol. 2)
   Includes bibliographical references and index.
   ISBN 0-8039-5604-5 (pbk.: acid-free paper).—ISBN 0-8039-5603-7
(cloth: acid-free paper)
   1. Social psychology. 2. Sex role. 3. Personality and situation.
4. Social exchange. 5. Symbolic interactionism. 6. Social
perception. I. Hollander, Jocelyn A. II. Title. III. Series.
HM251.H72 1996
302—dc20   96-10130

This book is printed on acid-free paper that meets Environmental
Protection Agency standards for recycled paper.

97 98 99 00 01 02 03 10 9 8 7 6 5 4 3 2 1

Acquiring Editor: Peter Labella
Production Editor: Astrid Virding
Designer: Lisa S. Mirski
Desktop Typesetter: Andrea D. Swanson
Cover Designer: Lisa S. Mirski
Print Buyer: Anna Chin

CONTENTS

CHAPTER 7

Conclusions: Reprising a Gender Lens on Social Psychology 149

To Philip Blumstein

Whose absence I feel acutely. And from whom I learned much more about gendered situations—and about friendship—than I thought possible.

—Judy

Whose kindness truly touched me, and whom I wish I had been able to know much better.

—Jocelyn

And to Jodi and Chris, with love and gratitude for the color and music they add to our lives—and for their bold defiance of gender expectations.

It is now over 20 years since feminist sociologists have identified gender as an important analytic dimension in sociology. In the intervening two decades, theory and research on gender have grown exponentially. With this series, we intend to further this scholarship, as well as ensure that theory and research on gender become fully integrated into the discipline as a whole.

Beth Hess and Myra Marx Ferree, in *Analyzing Gender* (1987), identified three stages in the study of women and men since 1970. Initially, the emphasis was on sex differences and the extent to which such differences might be based in biological properties of individuals. In the second stage, the focus shifted to individual-level sex roles and socialization, exposing gender as the product of specific social arrangements, although still conceptualizing it as an individual trait. The hallmark of the third stage is the recognition of the centrality of gender as an organizing principle in all social systems, including work, politics, every-day interaction, families, economic development, law, education, and a host of other social domains. As our understanding of gender has become more social, so has our awareness that gender is experienced and organized in race- and class-specific ways.

In the summer of 1992, the American Sociological Association (ASA) funded a small conference, organized by Barbara Risman and Joey Sprague, to discuss the evolution of gender in these distinctly sociological frameworks. The conference brought together a sampling of gender scholars working in a wide range of substantive areas with a diversity of methods to focus on gender as a principle of social organization. The discussions of the state of feminist scholarship made it clear that gender is both pervasive in society and operates at multiple levels. Gender shapes identities and perception, interactional practices, and the very forms of social institutions, and it does so in race- and class-specific ways. If we did not see gender in social phenomena, we were not seeing clearly.

The participants in this ASA-sponsored seminar recognized that although these developing ideas about gender were widely accepted by feminist sociologists and many others who study social inequalities, they were relatively unfamiliar to many who work within other sociological paradigms. This book series was conceived at that conference as a means to introduce these ideas to socio-logical colleagues and students and to help further develop gender scholarship.

As series editors, we feel it is time for gender scholars to speak to our colleagues and to the general education of students. Many sociologists and scholars in other social sciences want to incorporate scholarship on gender and its intersections with race, class, and sexuality into their teaching and research but lack the tools to do so. For those who have not worked in this area, the prospect of the bibliographic research necessary to develop supplementary units, or to transform their own teaching and scholarship, is daunting. Moreover, the publications necessary to penetrate a curriculum resistant to change and encum-bered by inertia have simply not been available. We conceptualize this book series as a way of meeting the needs of these scholars and thereby also encour-aging the development of the sociological understanding of gender by offering a *Gender Lens.*

What do we mean by a gender lens? It means working to make gender visible in social phenomena, asking if, how, and why social processes, standards, and opportunities differ systematically for women and men. It also means recogniz-ing that gender inequality is inextricably braided with other systems of inequity. Looking at the world through a gendered lens thus implies two seemingly contradictory tasks. First, it means unpacking the taken-for-granted assumptions about gender that pervade sociological research and social life more generally. At the same time, looking through a gender lens means showing just how central assumptions about gender continue to be to the organization of the social world, regardless of their empirical reality. We show how our often-unquestioned ideas about gender affect the worlds we see, the questions we ask, the answers we can envision. The *Gender Lens* series is committed to social change directed toward eradicating these inequalities. Our goals are consistent with initiatives at colleges and universities across the United States that are encouraging the development of more diverse scholarship and teaching.

The books in the *Gender Lens* series are aimed at different audiences and have been written for a variety of uses, from assigned readings in introductory undergraduate courses to graduate seminars and as professional resources for our colleagues. The series includes several different styles of books that address these goals in distinct ways. We are excited about this series and anticipate that it will have an enduring impact on the direction of both pedagogy and scholar-ship in sociology and other related social sciences. We invite you, the reader, to join us in thinking through these difficult but exciting issues by offering feedback or developing your own project and proposing it to us for the series.

About This Volume

The current volume presents a gendered analysis of social psychology, the study of the relationships between individuals and the social environments within which they act. A comprehensive understanding of social action is impossible without understanding how individuals perceive their environments, themselves, and others; how they assess and make decisions, judgments, and evaluations; how they negotiate the demands, stresses, and joys of everyday life.

Developing a gendered analysis of social psychology presents unusual challenges. Unlike many other fields in sociology, social psychology has directed a good deal of explicit attention to gender, or at least to sex differences. Most obviously, social psychologists have focused on gender differences in personality and behavior and have sometimes assumed that these differences are fixed, stable, and rooted in biological sex. Judy Howard and Jocelyn Hollander demonstrate, in contrast, that existing gender differences are not "natural" but are constructed through social processes. They show that social psychology has simultaneously failed to analyze gender and at the same time been deeply influenced by prevailing cultural assumptions about gender.

Howard and Hollander begin with an analysis of the major social psychological perspectives on gender. They then look closely at three social psychological theories—social exchange, social cognition, and symbolic interaction—showing how assumptions about gender, often accompanied by equally invisible assumptions about race, class, and sexuality, have shaped research in each tradition. The authors then apply the lessons learned from these analyses to the study of altruism and aggression, two venerable topics in social psychology. Application of a gendered lens shows how assumptions about gender have shaped the questions asked and the theories used to explain prosocial and antisocial behavior and, importantly, the often-ignored close links between these seemingly opposite forms of behavior. Howard and Hollander conclude with a case study, showing how a gendered analysis allows us to develop more nuanced and sociological understandings of the intersections between individuals and the societies in which they interact and live. This volume addresses a range of readers, using analytic terms and language that are accessible to upper-division undergraduates and beginning graduate students, yet also presents ideas that will be informative to scholars who are not familiar with developments in gendered analyses of social psychology.

We hope this book, and others in the *Gender Lens* series, will help the reader develop her or his own "gender lens" to better and more accurately understand our social environments. As sociologists, we believe that an accurate understanding of inequality is a prerequisite for effective social change.

Judith A. Howard
Barbara Risman
Mary Romero
Joey Sprague
Gender Lens Series Editors

On April 11, 1996, a few days before we wrote this preface, a 7-year-old girl named Jessica Dubroff, her father, and her flight instructor were all killed in a plane crash in Cheyenne, Wyoming. She was in the second day of her attempt to be the youngest person to fly across the United States. In the days following the deaths, the papers were filled with questions about this tragedy. Some pertained directly to the crash: Why did they fly in such bad weather? Why did they fly with an overweight load? Who was in charge of the controls when the plane crashed? Other questions ranged farther afield: Should Jessica have been allowed to fly solo at such a young age? A number of writers dug up information about Jessica's upbringing, suggesting that her mother, in particular, had raised Jessica in a questionable way, allowing her too much freedom.

This event and the reactions that followed it are the heart of social psychology: individuals taking actions, making decisions about what to do in particular situations, and other individuals responding, asking questions, making evaluations, forming judgments about what caused these actions and their consequences. Many of the questions the media raised about this event are crucial social psychological questions: Who were these actors and what abilities did they have? What sorts of factors did they consider in making their judgments about whether or not to fly? What social responsibilities did they have and did they carry these out appropriately? In short, who, if anyone, was to blame? Was the tragedy just an accident, or could it have been avoided?

Other unnamed, perhaps unrecognized, factors may have shaped the media coverage and the public's reactions, however. Is it relevant that Jessica was a young girl, not a boy? How does the fact that her 9-year-old brother was considering flying a plane over her funeral figure in? Why was her mother, rather than her father, such a pointed target of public commentary? The reactions to this tragedy, we suggest, were marked by the genders of the actors and the social norms and conventions associated with gender. Yet gender was never mentioned explicitly in any of the analyses we have read. In pointing to the omission of an explicit gendered analysis in the media and in suggesting that gender is one significant basis for reactions to this event, we illustrate the analytic method of this book. Social psychology is the study of human actors in social situations, circumstances shaped by their genders, races, economic conditions, ages, sexualities, and national backgrounds. Social psychologists have often failed to consider or look carefully enough at the complex ways in which the social positions of individuals shape their thoughts, feelings, and actions.

In this volume, we use a gender lens to analyze the three major social psychological perspectives—social exchange, social cognition, and symbolic interaction. Most social psychology texts are organized in terms of the many discrete topics of social psychology: perception, prejudice, social influence, attitudes, attribution, small-group dynamics, and so forth. In contrast, we organize this book in terms of these three major theories. A common set of assumptions and ideas underlies all of the research within a given perspective. Focusing on those assumptions and the types of research questions they lead to, as well as the types of research questions they avoid, thus generates a more comprehensive and more parsimonious analysis of the strengths and weaknesses of these traditions. At the same time, our analysis covers the major social psychological processes, such as perception, cognition, stereotyping, attribution, allocation of resources, social interaction, and impression management. We also offer a more extended analysis of two related forms of behavior—altruism and aggression. Throughout, we show how assumptions about gender, race, class, sexuality, and age (as in the case of Jessica Dubroff) fundamentally affect human thoughts, feelings, and actions. Daryl Bem and David Funder close their 1978 article, "Predicting More of the People More of the Time," with the note that their sequel, "Predicting All of the People All of the Time," has yet to be completed. We have not completed it either. We seek to convince the reader, however, that a gendered analysis facilitates a more nuanced and sociological understanding of the intersection between individuals and the societies in which they live.

We intend this volume to be useful to a wide and disparate set of readers. We hope there will be something of interest here for social psychologists who may not have thought a great deal about gender; for sociologists who may not have thought a great deal about social psychology; for students, both advanced undergraduates and graduate students, who are developing their own analysis of social interactions; and perhaps even for the curious general reader. This book encourages all of these readers to ponder how social positions affect the circumstances and actions of their own lives and the lives of others. These analyses may provoke social change. Thus we end with the words of Goethe: "If you treat an individual as he is, he will stay as he is. If you treat him as if he were what he ought to be and could be, he will become what he ought to be and could be." And, we add, so will she.

ACKNOWLEDGMENTS

Acknowledgements provide a rare opportunity to thank in print the people who sustain you. For us both, these are our friends and family. Judy thanks especially Carolyn Allen, Pat Novotny, Ellen Cooper, and Emily Warn for their steadfast friendship, and Jerry Baldasty for weekly breakfasts. Jocelyn thanks her parents, her brother, and her grandparents for their love and support, and their belief that she can do anything. We both thank Rachel Einwohner, Diane Lye, and Toska Olson for lots of good meals, good wine and port, and chances to complain.

We thank Kathleen Crittenden, Chris Halaska, David Newman, Jodi O'Brien, Barbara Risman, and Michael Schwalbe for their incisive and thoughtful readings of this manuscript. We thank Karen Hegtvedt, Peter Kollock, Susan McWilliams, and Mary Romero for their help in suggesting useful references. We thank our Sage editors, Mitch Allen in the early stages and Peter Labella in the later stages, for their unswerving support of our project and for their persistence in encouraging us to make our deadlines and the Sage staff to be flexible. We are especially grateful to our lens *madrina*, Joey Sprague, who read multiple versions of every chapter and offered wonderfully tactful and dead-on comments on this project from the moment it was an idea in our heads through the preparation of the final draft. She will pay a price—we promise to continue asking her advice on everything else we write.

The main thing that happens when you write a book, particularly when you approach the final stages, is that everything else in your life takes a back seat. With that in mind, we thank the remarkable group of women who produce the journal *Signs: Journal of Women in Culture and Society* for their patience with and tolerance of Judy's distractions while this book was being completed; and we thank Chris and Jodi for keeping us sane, well fed, well dressed, and playful throughout the 3-year gestation of this book.

Finally, we thank each other. Collaboration is a risky endeavor; it can be wondrous or disastrous. We are both grateful to have had such a careful, challenging, and supportive writing partner. From the most abstract conversations about theory to the most mundane wrangling about commas, working together was, and remains, a deep pleasure.

CHAPTER 1

Defining Social Psychology and Gender

A number of social psychology textbooks begin with the following story:

> On the night of March 13, 1964, at about 3:20 a.m., a woman named Kitty Genovese parked her red Fiat in the lot of the Long Island Railroad Station. She lived nearby in Kew Gardens, a quiet middle-class residential area of Queens. As she began the short walk home, sensing something wrong, she started running along a well-lit major boulevard. Milton Hatch heard the first scream. He looked out and saw Kitty Genovese kneeling on the sidewalk, a man standing over her. She screamed: "Help me! Oh God, he's stabbed me!" Hatch leaned out the window and shouted, "Let that girl alone!" Other windows opened and lights went on. The assailant, a man named Winston Moseley, fled in his car. No one called the police. No one went outside to help. She dragged herself along the street, but within 10 minutes the assailant drove by again, looking for her. He got out and stabbed her a second time. Still, no one called the police. The third and fatal attack occurred in the vestibule of a building a few doors from the woman's own entrance. Onlookers saw the assailant push open the building door. At 3:55 a.m. Harold Klein, a man who lived at the top of the stairs where she was murdered, called the police. The patrol car arrived within 2 minutes, but Kitty Genovese was already dead.

Why is this violent, disturbing story used to introduce students to the field of social psychology? We[1] begin by defining social psychology and presenting some of the traditional accounts of this murder as illustrations of the social psychological approach to social interaction.

What Is Social Psychology?

Social psychology is fundamentally concerned with the relationships between individuals and their social environments. From the perspective of social psychology, the failure of the 38 witnesses to Kitty Genovese's murder to intervene in the assault or even to call the police reflects the immediate social situations of these witnesses rather than, for example, a pervasive societal alienation.

For example, one explanation focuses on the effects of social influence on interpreting such situations. Many social situations, even emergencies, are ambiguous. It is not always clear precisely what is occurring and what, if anything, should be done. People look to others to assess whether there is an emergency, and if so, what to do about it. If no one else is doing anything, perhaps it is not an emergency; or if it is an emergency, perhaps there is no way to help. Social influence can occur also through social norms. Suppose the situation in question involves an assault, as in the Kitty Genovese murder, but in this case the assailant is known by the neighbors as Ms. Genovese's romantic partner. Are bystanders likely to intervene? Social psychological research suggests they are not. Social norms prescribe the privacy of intimate relationships, discouraging third parties from intervening in incidents involving family members or romantic partners (e.g., Shotland and Straw 1976).

Another explanation emphasizes emotional rather than cognitive factors. Social actors are concerned not just about what others might do but also about what those others might think about them. Bystanders to a possible emergency may feel "evaluation apprehension," concern about how others will evaluate their behavior. If no one else seems to be reacting to the situation in question, they may worry that they will appear foolish or even wrong in intervening. How many of us have hesitated to assist someone in a wheelchair, not sure whether the person needs help or how others might view us?

A third explanation addresses the acceptance of responsibility. Suppose Milton Hatch had seen a man attack Kitty Genovese outdoors in a field, where he and they were the only people present. Would he have done more than call out? Latane and Darley's (1970) theory of the diffusion of responsibility suggests that he might well have. In this situation, the responsibility to intervene would be focused entirely on a single bystander. In contrast, many of the 38 witnesses to Kitty Genovese's murder reported that they assumed others had already taken action; they diffused responsibility to the other bystanders.

Each of these three traditional social psychological explanations concerns the relationship between individuals and their social environments. *Social influence,* whether informational or normative, refers to the effect of other people's behavior on one's own decisions and actions. *Evaluation apprehension* refers to concern about the reactions of other social actors to one's own actions. The *diffusion of responsibility* points to the influence of a simple but significant feature of social environments—the number of other actors present—on individual action.

Other potentially relevant sorts of factors are overlooked by these traditional explanations, however. One of the most obvious social patterns is that Kitty Genovese was a woman and her assailant a man. Could this gender composition shape how witnesses responded? Would they have been more likely to intervene if both had been women? Or men? The gender of the witnesses themselves may also have been relevant. Interviews with the witnesses revealed one persistent pattern in their reactions. When the residents of an apartment were a woman and a man, the man was the one who decided whether to take action (or at least this is what the woman and man reported). Another potentially relevant factor is the socioeconomic circumstances of the neighborhood in which this occurred. Does an assault in a quiet, isolated, middle-class area evoke different responses from witnesses than an assault in a more lively, busy, commercial or working-class neighborhood? Or do the class backgrounds of the witnesses shape the sorts of responses they are likely to consider? The racial identities of the actors might also matter: Would the witnesses have responded differently if the assailant had been white and his victim black? Did it affect witnesses' responses that the assailant was, in fact, black? Would the racial identities of the witnesses complicate these patterns?[2]

In raising such questions, we are asking whether the social structural positions of the actors (i.e., their location in the various social hierarchies of race, gender, or socioeconomic status) have anything to do with their responses in this situation. Because social psychology, more than many disciplines, sees human behavior as rooted in social context, these are crucial questions. Nevertheless, many social psychologists have explored such questions in only the most limited way, if at all. This volume presents an analysis of social behavior that highlights the social structural characteristics of situations and human actors, focusing particularly on gender. We believe that gender is invoked by virtually all social behaviors and situations; therefore, gender must be a central component of theories and empirical research on social behavior. At the same time, however, we believe that it is impossible to analyze gender in isolation from other significant social positions, such as race, social class, sexual orientation, or age. As a simple example, imagine yourself walking down a deserted street near your home late one night. Suddenly you notice that there is someone else walking toward you. How would you feel if this person were an older white woman dressed in dirty clothes and pushing a shopping cart? What if she were young, Asian, and carrying a small child? What if she were wearing gang insignia? Would your reaction be different if this person were a man? What if the man were black, middle-aged, well dressed, and carrying a briefcase? What if he were young, white, with a shaved head and heavy boots? What if he were a school-age child carrying a lunch box?

As these hypothetical transformations show, it is impossible to analyze any one social position without considering others. No one has only a gender or only a race or only a class; our various social positions coexist, in our own experiences, in our perceptions of other people, and in their perceptions of us. Thus, although we focus on gender in this book, we consider it in the context of other social statuses.

We devote the rest of the chapter to introducing the key theories in social psychology and the key terms used to discuss gender. In the next chapter, we combine these emphases, discussing how gender has been conceptualized within social psychological theory and research. Later chapters present more detailed analyses and evaluations of the major social psychological theories, with a particular focus on how individuals and situations are shaped by gender, race, and social class.

Before we begin, however, it is crucial to point out an important distinction within the field of social psychology. Social psychology obviously concerns both social and psychological issues. But the theories, key questions, empirical research, and applied utility of the scholarship and knowledge generated by social psychologists diverge on the basis of whether those social psychologists work within a psychological or a sociological framework. The *psychological* approach takes the individual as the primary unit of analysis, evaluating differences in behavior as a function of personality, emotional makeup, and aptitude. Psychological studies of helping behavior, for example, have attempted to identify features of an "altruistic personality" or attributional style. The *sociological* approach, in contrast, emphasizes how social dynamics and social contexts shape cognition, emotional experiences, and behaviors. Sociological studies of helping behavior, as we have illustrated, focus on the constraints and opportunities for helping located in particular situations—the number of other people present, the social relationships between those people, their location in social structures, or the prevailing social norms about behavior in those situations. Moreover, psychological treatments of social psychology tend to be more topical and to draw on relatively narrow, specific theories of human behavior, whereas sociological treatments tend to be more conceptually driven and integrated with more general theories of human behavior.

We draw on both perspectives in our analysis of the field, using the sociological theories of social psychology to organize our discussion and the rich empirical traditions within psychology to illustrate our points. The key message of both perspectives, however, is the same: Social behavior always involves a reciprocal relationship between individuals and their social environments. To understand individual behavior, we must consider individuals in the social contexts in which they act.

Social Psychological Theories

Social psychology proceeds within a variety of conceptual frameworks. Primary among these are social exchange theory (and related theories, such as behaviorism and social learning), social cognition, and symbolic interaction. We organize this brief summary of the major social psychological theories around an illustration, the details of which may be familiar to many current and former college students.

Consider the following scenario, which we borrow from David Mamet's (1992) play *Oleanna*. A male college professor is on the phone in his office in the late afternoon. A female undergraduate student comes to his office for an appointment that he asked her to make with him. He keeps her waiting for a good 20 minutes while he has a long phone conversation with his wife about a house they are trying to purchase. Eventually, the professor turns to the student, invites her to sit down, and they discuss the student's poor performance on a recent exam and her confusion about the class material. She emphasizes her difficulties in understanding the main textbook, written by this professor, and the content of his lectures, which focus on all that is wrong with higher education. He stresses the importance of this material and urges her to try harder. She becomes increasingly more emotional and at one point begins to cry. He comes over to the sofa where she is sitting and consoles her. At the end of the appointment, he suggests that he will give her an A for the course if she comes in regularly and works with him on the material.

What is going on here? What would each of these three perspectives have to say about this interaction?

Social Exchange Theory

Social learning and social exchange theories both derive from the key principle of behaviorism, that humans are likely to repeat behaviors for which they are rewarded and to cease behaviors for which they are punished. We learn behaviors either by enacting them and directly experiencing their consequences or through observing the behavior of others and the consequences of those behaviors. Whereas social learning theory focuses on individual behavior, social exchange theory applies the principles of social learning theory to understanding social relationships. Every human relationship involves the exchange of resources, whether material, such as money, or intangible, such as status or affection. People tend to remain in mutually rewarding relationships. If the exchange relations are not mutually rewarding, a relationship is likely to be terminated by the disadvantaged partner. One key factor in such decisions is the availability of alternatives: People may remain in unsatisfying exchange relationships if the alternatives are even worse.

Social exchange theory would analyze the professor-student interaction in terms of what each actor contributes to and gets from the relationship. The professor is offering to contribute his time and expertise to the student. Although on the surface he may not appear to be getting much from the interaction, on closer inspection one could speculate that he gains a great deal. If the student agrees to the exchange, the professor receives the rewards of status enhancement that are implicit in the professor-student relationship. He may also gain personal satisfaction from helping a struggling student. From the student's perspective, the benefits may be more obvious than the costs. The student gains the advantage of individual tutoring, which presumably may help her do well in this class. She may gain some personal understanding from the professor, as well as the promised A. What the student gives to the exchange is her own time and the contribution of subservient behavior—that is, status acknowledgment. Does the professor have alternative sources of status enhancement? Presumably he does: Each of his students are potential sources. Does the student have alternative sources of the information she needs to pass this course? Presumably not. Not only is there just a single professor in charge of this course, but the text on which the course relies is written by the same professor. We can predict then that she will accept this exchange.

One important issue in exchange relationships is the operation of power. When one partner has greater control than the other over the available rewards and punishments, that partner has more relative power. Power implies that one partner is dependent on the other; whoever has the least to gain from the relationship is the more powerful partner, because she or he needs the relationship less. The power dynamics of the relationship portrayed in this situation are not straightforward. In the first act, which we have described above, the student is clearly dependent on the professor—for help with the course, for a grade, for her future. By the end of the play, however, the tables have turned, at least on the surface. The student has now charged the professor with sexual harassment, threatening his acquisition of tenure and potentially ruining his career—or so the playwright would have the audience believe. At this point, the student holds a degree of power over the professor, who is now dependent on her for the future of his career.

Our more detailed discussion of social exchange theory in Chapter 3 will allow the reader to apply the principles of social exchange more thoroughly to this interaction. For now, we note that social exchange theory facilitates the analysis of behavior in the context of social interaction. The answers it offers, however, emphasize situated, individual power. This perspective has tended to minimize the effects of those social structures that endow the professor with more institutional, systematic power than the student, such as the advantages associated with his occupation, his gender, his age, or his socioeconomic position.

Social Cognition

Thought is, of course, necessary for the calculation of exchanges, as well as for the capacity to learn through observation. Social learning and social exchange theories, however, do not fully explore the human capacity for thought. Social cognition, in contrast, emphasizes the ways in which we think about our social worlds. There are two fundamental premises of social cognition. First is the assumption of cognitive mediation: Thought intervenes between the environment and behavior. How we think about our environments shapes how we behave. This assumption implies that two different people in the same situation might behave differently, based on how they think about that situation. A second fundamental premise is that human cognitive capacities are limited. Because we cannot possibly perceive or use all of the available information in a given situation, we think as "cognitive misers," attending to and using only a portion of the available information.

This perspective distinguishes between the ways in which our thoughts are organized and the ways in which we process social information. Most important among the elements or building blocks of cognition are social schemas: organized, abstract frameworks of information. The need for cognitive efficiency encourages the development of cognitive categories such as social schemas as a way of organizing information. Repeated experiences with particular people, social roles, or particular situations allow us to develop what are essentially summaries of their "typical" characteristics, behaviors, and activities. We develop schemas about other people and ourselves (e.g., a "Woody Allen type"). We also develop schemas about social positions (e.g., gender or race stereotypes) and social roles (e.g., parental roles). And we develop schemas about various types of social situations, such as shopping at the grocery store, attending a play, or getting married.

The student-professor situation described above activates a number of familiar social schemas. First, an interaction between a professor and a student is itself scripted. Many of the details of this situation are predictable: They meet in the professor's office; the professor sits behind the desk, the student in a chair in front of the desk; the professor can interrupt the student, but the student cannot interrupt the professor. All of these are recognizable components of a situational script. Person and role schemas are evident as well. The professor is likely to have a "typical student" script, the student equally likely to have a "typical professor" script. (Indeed, many of us professors who have seen the play cringe when confronted with the schemas the general public appears to hold for college professors.) Student and professor are themselves social roles for which there are schematic cultural expectations. And important for this play, the gender of these actors is also the basis for social schemas. In short, there are a host of orderly, well-recognized expectations for the actors and the situation in which they find themselves.

These cognitive elements are used in several cognitive processes. Most important among these are attention, memory, and social inference. When we enter a situation, we must attend to some things in the environment and, by implication, fail to attend to others. We store some information into memory and, again by implication, neglect to store other information. When necessary, we retrieve some information from long-term memory, bringing it to immediate consciousness, and fail to retrieve other information. We use the available information to make a series of social inferences, such as decisions, judgments of probability, evaluations, and attributions of causality or assessments of the characteristics of other people. We use schemas in selecting what to attend to, what information to retain in memory, and what information to retrieve in making social inferences.

Note that people in different social positions and with different social experiences may develop systematically different schemas. Viewers of *Oleanna* who have a schema for sexual harassment presumably process the professor-student interaction quite differently from those who do not. Gender may also be associated with different understandings of the concept of sexual harassment: Some (most often, men) may view the situation from the perspective of the person accused of harassment; others (most often, women), from the perspective of the victim. These variations lead to systematic differences in the evaluations and judgments the viewers make about such situations.

Social cognition thus provides the tools to analyze precisely how social structures and social patterns affect everyday situated thought and in turn the daily behaviors of individuals—and also how individuals both contribute to and undermine social structures. Where this perspective is weak, however, is in specifying the ways in which these cognitive structures and processes are enacted in social interaction. This is the domain of symbolic interaction.

Symbolic Interaction

Symbolic interaction differs from social exchange and social cognition in emphasizing the everyday interactions and negotiations that constitute social life. Interaction relies on the human capacity to use symbols, a capacity that also enables the peculiarly human consciousness of self. Meaning itself is created through the manipulation of symbols in interaction. In other words, meaning is not inherent in the people or objects a person encounters but is created by the person perceiving them. This implies in turn that one of the main tasks of social interaction is literally to define the situation, to resolve the contradictions and inconsistencies between actors' individual understandings and interpretations of a situation into a common perspective that facilitates the accomplishment of their mutual goals.

Symbolic interaction also offers a useful framework for analyzing the student-professor situation described above. This is a richly textured interaction, one with a good deal of symbolic gesturing and negotiation. One of the more obvious symbolic gestures is that the professor makes the student wait for more than 20 minutes while he talks on the phone. He may be oblivious to the symbolic meaning of this behavior. Indeed, even the student may be unaware of the effects of this gesture. Nonetheless, this detail contributes importantly to the creation of status in this interaction. That he sits while she stands, that he dictates her moves around the office, are other gestures laden with symbolic meaning.

It is also clear in the second act that the professor and student do not agree on their definition of this situation. From the professor's perspective, he is making a generous offer to a student, one for which she should be grateful. From the student's perspective, he has stepped across some crucial boundaries, behaving toward her in a way that she interprets as sexual harassment. Their interactions are occasionally stilted and often awkward, attesting to the difficulties of negotiating a common framework. How the actors attempt to sustain this fairly involved interaction with these differing interpretations requires more detailed analysis; symbolic interaction provides a framework for this analysis.

Conclusion

Each of these three social psychological perspectives offers a distinct framework for analyzing complex situations. Social exchange theory focuses on the nature of the exchanges between the professor and student. What resources are exchanged between the two actors? What does each actor gain, and what does each actor contribute to the relationship? In what ways does each actor have power over or depend on the other? Social cognition focuses on the perceptions and thoughts of each actor about this situation. What sorts of cognitive expectations do the actors (and the audience) have about this situation and about themselves and each other? How do these expectations shape their perceptions and interpretations of the situation—and ultimately, their behavior? Symbolic interaction addresses the actual negotiations that occur between the actors. What symbolic gestures are used in this interaction? How does each actor define the situation, and how does he or she attempt to reach a common interpretation of what is going on? What happens if an actor is ultimately unsuccessful?

These three perspectives offer different approaches to the relationship between individuals and their social environments. Although they are often set up as competing theoretical interpretations, we believe it is more useful to understand them as different but not mutually exclusive ways of explaining social interaction. Although we maintain that some theories have more to offer than others (as we discuss in more detail in Chapters 3-5), we emphasize that all have both strengths and weaknesses and that in general it is useful to treat them as complementary rather than competing.

However, none of the three theories explicitly identifies particular features of the social environment as more or less significant. In contrast, we focus throughout this volume on the pervasive effects of gender, together with other social structural characteristics, in shaping the kinds of situations we find ourselves in, the resources available to us in those situations, and the patterns of behavior that result. In other words, we look at social psychology through a gender lens. Before we begin, however, we must specify what we mean when we talk about gender.

What Is Gender?

Over the last 30 years, social psychologists (and others) have become more and more interested in gender. But what exactly is "gender"? When we talk about gender, do we mean the biological characteristics of females and males, such as genes or genitals? Do we mean the social roles that men and women play— mother, father, breadwinner, caretaker? Or are we talking about personal characteristics, such as aggressiveness or nurturance?

Another source of confusion is that the relationship between *gender* and other terms is poorly defined. Some writers use the term *gender*, some discuss *sex*, and some examine *sex roles* or *gender roles*. Moreover, some authors use these words interchangeably, whereas others distinguish carefully between them. Our goal in the rest of this chapter is to untangle these confusions and spell out exactly what we mean—and do not mean—by the term gender. In this section, we define gender and compare it with related terms: *sex, gender role, gender stereotype, gender identity, sexuality,* and *sexual orientation*. We also define two other terms, *race* and *social class,* that we use throughout this book. Our discussion will help to illuminate precisely what we mean by a gender lens.

Sex

What is sex? When we fill out official forms, whether applying for a job, a driver's license, admission to college, or a credit card, we are usually asked to declare our sex by checking the box marked "male" or the box marked "female." How do we know which box to check?

The definition of sex seems straightforward: The term is generally used to refer to the biological characteristics that distinguish males and females, such as reproductive organs or chromosomes. Most people in this society think of sex as dichotomous and unchangeable. That is, they assume that there are only two boxes one can check, female and male, and that everyone falls into one (and only one) of these categories. Moreover, they assume that one always falls into the same category: Someone who checks the "female" box at age 20 will have checked the same box at age 10, and will check it at ages 50 and 85 as well.

However, these assumptions are not always correct. *Hermaphrodites*, for example, are people who are not easily classified as male or female: Their reproductive organs and chromosomal structures are ambiguous (Money and Ehrhardt 1972). For example, a child may be born with both male and female genitalia. Which box would this person check on official forms? Specialists estimate that up to 4% of the population may be intersexed in this way. In fact, Fausto-Sterling (1993) suggests that a more logical categorization scheme would actually include five sexes: males, females, and three types of hermaphrodites. *Transsexuals,* on the other hand, are people who have literally changed their sex—they have been surgically and hormonally altered so that they appear to be a sex different from that as which they were born. A well-known example is Jan Morris, a writer who began life as a boy, James, but who now lives as a woman, Jan. (Transsexuals are distinct from *transvestites,* who wear the clothes associated with the other sex.) Because transsexuals have the genetic structure of one sex but the physical appearance of another, they are also not easily classified as one or the other sex.

The belief in two sexes is an example of what Mehan and Wood (1975) have called an "incorrigible proposition": an unquestioned belief that cannot be proven wrong, even in the face of contradictory evidence. In this society, we believe that there are two, and only two, sexes, and when we encounter a situation that challenges this belief, such as a person who doesn't fit neatly into one of these two categories, we adjust the situation to fit our beliefs rather than adjusting our beliefs to fit the situation. In the case of hermaphroditism, for example, we "correct" the ambiguity by surgical or hormonal means and assign the person to one of our two categories rather than admitting the possibility of more than two categories.

How do we determine someone's sex? Most people would answer this question by appealing to biology: Males have penises and XY chromosomes, whereas females have vaginas, more prominently developed breasts, and XX chromosomes. In everyday life, however, we do not normally use these criteria to distinguish between males and females. Yet we rarely have trouble classifying those we meet as male or female:

> When encountering older children or adults for the first time, most of us do not usually examine their genitals to label their sex! Instead, we use their attire, movements, sex-related characteristics such as height or musculature, and their general style of self-presentation as cues to their sex. (Unger and Crawford 1992:17-18)

Thus assigning someone to a sex category is as much a social process as the application of physiological criteria. As we shall see in the next section, the way we ascribe sex is deeply intertwined with gender.

Gender

Gender is a slippery term. Most scholars would agree with the statement that gender has something to do with the social behaviors and characteristics associated with biological sex; however, there is substantially less agreement on exactly what this statement means.

Social scientists use the term gender in two different ways. Some use gender interchangeably with sex, suggesting that sex and gender are essentially the same thing. (Indeed, some argue that the term gender is meaningless and should be abandoned, because everything, they believe, reduces to sex.) These researchers might assume, for example, that women care for children (and are nurturing in general) because of their biological ability to bear children. This perspective sees gender as somehow essential to males and females; it is believed to be both innate and unchanging. For this reason, this approach is sometimes called the *essentialist perspective* on gender. Biology is believed to determine the social behaviors and characteristics of males and females.

Other scholars distinguish between sex and gender, using sex to refer to biological characteristics as we have described above but using gender to mean the culturally determined behaviors and personality characteristics that are associated with, but not determined by, biological sex. These writers do not assume that the relationship between sex and gender is direct or automatic. Rather, they believe that some mediating process, such as socialization, leads individuals to behave in gendered ways.[3] Thus different cultures may develop distinct notions of gender, which seem natural because they are associated with sex but that are socially, rather than biologically, driven. In contrast with the essentialist perspective described above, this nonessentialist perspective does not see gendered characteristics and behaviors as innate or unchangeable. It is this perspective that we adopt in this book, for reasons we detail below.

What does it mean to say that something is *gendered?* In this book, we use this phrase to mean that ideas about gender—assumptions and beliefs on both individual and societal levels—affect the thoughts, feelings, behaviors, resources, or treatment of women and men. Thus, to the extent that women and men dress, talk, or act differently because of societal expectations, their behavior is gendered. To the extent that an organization assigns some jobs to women and others to men on the basis of their assumed abilities, that organization is gendered. And to the extent that a professor treats a student differently because that student is a man or a woman, their interaction is gendered.

There are a number of variations on the nonessentialist perspective, which we discuss at greater length in Chapter 2. For now, we simply note that essentialist and nonessentialist positions are often at loggerheads. This is true not only in scholarly analyses but in the nonacademic world as well. For example, these perspectives were hotly debated at the United Nations Fourth World Conference on Women in Beijing, China, in 1995. At a preparatory meeting in New York City, former U.S. Representative Bella Abzug read the following statement:

> The current attempt by several Member States to expunge the word "gender" from the Platform for Action and to replace it with the word "sex" is an insulting and demeaning attempt to reverse the gains made by women, to intimidate us and to block further progress. We will not be forced back into the "biology is destiny" concept that seeks to define, confine, and reduce women and girls to their physical sexual characteristics . . .

The meaning of the word "gender" has evolved as differentiated from the word "sex" to express the reality that women's and men's roles and status are socially constructed and subject to change. In the present context, "gender" recognizes the multiple roles [filled] throughout our life cycles, the diversity of our needs, concerns, abilities, life experiences, and aspirations—as individuals, as members of families and households, and in society as a whole. The concept of "gender" is embedded in contemporary social, political, and legal discourse. . . . The infusion of gender perspectives into all aspects of UN activities is a major commitment approved at past conferences and it must be reaffirmed and strengthened at the Fourth World Conference on Women. (Abzug 1995)

As Abzug notes, the choice of perspective (here symbolized by the choice between the terms sex and gender) can have real consequences for women—and for men as well—when those perspectives are used to guide public policy.

Gender as Difference

In practice, research on gender—from any perspective—has tended to focus on differences between women and men. This tendency persists despite the fact that research shows very few significant sex differences (e.g., Maccoby and Jacklin 1974; Fausto-Sterling 1985). In fact, the distributions of women and men on most characteristics tend to be overlapping rather than separate. Nonetheless, many researchers continue to focus on differences rather than on the extensive similarities between the sexes or even on the extensive variations within each sex. This pattern of research reinforces the essentialist belief that there are large, stable, innate differences between the sexes and encourages biological explanations for those few differences that are resilient. Thorne, Kramarae, and Henley (1983) write that these studies mistake "description . . . for explanation" (p. 15) and warn that just because studies find differences between males and females does not mean that sex is the *cause* of the differences. For example, one analysis of gender differences in conversational patterns concluded that power, not sex per se, was the source of those differences (Kollock, Blumstein, and Schwartz 1985).

There are a number of reasons why researchers continue to prioritize sex differences. One of these reflects a pattern typical of human cognition. As we noted in the discussion of cognition above, human beings have a tendency to categorize information wherever possible. As an ostensibly dichotomous characteristic with highly visible social trappings (e.g., hairstyle and apparel), sex is a prime basis for cognitive categorization. The pervasive tendency to focus on sex differences rather than on similarities thus may derive partly from cognitive processes.

The persistent belief in sex difference in the face of contradictory evidence is also tied in part to the human quest for self-identity; we want to know who we are. This quest has a peculiar character, at least in Western culture: Knowing who we are implies knowing who we are not. Gender is one fundamental source of identity. Although there are several contradictory theories of how gender identity is created, most social psychologists concur that children learn at a very young age to adopt gender as a basic organizing principle for themselves and the social worlds they are learning about. In particular, children tend to regard gender as bipolar. "Children regard a broad range of activities as exclusively appropriate for only one sex or the other, and . . . they strongly prefer same-sex playmates . . . and gender-appropriate toys, clothes, and activities" (Bem 1993:111). As studies of gender stereotypes among adults reveal, gender polarization does not wane as children grow older. The cultural centrality of gender, together with the susceptibility of gender to a bipolar model, defines the contemporary social psychological approach to gender.

Perhaps as a result of these tendencies, researchers often expect to find sex differences. Social psychologists are not immune from popular essentialist beliefs about gender. These expectations often act as self-fulfilling prophecies, predisposing the researchers to focus on or even to elicit information that confirms their beliefs. Many studies have shown that experimenters' hypotheses affect research findings. According to Weisstein (1970),

> These studies are enormously important when assessing the validity of psychological studies of women. Since it is beyond doubt that most of us start with notions as to the nature of men and women, the validity of a number of observations of sex differences is questionable, even when these observations have been made under carefully controlled conditions. Second, and more important, [these studies] point quite clearly to the influence of social expectation. In some extremely important ways, people are what you expect them to be or at least they behave as you expect them to behave. (p. 215)

The biases that have plagued social psychology were apparent as early as 1910, when psychologist Helen Thompson Wooley commented, "There is perhaps no field aspiring to be scientific where flagrant personal bias, logic martyred in the cause of supporting a prejudice, unfounded assertions, and even sentimental rot and drivel, have run riot to such an extent as here" (Wooley 1910:340).

Another reason for social psychology's focus on sex differences has to do with the structure of the field itself. Over the past century, psychology and sociology (like other sciences) have become more and more reliant on statistical tests. These tests are designed to identify significant differences between groups and therefore shape a search for differences rather than similarities (Unger and Crawford 1992:12). Moreover, even if a difference is *statistically* significant (i.e., unlikely to have occurred by chance), it may not be *substantively* significant (i.e., meaningful). For example, Eagly and Carli's (1981) review of the literature on social influence found that even though sex differences were often statistically significant, they explained less than 1% of the variance in influenceability and thus contributed very little to understanding influenceability. Reviews of other sex differences have found similar patterns of statistically, but not substantively, significant effects (Deaux 1984).

Researchers may also have a difficult time disseminating the results of studies that find no evidence of sex differences. Findings of similarity are not "newsworthy"; academic journals are much less likely to publish such studies. Newspapers and other media are similarly disposed: Whereas reports of sex differences in math abilities garner headlines and newsmagazine cover stories, reports of similarity are relegated to short, unobtrusive articles, if indeed they are reported at all (Eccles and Jacobs 1986). Thus, even if the majority of research projects were to find no significant differences between women and men, *published* research might actually consist of only those few studies that do find differences.

Sex differences research also tends to ignore the fact that *different* often means *unequal*. In other words, such research tends to ignore power relationships. Carrigan and his colleagues write that in the study of gender, "relations have been interpreted as differences. The greater social power of men and the sexual division of labor are interpreted as 'sexual dimorphism' in behavior. With this, the whole question of social structure is spirited away" (Carrigan, Connell, and Lee 1987, pp. 75-76). Even when research considers power differences between genders, it rarely looks at power differences within genders—that is, it ignores very real differences among women and among men, homogenizing each category as though gender is the most important differentiating feature (Fine and Gordon 1989).

Research on gender differences also ignores the fact that behavior is specific to situations, depending on factors such as the structure of the social context or the attitudes and expectations of others in that context. For example, one study found that women's behavior in a simulated job interview depended on the perceived gender stereotypes of the interviewer. When the research participants believed the interviewer to hold traditional views of women, they behaved in a more stereotypically feminine manner (von Baeyer, Sherk, and Zanna 1981). These women altered the femininity of their behavior to best achieve their goals in the interview. Individuals' behavior may change significantly from one situation to the next, and the results of a psychological study may depend on which situation is examined.

Indeed, the experimental laboratory itself affects the expression of gender. Although it purportedly allows scientists to study gender in an objective context, the laboratory is in fact a specific social setting that affects the respondent as do all social contexts. The laboratory is no more neutral than any other situation.

Thus it is important to exercise caution when interpreting research reports of sex difference. Findings of difference may be due not so much to meaningful differences in the abilities or behavior of women and men as to a host of other factors, including the norms of publishing and research and the biases of researchers. On the other hand, just because these reports of sex differences may be misleading does not mean that they should be ignored. The belief that males and females are fundamentally different is widely shared among Americans and, indeed, among most peoples of the world. These beliefs, regardless of their validity, influence our identities, thoughts, and behaviors and may cause men and women to behave differently (gender difference) even if no underlying difference in ability (sex difference) exists. In other words, these beliefs have material consequences regardless of their basis in fact. Thus we contend that sex differences research must be taken seriously—if only to understand how essentialist beliefs shape social psychological research and social life. We suggest that readers keep these issues in mind as they proceed through the next chapters. For now, however, we return to our definitions of key terms.

Gender Role

Another common term in social psychology is gender role, which is often used interchangeably with sex role. Sociologists use the term *role* to refer to "a set of prescriptions and proscriptions for behavior—expectations about what behaviors are appropriate for a person holding a particular position within a particular social context" (Kessler and McKenna 1978:11). The term gender role, then, refers to the characteristics and behaviors believed to be appropriate for men or for women. People expect that others will behave in accord with their gender role, and they punish those who violate these expectations.

The concept of gender role has been strongly criticized, however. For example, some note that these roles are based on the theorist's ideas of what people should be like rather than on what people really are like (Carrigan et al. 1987). Most people's lives, in fact, do not conform to what gender roles prescribe. Moreover, talking about "the male gender role" and "the female gender role" also ignores the very real variation among women and among men, and overlooks the substantial overlap in the characteristics and behaviors of males and females.

Perhaps more important, the concept of gender roles ignores issues of power and inequality. Gender role theory describes the relationship between women and men as one of difference and complementarity: The sexes are "separate but equal," and both roles serve important functions in society. But in fact male and female "roles" are not equally valued and are not necessarily "functional" for everyone. The concept of roles masks, for example, that women have traditionally been legally subservient to men in the family. Until relatively recently in the United States, women could not own property or enter into a contract, and men were (and still are in some states) legally allowed to rape and beat their wives. These are not the hallmarks of an equal relationship, a fact that is hidden by role terminology (Carrigan et al. 1987; Lopata and Thorne 1978). As a result of these critiques, many scholars have discarded the terms sex role and gender role. However, we discuss these terms here because they are still very much a part of both popular and social psychological discourse.

Gender Stereotype

Stereotypes are "strongly held overgeneralizations about people in some designated social category" (Basow 1992:3). For example, many Americans have stereotypes about athletes, professors, or police officers. These beliefs are "not necessarily based on fact or personal experience, but applied to each role occupant regardless of particular circumstance" (Kessler and McKenna 1978:12). Unlike roles, stereotypes do not imply that individuals should conform to particular expectations for behavior. Nor do they suggest that these beliefs are useful, either for individuals or for societies. Because stereotypes are oversimplifications, they may be inaccurate for a group as a whole, as well as for any particular member of that group.

Gender stereotypes, then, are beliefs about the characteristics of women and men, including their physical characteristics, typical behaviors, occupational positions, or personality traits. Reflecting the assumption that sex is dichotomous, stereotypes for women and men often involve polar opposites. For example, "Traits related to instrumentality, dominance, and assertiveness . . . are believed more characteristic of men, while such traits as warmth, expressiveness, and concern for other people are thought more characteristic of women" (Deaux and Major 1990:95; see also Rosenkrantz et al. 1968). Such polarizations serve to increase the perception of difference between women and men, and mask the ways in which they are similar.

This does not mean that stereotypes paint all women or all men as the same. Indeed, stereotypes for certain subgroups of men and women, such as business-women, homemakers, or blue-collar working men, are common. Stereotypes may also vary by race, ethnicity, or class, as we discuss further in Chapter 4. However, these variations are accommodated as subtypes subsumed under the more general stereotypes of women and men. The fact that we create subtypes rather than modifying our dichotomous view of gender suggests our deep investment in the idea of gender differences.

Gender Identity

The term gender identity refers to one's inner sense of oneself as female or male; it is a major part of one's self-concept. Gender identity develops during very early childhood, and once established, it is quite resistant to change (Kessler and McKenna 1978:9). Gender identity tends to be dichotomous—people gener-ally think of themselves as male or female, not something in between. This is probably due to our "incorrigible proposition" that there are two, and only two, sexes. Kate Bornstein (1994), a male-to-female transsexual, writes that

> I know I'm not a man—about that much I'm very clear, and I've come to the conclusion that I'm probably not a woman either, at least not according to a lot of people's rules on this sort of thing. The trouble is, we're living in a world that insists we be one or the other—a world that doesn't bother to tell us exactly what one or the other *is*." (p. 8)

Gender identity is a subjective feeling; it cannot be determined without asking a person directly. Gender identity may or may not be congruent with someone's sex or gender, and it is unrelated to sexual orientation. Transsexuals, for example, generally go through sex-change operations because they feel that they do not "fit" their biological sex. Jan Morris (1974) describes her gender identity in this way: "I was born with the wrong body, being feminine by gender but male by sex, and I could achieve completeness only when the one was adjusted to the other" (p. 26). Like many other transsexuals, however, Morris ultimately found that it was easier to change her body than her social identity.

Although everyone has a gender identity, the salience of this identity may vary among people. For example, women are more likely than men to spontaneously mention gender when asked to describe themselves (Deaux and Major 1990:93). The salience of gender identity may also vary between situations: A woman alone in a group of men, for example, is likely to find her gender to be more salient than when she is in a group of other women (Cota and Dion 1986). Indeed, group identity is generally more salient for those in any kind of subordinate position, indicating the relevance of social position and power to identity.

Sexuality

Sexuality is a fuzzy term, often used to refer to a group of related concepts, including sexual behavior (what you do), eroticism (what turns you on), sexual orientation (who turns you on), or desire to engage in sexual activity. A discussion of sexuality may seem out of place in a book focusing on gender and social psychology. Nonetheless, sexuality is often associated with gender, although the two are not equivalent. This association probably results from the popular essentialist belief that gender is the natural outgrowth of biological sex. Because sexuality is also believed to be biologically driven, gender and sexuality are often thought to be directly related (Schwartz and Rutter, forthcoming).

As with gender, however, there are other perspectives on sexuality. Like other activities, sexual behavior has a social and symbolic component. Consider the activity of a woman baring her breasts. Now vary the social context: How would this action be interpreted if the woman is in her lover's bedroom, her doctor's consulting room, or a public place? Now take the last location, a public place, and vary the reasons for her action: She is participating in a public demonstration, performing at a strip joint, or breast-feeding her baby. It is the social context, not the activity itself, that leads us to impute meaning to the woman's action as being erotic, clinical, political, exhibitionist, or maternal. The meaning of sexual behaviors varies by situation, and we evaluate behavior on the basis of goals and motivations. Meaning also varies by culture: In some societies, women's breasts are always bare and thus do not elicit the charged interpretations that they do in our own culture. Sexual meanings are thus socially constructed, not inherent in an activity.

Similarly, sexuality is not innate in individuals. For evidence, we can point to the fact that expectations for the sexual behavior of men and women vary historically and cross-culturally. Traditional Western dating scripts, for example, expected men to be more physical and aggressive and women to be more passive and emotional in sexual situations. Although it might appear that these expectations have changed (and they have, to varying extents among different social groups and regions), they have not entirely disappeared. Men, for example, are still expected to take the lead in sexual situations, and women who violate gender expectations by being sexually assertive risk being labeled "pushy," "aggressive," or worse. However, other cultures have very different expectations for women and men. For example, Ford and Beach (1951) report that women are expected to be the sexual aggressors among societies such as the Maoris and the Trobriand Islanders. Sexual behavior is thus guided by social factors as much as by biology.

What, then, is the relationship between sexuality and gender? Expectations for "appropriate" sexual behavior and characteristics differ by gender; sexuality becomes a way of expressing gender. For example, Lillian Rubin's (1976) study of U.S. working-class families found that women were expected to be sexually passive and inexperienced, whereas men were expected to be more dominant, experienced, and adventurous. And as the next section points out, there are also expectations about whom we perform sexual behaviors with. An important point, however, is that this society's construction of sexuality helps maintain the existing gender hierarchy. The definition of men as aggressive and women as passive reinforces men's power over women and women's dependence on men. Popular culture's ideology of love and romance also reinforces gender inequality: For example, Cantor (1987) found that in popular media "women are usually depicted as subordinate to men and passive-dependent. . . . The basic message is that sexual relationships are all-important in women's lives" (1987:190). Thus, when women attempt to meet cultural expectations about heterosexual relationships, they contribute to their own subordination. However, the examples provided by other cultures show us that this pattern is not innate in human beings.

Sexual Orientation

Sexual orientation, the match between one's sex and the sex of one's (desired or actual) sexual partners, is one component of sexuality. Like sexuality more generally, sexual orientation is part of gender expectations. For example, the expectations for a "real man" include heterosexuality. Think of male icons such as James Bond, Indiana Jones, or Rocky: Besides being strong and daring, these characters were all attracted and attractive to beautiful women. Thus, in this society, "Mainstream masculinity is heterosexual masculinity" (Carrigan et al. 1987:83; see also Connell 1987, 1995). This version of masculinity is a yardstick against which all men are measured: "The homosexual-heterosexual dichotomy acts as a central symbol in all rankings of masculinity. Any kind of powerlessness, or refusal to compete among men readily becomes involved with the imagery of homosexuality" (Carrigan et al. 1987:86). A similar argument can be made for women: Mainstream femininity entails heterosexuality, and any deviation from feminine norms risks "accusations" of lesbianism (Rich 1980), a status to which many people attach stigma. Thus sexual orientation is integrally related to gender. Sexual orientation is one of the ways in which gender is performed, while at the same time, gender incorporates and depends on sexual orientation.

Like sex and gender, people tend to think of sexual orientation as dichotomous: One is either heterosexual or homosexual. But sexual orientation is better described as a continuum, with many possible variations between the two poles. Some people (bisexuals) are attracted to people of both sexes. Some people are attracted to people of one sex but maintain relationships with people of another; these people cannot be easily classified. Many people who define themselves as heterosexual, in fact, have had some sort of homosexual experiences (Blumstein and Schwartz 1983:43). It should be noted that sexual orientation is distinct from gender identity. Although some people think that those who prefer same-sex partners must be "confused" about their own gender identity, this is not the case. In fact "most gay men and lesbian women have no confusion about their gender identity; they simply prefer sexual partners of the same sex" (Vander Zanden 1990:358).

What is the source of sexual orientation? Debate rages in the scientific community and the popular press about whether sexual orientation is genetically or environmentally determined; at the moment, there is no consensus on the answer. One thing is certain, however: Like sexuality, the meaning of sexual orientation is socially constructed. Homosexuality is not everywhere as stigmatized as it is in the United States: Many past and present societies of the world, including the ancient Greeks and the modern Sambia of New Guinea, condone and practice both heterosexuality and homosexuality in some forms (Ford and Beach 1951). Moreover, the meanings of homosexuality and heterosexuality vary depending on the social context, even within the United States. Childhood sexual play, for example, is interpreted very differently from adult relationships. Or to give another example, the same man who might never consider engaging in homosexual activity in everyday life might practice it within an all-male prison context. Like the meaning of sexuality more broadly, the meaning of sexual orientation varies depending on context, goals, and motivations.

Crosscutting Social Positions

We argue throughout this book that gender cannot be adequately understood without analyzing its intersections with other social statuses. Thus we conclude this chapter by briefly discussing two particularly important statuses, race and social class. Ideally, research and writing would consider all of these statuses—gender, race, social class, sexual orientation, age, and others—simultaneously, to understand how they collectively contribute to an individual's experiences. Where research allows, we do address their simultaneity. However, social psychology (and the social sciences more broadly) have generally addressed these statuses separately, and so we are forced to discuss them separately at many points in this book. It is our hope, however, that eventually there will be an adequate vocabulary with which to talk about the simultaneous experience of these social positions.

Race

Race is "a social definition of a social category of people, typically based on visible physical characteristics, such as skin color, stature, and facial features" (Rothman 1993:6). Racial groups are generally broader categories than ethnic groups, a term that refers to people who share a common culture, including language, religion, and customs.

For those of us who have lived all our lives in the extremely race-conscious United States, it may be difficult to imagine a world in which race is not a central defining feature of individuals. But in fact, "race was first employed as a means of categorizing human bodies in the late seventeenth century, and it was only in the eighteenth century . . . that there began to be made what were taken to be authoritative racial divisions of human beings" (Nicholson 1994:85). People did notice physical differences between themselves and others, of course. But these differences were not used "to 'explain' basic divisions among human populations as the concept of race increasingly did from the late eighteenth century on" (Nicholson 1994:85-86).

Race is popularly thought to be a biological attribute based on genetic ancestry and clearly identifiable by physical features. "In the United States, we tend to see race as a simple, unambiguous matter of skin color alone and to judge everyone as belonging to one and only one group" (Healy 1995:24). But when we look more closely at the use of race, the definitions become less clear. "Skin color, for example, varies in shades from one extreme to the other, and there are no clear or definite points at which 'black' skin color stops and 'white' (or brown or yellow or red) color begins" (Healy 1995:23). And why is skin color so important?

> There are clear physical differences between human beings and some of these differences are inherited. But the question of why some physical differences, and not others, become matters for social discrimination and prejudice has nothing to do with biology. Racial differences, therefore, should be understood as *physical variations singled out by the members of a community or society as socially significant.* Differences in skin color, for example, are often treated as significant in this way, whereas differences in color of hair are not."
> (Giddens 1991:301)

Contrary to popular belief, even genetic makeup does not distinguish between members of different racial classifications. In fact, there is more genetic variation within races than between them (Begley 1995). Race is thus a social and political phenomenon, not a biological one.

Racial identity is also malleable, on both a societal and an individual level. As a society, the United States has often seen changes in racial classification. For example, the U.S. census has at different times in the past categorized Japanese Americans as "nonwhite," "Oriental," or simply "other." More recently, members of this group have been classified as a specific ethnic group under the general category defined as "Asian and Pacific Islanders" (Omi and Winant 1986:3). Another example is the term *Hispanic,* which was created by the federal Office of Management and Budget for the 1980 census and which includes an economically, racially, and culturally heterogeneous group of people who, "far from being unified . . . are divided along ethnic or racial lines" (Forbes 1992:65). Giménez (1992) writes that

> for a substantial proportion of these populations this origin makes no sense either in terms of their actual ancestry (which may be Native American, Northern, Eastern, or Southern European, African, or Asian) or in terms of their historical understanding of who they are as citizens of a given country or as descendants of Latin American immigrants. (p. 12)

Similarly, Eastern and Southern Europeans were not considered "white" when they first began to immigrate to the United States in large numbers; a century later, this classification has changed. On an individual level, people's racial identities can shift based on their situations and experiences. A light-skinned African American person might "pass" for white in certain situations but claim a black identity in others. A Jewish person might consider herself or himself white compared to black people but Jewish as compared to other whites. According to the Nazis, having a Jewish grandfather was sufficient to brand one as Jewish; Orthodox Jews, however, would not consider such a person Jewish. Many people—probably most—have a mixed heritage, yet in everyday life they are classified as belonging to only one racial group. (Note the similarity here to gender classification; in both cases, ambiguous persons are assigned to one category that may not accurately represent their own identity.) Clearly, race is a social concept and is not as fixed and definite as is generally believed.

Thus race is not the clear-cut biological phenomenon most people believe it to be. In fact, many scientists have argued that the term is meaningless and should be abandoned. It is indisputable, however, that race has a social and political reality regardless of its scientific status. People believe that race is real, and societies and individuals allocate rewards and power based on racial classification. In other words, "racial distinctions are meaningful because we *attach* meaning to them, and the consequences vary from prejudice and discrimination to slavery and genocide" (Pitchford 1992:1617). As a result, racial classification must be taken seriously, despite its tenuous grounding in biology.

Like gender, racial classification is fundamentally about difference, although in the case of race there are many possible differences, not just two. Smedley (1993) articulately summarizes the pervasiveness of difference:

> Race in the American mind was and is tantamount to a statement about profound and unbridgeable differences. In whatever context race comes to play, it conveys the meaning of nontranscendable social distance. This sense of difference is conditioned into most individuals early in their lives and becomes bonded to emotions nurtured in childhood. In the United States, it is expressed in all kinds of situations and encounters between peoples. It is structured into the social system through residential separation, differential education, training, and incomes, and informal restrictions against socializing, intermarriage, and common membership in various organizations, including, most visibly, the church. It is reflected in virtually all media representations of American society and in institutional aspects of culture such as music, the arts, scientific research, educational institutions, politics and political forms, businesses, the theater, television, music, and film industries, and recreational activities. It provides the unspoken guidelines for daily interaction among persons defined as of different races, especially black and white. It sets the standards and rules for conduct, even though individuals may not always be conscious of this fact. (p. 21)

As with gender, a focus on differences has guided social psychological research about race. The vast majority of empirical research on race investigates only the possibility of difference and accepts race as the explanation for any differences found between people categorized as belonging to different races. Our discussions of race in the following chapters, in contrast, are premised on the assumption that race (like gender) is a social phenomenon and is something that must be explained, not an explanation in itself.

Social Class

Social class refers to an individual's location in the economic system of a society. Unlike race or gender, it is based in part on a material reality: economic resources. How a person's class position is measured varies but often includes factors such as occupation, income, and education. According to Marx (1974), class position is determined by a person's relationship to the "means of production," such as machinery, offices, or money: Does the person own the means of production (a capitalist), or does the person sell his or her labor to capitalists to earn a living (a member of the working class)? Whereas gender and race are considered ascribed statuses (i.e., based on relatively fixed characteristics of individuals), class is considered an achieved status, based on the individual's own behavior and permitting more mobility between groups. We note, however, that neither of these classifications is definitive. We discussed earlier the fact that both gender and race are more malleable than they appear; we also contend that class is more constrained than is generally believed. Many Americans accept the ideological position that people can "pull themselves up by their bootstraps" if they simply try hard enough; in fact, one's class position is driven as much by current and historical family circumstances as by individual ability or effort.

Social class is important not only because it determines one's financial position but also because it influences other factors such as prestige, power and authority, control over resources, and possibilities for advancement. Although class is often discussed as simply a matter of economics, it has important ramifications for self-concept. In "A Question of Class," Dorothy Allison (1994) describes how her childhood of extreme poverty affected her identity:

> When I was six or eight back in Greenville, South Carolina, I had heard that same matter-of-fact tone of dismissal applied to me. "Don't you play with her. I don't want you talking to them." Me and my family, we had always been they. Who am I? I wondered . . . Who are my people? . . . What may be the central fact of my life is that I was born in 1949 in Greenville, South Carolina, the bastard daughter of a white woman from a desperately poor family, a girl who had left the seventh grade the year before, worked as a waitress, and was just a month past fifteen when she had me. That fact, the inescapable impact of being born in a condition of poverty that this society finds shameful, contemptible, and somehow deserved, has had dominion over me to such an extent that I have spent my life trying to overcome or deny it. I have learned with great difficulty that the vast majority of people believe that poverty is a voluntary condition. (pp. 13-15)

Class position is related to race and gender. Racial minority group members are overrepresented in the ranks of the working class and the poor. Women of any race living without a man are also more likely to be poor; association with a man is often what makes the difference between social classes for women (and children).

Before concluding this section, we must make one final point that applies equally to all of the social positions described above—gender, sexual orientation, race, and class. It is obvious that these statuses affect the experiences of those who are in the subordinate categories of each group—women, homosexuals, people of color, poor people. It is much less obvious, however, that these statuses also affect the lives of those who are not subordinate:

> In the same way that both men's and women's lives are shaped by their gender, and that both heterosexual and lesbian women's experiences in the world are marked by their sexuality, white people and people of color live racially structured lives. In other words, any system of differentiation shapes those on whom it bestows privilege as well as those it oppresses. (Frankenberg 1993:1)

Privilege is often invisible to those who enjoy it, because to them it is simply the normal state of affairs. Privilege "makes life easier—it is easier to get around, to get what one wants, and to be treated in a way that is acceptable" (Rosenblum and Travis 1996:139). For example, white people driving a fancy car generally are not suspected of having stolen it, as people of color often are. Men, for the most part, do not consider their safety when deciding whether to walk to the grocery store after dark, as women often do. Heterosexuals do not need to consider whether their jobs or friendships with coworkers will be threatened if they place a photo of themselves with their romantic partner on their desk or in their locker at work, as homosexuals often do. Upper-class people do not have to decide between taking their sick child to the doctor and feeding their families, as poorer people sometimes do. In each case, the advantages of privilege may not be noticed by those who enjoy it—but they are real nonetheless. Thus each of the social statuses we discuss is in effect a system of hierarchy and difference that permeates the lives of all people—those who are privileged by it as well as those who are not.

A Gender Lens

To conclude this chapter, we return to the metaphor of the *gender lens*. What do we mean by this term? What can we see through the gender lens that we cannot see without it?

Throughout this book, we emphasize two points. First, we argue that social psychology has simultaneously ignored and been deeply influenced by gender. Social psychologists have assumed that situations and behavior are gender neutral; yet they have nonetheless allowed prevailing cultural assumptions about gender to affect the questions they have posed and the answers they have provided. Most obviously, as we discussed earlier, social psychologists have focused on gender differences in personality and behavior and have often assumed that these difference are fixed, stable, and rooted in biological sex.

Our second argument in this book is that although gender differences may exist, they are not the same as sex differences. In other words, just because women and men may appear to behave or think differently does not mean that they have different innate characteristics or abilities. Instead, these differences may be (and, we believe, generally are) constructed through social processes. Thus, in a sense, we are arguing that these differences are not as meaningful as people—both social psychologists and laypeople—believe they are.

This does not mean that we should ignore these differences, however. If that were the case, there would be no reason to write (or read) this book. On the contrary, these ideas about gender deeply affect people's thoughts and behaviors and are central to the ways in which resources, power, and status are distributed in most (if not all) societies. In other words, despite its lack of grounding in sex, gender has real, material consequences for people's lives. For this reason, it is crucial to understand gender and the role it plays in the social world. Only through such an understanding can we hope to address the pervasive and deeply damaging social problems (discrimination, violence, injustice, and so on) that continue to plague our society.

Looking at the world through a gender lens, then, means recognizing and analyzing the central role that gender plays in social life. More concretely, it implies two seemingly contradictory tasks. First, it means unpacking the taken-for-granted assumptions about gender that pervade social psychology and, more generally, social life. We must show how the terms we use to discuss gender (such as gender role) naturalize inequality and perpetuate gender difference. We must question the truth of these assumptions and, where warranted, reveal them as the illusions they are.

At the same time, looking through the gender lens means showing just how central these assumptions about gender continue to be to the perception and interpretation of the world, regardless of their grounding in reality. We must show how our unquestioned ideas about gender affect the world we see, the questions we ask, and the answers we can envision. In other words, we must show how deeply the social world is gendered and how far-reaching the consequences are. Looking at social life through the gender lens means asking where gender is overemphasized and where it is ignored; it means making the invisible visible and questioning the reality of what we see.

In the remainder of this book, we use this gender lens to look more closely at social psychological theory and research. In Chapter 2, we present the major social psychological perspectives on gender, elaborating at the same time historical trends in social psychology. In Chapters 3 through 5, we look more closely at the three social psychological theories described above, showing how assumptions about gender have shaped research in each tradition. In the subsequent chapters, we apply these theories, through a gender lens, to the topics of altruism and aggression, showing the fundamental ways in which assumptions about gender have shaped the questions asked and the theories developed to explain these forms of social behavior.

Notes

1. *We* can be a slippery and ambiguous word. It is not always clear whether it is meant to refer to the speaker alone, to one or more of the social groups to which the speaker belongs, or to all humans in general. In this book, we use the term with caution. Unless otherwise specified, we use *we* to refer either to the two of us as authors or to human beings more generally. We try to ensure that the context will make clear which of these meanings is intended.

2. For an incisive analysis of the response to this crime, see Chapter 2 in Cherry (1995).

3. Indeed, some authors also argue that sex itself is a social construction (Kessler and McKenna 1978; Scott 1988). According to this view,

    > Society not only shapes personality and behavior, it also shapes the ways in which the body appears. But if the body is itself always seen through social interpretation, then sex is not something that is separate from gender but is, rather, that which is subsumable under it. (Nicholson 1994:79)

CHAPTER 2

Conceptions of Gender
in Social Psychology

As we noted in concluding Chapter 1, social psychologists have simultaneously ignored and been deeply influenced by gender. Existing patterns of relationships between women and men have been taken for granted. Until fairly recently, social scientists regarded traditional sex role arrangements as nonproblematic, often assuming that such patterns were biologically inevitable. Many studies used only one sex—almost always men—as respondents and assumed either that the processes being studied were so general that they would apply to all humans or that women's behavior would be the opposite of men's behavior. Male behavior was taken as the norm.

In this chapter, we trace and evaluate this social psychological treatment of sex and gender. Our discussion loosely follows the historical development of social scientific theorizing about gender, moving from essentialist perspectives through socialization to social constructionist and structural explanations of gender. These four perspectives underlie contemporary social psychological research, to varying degrees, and cut across the three social psychological theories we present in Chapters 3 through 5. These four perspectives propose radically different explanations of gendered behavior, the causes of gender inequality, and therefore the ways in which these (and other) inequalities might be reduced. As we elaborate in the following text, these perspectives reflect the sociopolitical and historical climates in which they were generated. Because these sociopolitical climates have also shaped prevailing accounts of race, class, and other social positions, we weave these accounts together as fully as possible.

Essentialist Approaches

As we discussed in Chapter 1, an *essentialist* approach to gender maintains that innate, stable differences between the sexes shape divergent social behaviors. This approach was prevalent among social psychologists (and social scientists more generally) in the first half of the 1900s. Thus, when two psychologists, Helen Thompson Wooley and Leta Stetter Hollingworth, published results in the early 1900s showing that women and men were virtually equal in a broad range of abilities (cited in Bem 1993), others took it on themselves to refute these findings. Terman and Miles (1936), for example, developed an "M-F Test" that was intended to assess individuals' own masculinity or femininity. The test items were selected explicitly to distinguish between men and women. Respondents earned femininity points for agreeing that they "nearly always prefer for someone else to take the lead," for example, and they earned masculinity points for disliking nursing. (Women who did not score high on the femininity pole of this dimension and men who did not score high on the masculinity pole were thought to have homosexual tendencies; this is another example of stereotypes about social groups.) Underlying this test were the related assumptions that masculinity and femininity are the opposite poles of a single dimension and that masculinity and femininity are virtually synonymous with being male and female. This M-F Test is based on an essentialist understanding of sex and gender. For the next several decades, this conviction of natural gender difference prevailed.

Although the essentialist perspective is less explicit in more recent social psychological research, the underlying assumptions are often consistent with essentialism. One example is the common use of sex as a variable representing gender. In these studies, respondents are simply categorized as females or males, and any differences found between the two groups are labeled as "gender differences." This approach treats sex and gender as one and the same; sex-gender is conceptualized as a stable, innate, bipolar property of individuals. Much of this research is unreflective about the nature of gender as a social category. "Sex-as-variable" research leaves sex differences untheorized and other social and contextual factors unexplored. The implication is that sex itself is a sufficient explanation for behavior—an assumption that is the heart of the essentialist view of sex and of gender.

Take, for example, the substantial body of research on sex differences in mathematical ability. The conventional belief is that men have greater abilities in math than do women. For many years, empirical research on mathematics skills appeared to confirm this assumption of male superiority; study after study found that men outperformed women on math tests, beginning in the seventh grade. These studies were used to bolster the claim that men have superior cognitive abilities (ignoring the parallel finding that women have superior reading skills during the same developmental period). These studies treat gender differences as sex differences.

When researchers began to consider the social contexts in which these differences occurred, however, the sex difference in math performance all but disappeared. Social factors, such as the expectation that boys will take more math classes than girls and the perceived importance of such classes for future careers, as well as the actual number of math classes taken, provide a more adequate explanation for the observed differences than do the relative math abilities of girls and boys (Fausto-Sterling 1985). Recent newspaper reports that girls' math and science ACT scores are rising because they are taking more advanced courses in these subjects in high school underscore the importance of these contextual factors. In their attention to the social context of patterns ostensibly associated with sex, these more recent studies *analyze* gender rather than treating it as an unproblematic variable.

Sex-as-variable research implies that sex and gender are isomorphic. Gender and sex are not identical, however. Whereas sex category is usually constant and dichotomous, gender is fluid and dependent on social contexts. There is substantial overlap between women and men on virtually all personality traits and behaviors. Although dominance is a stereotypically "masculine" trait, for example, some women are more dominant than some men. And in some situations, most women are more dominant than most men (e.g., gendered contexts, such as cooking or child care). Using sex as an indicator of gender is thus misleading. Measures of masculinity and femininity are more appropriate indicators of the personality components of gender.

The social psychological research on race, echoing research on gender, also began with a deeply essentialist set of assumptions. Characteristics correlated with racial categories were assumed to be innate and irreversible; this legacy has been most striking in the considerable research on the relationship between race and intelligence. Strains of essentialism continue to the present day (e.g., Herrnstein and Murray's *The Bell Curve* [1994], one of several contemporary books that argue both that racial differences in intelligence do exist and are based in genetics). This literature has been criticized on precisely the same grounds; interactional, cultural, and structural factors provide more adequate explanations of human behavior.

Thus many social psychologists have pursued other approaches. We continue to refer to essentialism in the next several chapters, despite these problems, because essentialist assumptions continue to shape some social psychological research and much popular discourse on both race and gender. We turn now to a socialized approach to gender, the perspective that dominated social psychology during the 1960s and 1970s. We devote considerable attention to this approach, because it has been particularly influential in shaping social psychological research on gender, race, sexuality, and class.

Socialization Approaches

Sparked in part by the social movements of the late 1960s, the focus of the social psychological study of gender shifted from biology to socialization. New empirical investigations found that women and men were more similar than different on most social psychological dimensions. Researchers began to consider social processes and factors other than biology that might account for those gender differences that were observed. According to the socialization perspective, children are not innately gendered but, rather, learn gendered behavior from their environment through a variety of processes, including modeling and imitation (Bandura 1977), the gender-specific application of rewards and punishments, or the intrapsychic processes facilitated by parenting practices (Chodorow 1978). (These processes of social learning are discussed in more detail in Chapter 3.) Through these processes, children learn to internalize prescriptions and proscriptions (i.e., "dos and don'ts") for being appropriately masculine and feminine according to the norms of their society. These processes result in gendered personalities and patterns of behavior. Thus gender differences are believed not to be essential but, rather, the result of social and cultural forces.

Two implications of this approach are notable for our purposes. First, a socialization perspective on gender can more easily account for diversity within genders. For example, differences in the gendered behaviors of black and white women or upper-class and working-class men, can be explained by the systematically different socialization environments they may have experienced as children. Second, the socialization perspective suggests that change in gendered behaviors and personality characteristics is possible, if a society and its members choose to modify socialization practices. Both of these implications stand in stark contrast to the assumptions of essentialism, which assumes that all women and all men are fundamentally alike as a result of biology and that therefore change in gender patterns is impossible.

From a socialization perspective, gender differences in personality and behavior are created and become ossified in childhood; the implication is that behavior throughout one's adult life follows unproblematically. Gender thus is viewed as operating at the level of individual personality but in the service of more general social control. Through socialization, girls and boys learn to behave in ways that sustain the social order when they are women and men. In this section, we focus on the adult consequences of this socialization (although there is a substantial literature on the gender socialization of children). We begin by discussing what is learned during socialization—that is, cultural stereotypes about the characteristics of women and men.

Gender Stereotypes

As we noted in Chapter 1, *stereotypes* are primarily descriptive; they detail what members of particular categories are believed to be like. Stereotypes also have prescriptive power. Beliefs sometimes shade into normative "oughts" and "ought nots." Stereotypes about gender are particularly likely to carry prescriptive, as well as descriptive, elements. In addition, members of different groups often differ in their conceptions of selves and of others. Much of what we discuss next concerns the stereotypes held by those in dominant social positions, although where research is available, we address stereotypes held by both dominant and subordinate groups. (Much of the material presented here derives from the social cognitive perspective, which we elaborate in more detail in Chapter 4.)

The conceptions of gender we learn through socialization shape both our definitions or senses of self and our perceptions of others. In the sections that follow, we begin by discussing gendered personality—perceptions of self in terms of gender—and then move into gendered stereotypes about others. Until fairly recently, gender stereotypes have been conceived primarily in terms of personality. Deaux and Lewis (1984) demonstrate that gender stereotypes are a good deal broader than personality, including role behaviors, physical characteristics, and occupations in addition to personality traits. Stereotypes include "type of dress and bodily adornment, codes of sexual etiquette, styles of self-presentation, patterns of sexual behaviors, [and] rules for social interaction in various settings" (Spence, Deaux, and Helmreich 1985:153). The variety of social characteristics that compose gender stereotypes attests to the fact that gender is much more than biology.

Personality: Masculinity and Femininity. *Personality* refers to characteristics of individuals and is conceptualized as stable and inherent. For this reason, personality is the component of gender stereotypes that comes closest to an essentialist perspective. There has been extensive research on personality correlates of sex, or masculinity and femininity, the traits, behaviors, and interests believed to be associated with males or females in a particular culture.

As we have noted, early measures of personality were based on an essentialist understanding of gender (e.g., Terman and Miles's [1936] M-F Test). Later researchers, however, conceptualized masculinity and femininity as socialized characteristics learned through cognitive and emotional development. Beginning in the 1970s, researchers began to demonstrate that masculinity and femininity are two independent dimensions; that is, one's score on a masculinity scale need not be associated with one's score on a femininity scale. Scales such as the Bem Sex Role Inventory (e.g., Bem 1974; Spence, Helmreich, and Stapp 1974) treated masculinity and femininity as separate dimensions, allowing an individual to be categorized as highly masculine, highly feminine, both, or neither.

Those individuals who have high, approximately equivalent scores on both the masculinity and femininity scales are labeled *androgynous.* The concept of androgyny (derived from the Greek roots *andro* [male] and *gyn* [female]) captured both academic and popular attention in the 1970s. Some suggested that androgyny was an ideal state: Androgynous individuals should have a wider variety of skills and characteristics at their disposal than primarily masculine or primarily feminine people and would therefore be able to deal with a broader range of situations (e.g., Bem 1975). Indeed, research showed some evidence of the greater mental health of androgynous individuals (Heilbrun 1973).

In the end, however, the concept of androgyny (which long predates social psychology) fell out of academic favor. In that it treats masculinity and femininity as if they were equal, the concept of androgyny is insensitive to the power differences that mark gender. Moreover, this concept reproduces the very gender polarization it seeks to unsettle, treating masculinity and femininity as conceptual givens; this tendency is characteristic of the socialization perspective more generally. Many contemporary scholars recognize that behavior is determined by situational factors as much as by the traits reported on personality inventories.

Some scholars have attempted to resolve these problems by labeling these dimensions as *expressiveness* (e.g., aware of feelings of others, expresses tender feelings, tactful) and *instrumentality* (e.g., objective, competitive, makes decisions easily). As with masculinity and femininity, these traits are related to sex category, but the correlations are small. Carol Gilligan's (1982) research on interpersonal moral orientations and behaviors does show empirical support for gender differences in these behaviors: She finds that women show a markedly greater sensitivity to interpersonal dynamics, whereas men use rules and responsibilities as guides to moral behaviors. Gilligan's explanation of these differences relies almost completely on very early childhood socialization. Although Gilligan herself does not espouse biological determinants of these patterns, both her own writing and the use of her work in subsequent research of others comes close to an essentialist position whereby these gendered patterns are so pervasive and persistent as to seem "natural." Nonetheless, there is considerable variation within the sexes on both expressiveness and instrumentality; women vary widely in how often they engage in expressive behaviors, and men vary widely in how often they engage in instrumental behaviors. Because of this variation, there is also a good deal of overlap between women and men in these characteristics; some women, for example, behave instrumentally more often than some men.

The various measures we have discussed refer primarily to assessments of one's own gender. Conceptions of the gendered characteristics of others, as we have suggested, are also prevalent. Despite both the variation among women and among men and the overlap between women and men on these characteristics, early empirical studies of gender stereotypes found widespread agreement about the personality characteristics of men and women across respondents of different ages, educational levels, religions, sexes, and marital statuses (Broverman et al. 1972). Respondents rated men highly on instrumental attributes and rated women highly on expressive attributes. Despite the social and political changes that have occurred since many of these studies were carried out, these stereotypes have changed very little (e.g., Smith and Midlarsky 1985; Spence and Savin 1985).

Intersecting Stereotypes. The studies we have described so far imply that stereotypes of women and of men can be described independent of the racial, class, and sexual positions of women and men. Other studies, however, demonstrate that this assumption is wrong. Stereotypes about women and men differ on the basis of the race, ethnicity, social class, sexual orientation, age, and other social locations of both the perceiver and of the target of the perception. Landrine (1985) reports, for example, that middle-class white students rate white women as more dependent, emotional, and passive than black women and rate poorer women as more dirty, hostile, inconsiderate, and irresponsible than wealthier women. Romer and Cherry (1980) observe that black children perceive women and men as fairly similar in expressiveness, reflecting in part that these children also describe men as extremely expressive. Social class qualifies these patterns. Black middle-class children view men as more competent than women; black working-class children see women and men as similarly competent, because they perceive men as relatively less competent than do black middle-class children. Combining these perceptions of expressiveness and competence suggests that black children and children from working-class backgrounds perceive fewer gender differences than do white children and children from middle-class backgrounds.

Historical and sociopolitical contexts are important influences on prevailing images of these intersecting social categories. Patricia Hill Collins (1990) comments on the images of black women prevalent at different historical moments in the United States. Images of black women as mammy (generated through slavery and dominant during the following century, during which black women were disproportionately likely to work as domestic servants); as Jezebel, the sexually aggressive black woman (an image also generated during slavery); and as welfare mother or irresponsible breeder (a more recent image constructed in the context of the post-World War II welfare state) all served symbolic functions in maintaining the oppression of blacks and of women.

Chow's (1985) analysis of stereotypes of Asian American women also points to historical and cultural influences. Chow suggests that Asian cultures tend to reinforce "feminine" characteristics (as defined by Western norms) for both women and men (a suggestion supported by Fong and Peskin's [1969] empirical findings that Chinese-born American men and women exceed American norms on femininity). An anti-Asian political context prevalent in the United States during the early 1900s and again during World War II also deepened the prevailing perceptions of Asian women as sexual commodities and of Asian men as desexualized (Espiritu 1996).

Thus it is crucial to recognize the varying perceptions of and about different social groups. Socialization is always only partial, but at the same time, it is the rare individual who is not exposed to and influenced by the values and perspectives expressed by a dominant culture. We can speculate that Japanese Americans, African Americans, or European Americans living in the United States during World War II had different perceptions of the attributes of Asian women and men, for example, and at the same time all of them were likely influenced to varying degrees by media portrayals of these groups.

Although gender, race, and class positions are not separable, they have been treated quite differently by social scientists. Ferree and Hall (forthcoming) offer an insightful analysis of differential approaches to gender as opposed to race or class in introductory sociology textbooks. They assert that gender is most often explained in terms of socialization; socialization is treated not as a reflection of structural sources of gender inequality but, rather, as an explanation in its own right. The sources of socialization receive little attention.

Race and class, on the other hand, are treated quite differently. Contemporary textbook discussions of race emphasize the arbitrariness of racial categories rather than essential differences. To be sure, the concept of the "culture of poverty," a theory of racial and class differences that relies on socialization, is alive and well in both sociology texts and political discourse. Nonetheless, there is considerably more debate about the idea of a culture of poverty than about the socialization of gender. Moreover, discussions of race socialization are as likely to address the learning of prejudice by dominant group members as the learning of subordination by racial minorities. In contrast, there is virtually no discussion of why and how men learn to discriminate against women. Thus the socialization of gender is often the major explanation of gender difference, and gender is analyzed primarily in terms of difference rather than of inequality. In contrast, race and class are more likely to be analyzed in terms of systematic and structured inequalities.

Gender Prescriptions and Gender Roles

Gender socialization is also prescriptive. Gender stereotypes carry prescriptive implications, manifested in *gender roles*—prescriptions for two opposite sets of behaviors and characteristics, one believed to be appropriate for women and the other appropriate for men. In Chapter 1, we outlined some of the criticisms of the concept of gender role: It ignores the differences within each gender and the considerable overlap between genders. Moreover, gender roles are often unrelated to how people actually behave. We do not mean to imply that most people do not conform in various ways to prescriptions about gender; even ostensibly "progressive" parents determined to avoid traditional gender socialization continue to "girl" and "boy" their children in some ways. This speaks to the power of social norms. Nonetheless, some parents also consciously undermine the prescriptions of gender. And people of a wide variety of political orientations often violate the conventions of gender in their everyday behavior.

Despite these critiques, the "gender-as-role" approach continues to be influential. Why? The concept of gender role reinforces the normative power of gender. Spence et al. (1985) note that in marking the differences between women and men, normative expectations of gender preserve (white middle-class) men's generally dominant position over women and their greater access to economic and political resources. The concept of gender role is rooted in a fundamentally functionalist understanding of gender difference as integral to maintaining a smoothly functioning society. The prescription of reproductive tasks such as childbearing and child rearing for women and the prescription of productive tasks such as wage labor for men legitimizes a division between private and public spheres that entrenches women's subordination and men's domination.

Stacey and Thorne (1985) offer a telling contrast between gender and other significant social positions, noting the absence of concepts such as "class roles" or "race roles." Presumably, sociologists are sufficiently aware of (or at least cautious about) race- and class-based social inequalities to avoid language that would suggest that social order depends on such inequities. The concept of gender role, in contrast, prescribing the allocation of women and men to different types of work, implies that gender inequalities are part of the foundation of social order.

Consequences of Gender Stereotypes and Prescriptions

Gender socialization does have serious negative repercussions for individuals, although few social psychologists have explored these consequences. Bem (1993) maintains that the rigid, polarized conception of gender means that the everyday behavior of women and men often violates these prescriptions. These violations generate deep insecurity, motivating adults to strive to be "real women" and "real men."

Bem speculates that in this androcentric world, the consequences of this rigidity are particularly difficult for men. Joseph Pleck and his colleagues have studied the effects of "masculinity ideologies," "beliefs about the importance of men adhering to culturally defined standards for male behavior" (Pleck, Sonenstein, and Ku 1993:85; see also Connell 1995; Carrigan, Connell, and Lee 1985). Believing in the ideal of masculinity can be damaging: Endorsement of masculinity ideology is correlated with problem behaviors among adolescent males, including drug and alcohol abuse, educational troubles, being picked up by the police, and coercive sexual behavior (Pleck et al. 1993). As Bem (1993) summarizes,

> It is males who are made to feel the most insecure about the adequacy of their gender. It so thoroughly devalues whatever thoughts, feelings, and behaviors are culturally defined as feminine that crossing the gender boundary has a more negative cultural meaning for men than it has for women—which means, in turn, that male gender-boundary-crossers are much more culturally stigmatized than female gender-boundary-crossers. At the same time, andro-centrism provides such an unreachable definition of what a real man is supposed to be that only a few men can even begin to meet it. (pp. 149-50)

Ideologies of masculinity are likely to have negative consequences for women as well as men: Among the more obvious are violence against women, pervasive wage inequities in the paid labor force, and persistent disparities in the allocation of domestic labor.

Ideologies about femininity can also be damaging. Fox's (1977) work on the "nice girl" ideal of femininity suggests that adherence to this ideology can be harmful to women: Women are discouraged from being in public alone or without "appropriate" supervision; they are channeled into jobs consistent with the nice girl image, jobs that call for nurturance, service, or emotional behavior and that, not coincidentally, are poorly paid. Similarly, ideologies of femininity are likely to harm men as well as women; as one example, if parenting is viewed as something women do, it becomes difficult for men to experience sustained involvement in and commitment to parenting.

At the same time, of course, gender stereotypes and prescriptions signifi-cantly advantage some social groups. As we have suggested, prevailing concep-tions of masculinity and femininity allocate a great deal of power and privilege to men. Indeed, gender nonconformity may have more serious consequences for men than for women precisely because it threatens to undermine this pattern of male domination; women's nonconformity is less threatening because women as a group have less social power. These advantages of gender are not shared seamlessly by all men or suffered seamlessly by all women, however; hierarchies of race and class modify the consequences of gender. For example, do cultural ideals of masculinity harm poor men of color differently and possibly more than affluent white men? Do cultural ideals of femininity harm lesbian mothers differently and possibly more than heterosexual married mothers?

In summary, socialization approaches to gender have produced valuable insights into the content and sources of gender. Nonetheless, they suffer from significant problems. This perspective emphasizes that gender is learned rather than innate, but it continues to define gender in terms of dichotomous difference. The distinction between innate and learned characteristics is in some senses merely semantic; gender socialization is conceptualized as so deep-seated that it persists throughout the life course. Thus, in practical terms, gender is still believed to be internal and unchangeable. These approaches have also overlooked or at least minimized situational and cross-cultural variations in gendered behavior. These concerns are addressed by the next perspective we discuss, the social constructionist approach to gender.

Social Constructionist Approaches

According to social constructionism, social reality is created through human action and the interpretations of those actions. Social phenomena can be interpreted in a wide variety of ways; the meaning of objects or behaviors is not inherent. Interaction cannot proceed, however, until those involved agree, at least provisionally, on a common interpretation of the situation in which they interact. Through interaction, we negotiate particular interpretations; that is, we create meaning. Through talk, through participation in the rituals of social interaction, through our active engagement with the symbols and material realities of everyday life, we literally create what we recognize as real. A minimum common understanding of shared rules and realities is necessary to sustain human communication and interaction, and ultimately, societies.

The first analysis to frame gender in this way was Garfinkel's (1967) now classic case study of a transsexual named Agnes, who appeared male at birth but underwent sex reassignment surgery after she began to develop female secondary sex characteristics at puberty. The focus of Garfinkel's analysis was not Agnes's transsexuality but the ways in which her case illustrated the performance of gender. Because she wanted to "pass" as a woman, Agnes took great pains to appear and behave in feminine ways. Garfinkel argues that Agnes's efforts to become "female" in a social sense reveal the strategies that "real" women use to construct and maintain their gender identity: dressing in an appropriate "feminine" manner, dieting, wearing makeup, holding a "female" job, and so on. In essence, Agnes had to learn in adulthood what most women learn as children: how to manage their self-presentation to appear appropriately feminine. Thus Agnes's efforts illuminate the strategies of "normal" females, strategies that are so taken for granted that they are invisible.

Garfinkel argues that these strategies revolve around eight "facts," or assumptions, regarding gender in this culture:

1. There are two, and only two, genders (female and male).
2. One's gender is invariant. (If you are female/male, you always were female/male, and you always will be female/male.)
3. Genitals are the essential sign of gender. (A female is a person with a vagina; a male is a person with a penis.)
4. Any exceptions to two genders are not to be taken seriously. (They must be jokes, pathology, etc.)

5. There are no transfers from one gender to another except ceremonial ones (masquerades).
6. Everyone must be classified as a member of one gender or another. (There are no cases where gender is not attributed.)
7. The male/female dichotomy is a "natural" one. (Males and females exist independently of scientists' [or anyone else's] criteria for being male and female.)
8. Membership in one gender or another is "natural." (Being female or male is not dependent on anyone's deciding what you are.) (Kessler and McKenna 1978, pp. 113-4)

Garfinkel contended that gender is not "natural" but is instead accomplished through everyday behavior.

Televised interactions offer an unusually pointed example of this process, because they are deliberately designed to be engaging and interpretable modes of communication. In an analysis of the interactions on the television dating game show *Studs*, Hollander (1995) shows the rich interactional dynamics of performing both gender and sexuality. Some highlights: "Dates" (the women) sit demurely on the stage, whereas "studs" (the men) run onstage and engage in physical clowning; the women's clothing emphasizes feminine curves, whereas the men's emphasizes masculine strength; the women sit with legs crossed and close together, their arms close to their bodies, whereas the men sit with legs wide apart or crossed knee to ankle; the stories they tell enact the "nature" of women as sexually reluctant and of men as sexually aggressive; their verbal comments on what sort of date they might want establish their heterosexual "normality." In short, they perform gender, and appropriate gender, through a rich repertoire of actions. Their behaviors literally sustain the social reality of gender.

Kessler and McKenna (1978) go even further and argue that not only gender but the very idea of two distinct sexes, is socially constructed. They note that there are a considerable number of people who do not fit easily into the categories male and female. Examples include "intersexed" individuals (who are born with both female and male physical characteristics), *berdaches* (who are physically assignable to one sex but who take on the social behaviors and characteristics of the other), and transsexuals (who move from one sex category to another). Kessler and McKenna use these examples to demonstrate that sex is not dichotomous. Our cultural belief in two (and only two) sexes, however, leads us to categorize these people as "really" one or the other sex. Transsexuals might seem to violate Garfinkel's "facts" about gender, but in fact they reaffirm it. By engaging in sex reassignment surgery, they change not gender but genitals; they alter sex to conform to gender. In a society that tolerated a lack of correspondence between genitals and gender, there would be no transsexuals, and no need for such surgery.

This approach to gender differs significantly from the essentialist and socialization approaches. Deaux (1984) criticizes these latter approaches for "the static nature of the assumptions—that sex-related phenomena are best approached either through biological categories, via stable traits, or in terms of relatively stable stereotypic conceptions" (p. 113). She suggests that attention "be directed toward more active interaction sequences, toward the processes through which gender information is presented and acted upon" (p. 113)—the choices women and men make and the processes of interaction. Gender is not only something society imposes on individuals; women and men themselves enact gender, and in doing so, they choose certain behavioral options and ignore others. This perspective challenges the naturalness of gender difference, maintaining that all significant social characteristics are actively created, rather than biologically inherited, permanently socialized, or structurally predetermined.

In other words, gender is constructed in part through performance. "Doing gender" means behaving so that whatever the situation, whoever the other actors, one's behavior is seen in context as gender appropriate. To be sure, women and men do take actions that contradict norms for their gender; what is important is that the balance of one's actions is perceived as conforming. West and Zimmerman (1987) argue that one driving force behind gender performance is the threat of being held accountable for one's behavior:

> A person engaged in virtually any activity can be held responsible for performance of that activity as a woman or a man, and their incumbency in one or the other sex category can be used to legitimate or discredit their other activities. (p. 136)

Thus female college professors, for example, are often expected to be more nurturing than male professors in their interactions with their students. When they fail to conform to this expectation—an expectation that has no relationship to their position as college professor—students may express their dissatisfaction through their evaluations of these professors. To the degree that a society is organized in terms of what it understands as essential differences between women and men, doing gender is thus unavoidable.

Erving Goffman (1977) provides an apt example of the ubiquity of doing gender, noting that public bathrooms (at least in the United States) are segregated on the basis of gender. This is despite the fact that "both [ladies and gentlemen] are somewhat similar in the question of waste products and their elimination . . . there is nothing in this functioning [of sex-differentiated organs] that biologically recommends segregation; that arrangement is a totally cultural matter" (pp. 315-6). In other words, bathroom segregation creates gender difference for social, not biological, ends. Lest one doubt this claim, consider the absence of gender-typed bathrooms in most private homes. Every time we enter a gender-appropriate bathroom, we do gender. We even do gender when we enter the "wrong" bathroom, if we express embarrassment or otherwise indicate this is not something we would normally do (a not uncommon occurrence during short intermissions when there are long lines outside women's bathrooms and none outside men's bathrooms). Should individuals occasionally lapse, social institutions enforce gender segregation: Witness the arrest of a woman for using the men's bathroom several years ago at a concert in Houston.

The social constructionist conceptualization of gender helps reconcile the empirical findings that women and men are more similar than different on most traits and abilities with the common perception that they seem to behave quite differently. Women and men may have the same abilities, but because they face different societal constraints and expectations, they often make different choices from this repertoire of options. Gender expectations can thus act as *self-fulfilling* prophecies. Suppose an employer interviewing a woman for a position in his firm holds traditional views about women and he makes these opinions clear in his behavior. The woman being interviewed is likely to respond by behaving in a "feminine" way, whether or not those behaviors reflect her usual behavior, thus confirming the employer's gender expectations (Snyder and Skrypnek 1981).

These cumulative performances of gender create the gendered institutions of contemporary society. Brines (1993), for example, demonstrates how husbands' and wives' contributions to housework serve as gender performances: "Among couples whose earnings arrangement seriously deviates from the gender norm, housework is used symbolically to reassert [the respective partners'] 'essential' masculinity or femininity" (p. 302; and see Chapter 3 of this volume). Individual husbands and wives thus perform gender through their allocation of household work. Summed across the members of a society, these performances reproduce the division of public and private labor and maintain the subordination of women.

Performances of gender are also performances of other intersecting social positions. Pate (1995) shows how seemingly minor "acknowledgment rituals"—the nod of a head or verbal "hello" when passing a stranger in public—among members of various minority groups simultaneously reinforce both intraminority group solidarity and the boundaries between minority and majority groups. Importantly, these rituals are strikingly more frequent among African American men than among African American women or women and men of other racial groups. These patterns likely reflect the markedly visible and virulent racial discrimination against African American men.

Doing gender is also doing sexuality. Herbert (1995) shows the performance strategies of women in the U.S. military as they attempt to avoid being perceived as too masculine, on the one hand, and too feminine, on the other. Over half of the women in her study identified being labeled a lesbian as the primary penalty of being perceived as too masculine. The penalties of being perceived as not masculine enough include career limitations and being judged an inadequate soldier. Although these dilemmas are magnified among women working in a traditionally masculine institution, they are only an exaggeration of the interactional and structural difficulties facing other women and men who are not performing gender according to cultural norms.

As these examples illustrate, doing gender reaffirms the social arrangements based on sex category as normal and natural and thus legitimates the prevailing social order. Differences between women and men created through these processes can be portrayed as fundamental and enduring, as essential. Doing gender is how social interaction sustains broader, macrolevel systems of gender hierarchy. This implies in turn that doing gender "wrong" may be the interactional foundation for social change in gender relations. It is important to note, however, that those who contest norms are often held accountable as individual actors;

responsibility is attributed to the actors rather than to the norms they contest. In this exceedingly individualistic society, persistent and coordinated efforts are necessary to pose effective challenges to social institutions.

The social constructionist approach emphasizes the social context of gendered behavior. Unlike traditional experimental social psychology, which isolates elements of social life in the supposedly neutral context of the laboratory, this perspective focuses on interactions among individuals in their specific social situations. Many aspects of the situation are influential: the expectations of those with whom one interacts, the differential opportunities for interaction, and the differential rewards and punishments for behavior accorded to women and men. Thus the distinctive contribution of the social constructionist approach is its attention to the relationship between the person and the situation. "Gender is pervasive, but gender effects do not reside solely in either person or situation" (Spence et al. 1985:172). This, of course, is the mission of social psychology—to articulate the interface between individual and society.

We do not want to overstate the power of the social constructionist approach to gender, however. In its emphasis on individual agency, this approach minimizes the constraints of social structures and the effects of power inequities. Action is always situated somewhere. The particularities of actors' genders, class positions, races, and sexualities have direct material consequences for the range of actions they can envision, let alone perform. Although almost all actors have some degree of choice among potential behaviors, some people have a good deal more choice than others. The emphasis on agency comes at the cost of recognition of the reality of institutional and interpersonal constraints—that is, of social hierarchies. This brings us to the fourth perspective on gender, a structural account.

Structural Approaches

Gender is one basis for the systematic allocation of resources; in other words, gender is one form of social structure (Risman, forthcoming). In previous sections of this chapter, we have considered how gender operates as a microlevel structure, shaping interactional expectations and possibilities. Gender is also a basis for the macrolevel allocation of material resources and opportunities. Women and men who seek to establish equitable divisions of labor in their relationships, for example, must battle the structural arrangements of day care, parental leave policies, pay inequities, and gender-segregated labor, as well as the gender-differentiated expectations of parents, employers, teachers, and children themselves. At the same time, as detailed in the previous section, social structures are also continually negotiated and redefined through individual action and interaction (Howard 1994). A structural approach to gender, then, examines the gendered distribution of resources in social institutions (from small groups, such as families, to large organizations, to society itself) and demonstrates how those resources shape gendered behaviors. The structural approach has not been prevalent in social psychology; hence our discussion of this perspective is considerably shorter than that of other perspectives. As we argue in subsequent chapters, however, we believe that a comprehensive understanding of social behavior is impossible without serious analysis of the relationships between individuals and social structures. Social psychologists must consider the myriad ways in which the social organization of gender (and race, class, and sexuality) shapes both the microlevel interactional possibilities and the macrolevel material resources of women and men.

Returning to the principles of socialization, we might ask, for example, why it is that certain behaviors are rewarded when they are performed by boys and punished when they are performed by girls? Why are the sorts of behaviors girls are encouraged to perform valued less than the sorts of behaviors boys are encouraged to perform? Why are there many fewer female than male role models in prestigious, societally rewarded positions and many more female than male role models in less rewarded positions? Turning to the principles of the social constructionist approach to gender, we might ask whether all actors have the same degree of behavioral choice and control. Do all actors bring the same resources to their social interactions? What are the effects of what Kanter (1977) calls "tokenism," interactional strategies whereby men in the numerical majority in institutions such as corporations ostracize and stigmatize the few women who are successful in entering these arenas? A structural approach emphasizes the profound effects of a pervasive system of male dominance, whereby men as a category have systematic advantages over women as a category. Note, too, that men have these advantages whether or not they consciously desire them; this is, of course, one aspect of a social structure.

Moreover, gender does not operate independent of other significant social structures. At the same time that men as a class have advantages over women as a class, whites—both women and men—have advantages over members of other racial categories; those who have substantial economic resources have considerable advantages over those who are poor. Because these systems are inextricably interconnected, the advantages that gender stratification accords to men accrue significantly more to some men (i.e., those who are white, wealthy, or both) than to others. The intersections between these various structures make social hierarchy extremely complex: The dynamics of interactions between gay Latino men and poor white women or between straight, wealthy black men and older lesbians are not straightforward. Gender intersects with other social hierarchies, affecting social psychological phenomena from cognitive structures to the dynamics of social interaction to macrolevel institutions and collective actions.

In summary, from a structural perspective, observed differences between women and men, whether in personality characteristics, interactional styles, educational levels, or income, are attributable to the differential access of women and men to material and social resources rather than to deep-seated traits or biological factors. The weakness of the structural approach, however, is its minimization of the role of everyday behavior in creating, sustaining, and transforming social structures. We suggest that the structural and social construction approaches are complementary. Everyday behavior is always enacted within the structural constraints and possibilities associated with actors' locations in significant social systems. We close this discussion of the various social psychological approaches to gender with the observation that a combination of social construction and structural perspectives seems to us to offer the most incisive lens for analyzing contemporary social life.

Conclusions

We have presented four theories of gender prominent in social psychological research. We have emphasized the construction of gender through social interaction and at the same time the importance of the location of human actors in particular social structures. We have been particularly critical of essentialist understandings of gender, whether these are based on assumptions about biological determinants of gender or on theories of socialization that treat gender-related characteristics as virtually unchangeable. We have suggested that essentialist approaches to gender, sexuality, race, socioeconomic position, or any other human attribute are not consistent with a wealth of empirical research. On the other hand, most cultures and societies have treated these categories and positions as if they were essential, innate, and stable. Accordingly, these systems have been the bases for the allocation of resources, both material and nonmaterial, across human history.

As the subsequent chapters make clear, there are consistent historical patterns in the treatment of gender, race, class, and sexuality in social psychological research. Research on gendered patterns of social behavior began to increase in the 1970s and has continued at a fairly consistent rate through the mid-1990s. Many researchers attended to the hierarchical relationships between the sexes—to inequality and power as well as to difference. These developments were not unrelated to the fact that more women began to earn doctorates and to conduct research in these areas.

In contrast, research on racialized patterns of social behavior was prominent in the 1970s but began to drop off during the 1980s and continues to decline. The progress in incorporating more women into research, both as scholars and as participants, has not been paralleled in the study of race. Only 5% of the 1995 membership of the American Psychological Association, for example, identified themselves as racial or ethnic minorities. A recent study shows a marked decline since 1974 in the proportion of published social psychological articles that include African Americans as respondents (Graham 1992). Patterns of research on social class are similar to those of research on race, except that the drop during the 1980s is even more precipitous. Not only is social class rarely a focus of research, but the class position of research respondents is rarely assessed. Even in research that attempts to disentangle the effects of race and social class, only one quarter of the relevant studies report the social class positions of the respondents (Graham 1992). The importance of socioeconomic position for explaining social behavior has been acknowledged primarily at the margins of social psychology (see Archibald 1978; Bramel and Friend 1981; Reid 1993; Wexler 1983), although there have been a few experimental studies (Howard and Pike 1986; Romer and Cherry 1980) and more rarely, book-length treatments (Argyle 1994).

Considering these patterns together, the inescapable conclusion is that the real-world political vitality of particular social communities plays a central role in determining research agendas. Patterns of research that address gender mirror the sustained recent sociocultural awareness of gender. Patterns of research that address race mirror the heights—and the depths—of the civil rights movement and its successors. Patterns of research that address sexual orientation mirror the recent ascent to the national stage of the lesbian and gay community.

Thus we exhort the reader to evaluate what we report here as critically as the phenomena we critique. Throughout this chapter, we have directed our comments and criticisms toward both the central theories and ideas of social psychology and the actual practices of the discipline of social psychology. We discuss these disciplinary practices because the lessons of social psychology apply as strongly to the discipline itself as to other arenas of social life. Social context shapes all social behavior, including the production of social psychological scholarship. We turn now to that scholarship.

The four approaches we have reviewed—essentialist, socialization, social constructionist, and structural—trace the evolution of social psychology's conceptualizations of gender over the last century. In general, this evolution has been productive: Each advance has brought new insights into the sources and content of gender. In the remainder of this book, we examine specific areas of social psychology in greater depth. We begin by analyzing the three dominant theories in social psychology—social exchange, social cognition, and symbolic interactionism—and then discuss two related topics, aggression and altruism. In each chapter, we describe in detail how research in the area has dealt with gender and related social systems and how further attention to gender can illuminate our understanding of both social psychology and gender.

CHAPTER 3

Social Exchange
and Related Theories

Every day, we make innumerable choices about how we will behave. We choose what we eat, what we wear, to whom (if anyone) we talk, what we do with our time. We may also make decisions about how we spend whatever money we have, what books we read or what films we see, and with whom we form or maintain intimate relationships. Why do we make the choices we do? Why do we often make the same choices day after day—to wear certain types of clothes, to talk with particular friends, or to buy particular products? This chapter discusses three theories—behaviorism, social learning, and social exchange— that share a common perspective on such questions. Each theory assumes that human behavior is driven by the pursuit of rewards, whether material (such as money, food, or physical pleasure) or symbolic (such as status, prestige, or love). Humans behave in ways that they expect will bring them such rewards and avoid behaving in ways that they expect will bring punishments—negative events such as pain, hunger, loneliness, or loss of status.

This chapter surveys these three theories, focusing on their treatment of gender. We begin with brief reviews of behaviorism and social learning theory, both of which have been very influential in psychology. We conclude with a more extended discussion of social exchange theory; this is arguably the dominant social psychological perspective in sociology and is gaining currency throughout the social sciences. We combine these three theories in a single chapter because of their shared reliance on the assumption that human behavior is driven by rewards and punishments.

Behaviorism

Behaviorism was the dominant paradigm in social psychology for the first half of this century. Although it has in large part been superseded by more recent theories, we discuss it here because its principles form the basis for both social learning and social exchange theories. Behaviorism grew out of animal research. Scientists found that animal behavior could be changed by a process they called *reinforcement*—the association of a particular behavior with specific consequences, either positive (such as receiving food) or negative (such as experiencing electric shocks). Behavioral psychologists (e.g., Watson 1924; Skinner 1938) suggested that the same principles could explain human behavior as well.

The key to understanding behavior, according to these theorists, lies in the consequences that follow from the behavior. But how do people know what the consequences will be before they occur? By looking back at the consequences that have been associated with the action in the past. If we have found that a certain behavior has been associated with rewards in the past, we tend to repeat it; similarly, if we have found that a behavior has been associated with punishments, we avoid repeating it.

It is crucial to note that behaviorist theory focuses on *behavior*, not on thought or feeling. According to behaviorism, the environment affects behavior *directly*, without intervening processes such as thought or feeling. These thoughts and feelings may occur, but they are simply by-products of the effects of the environment on behavior (Skinner 1974) and do not cause behavior (Skinner 1974; Molm 1981). In contrast, most other social psychological theories assume that thought and emotion mediate between the environment and individual behavior.

Behaviorism's Treatment of Gender, Race, and Class

Behaviorism has paid almost no attention to social statuses such as gender, race, or class. The theory postulates that all creatures—animals and humans, males and females, whites and people of color, poor and rich—operate according to the same behavioral principles. Gender is therefore not considered relevant to behaviorist questions.

Is it even possible to integrate gender into a behaviorist model? If researchers were interested in including gender in their theories, we suggest that the integration might take the following form. Behaviorists could expand on their insight that consequences are the real causes of behavior, using this principle to explore gender differences and similarities in behavior. Experiments could be devised to assess whether gendered patterns of behavior (such as nurturance or aggression) could be produced in a similar fashion in males and females by modifying patterns of reinforcement. For example, might men behave nurturingly and women aggressively if they were rewarded for these behaviors? Moving out of the laboratory, behaviorists could examine the environmental conditions that differentially affect men and women and theorize about how these might affect behavior. For example, men might behave aggressively because, over time, they have been rewarded for displaying aggressive behavior. Women, on the other hand, might not behave aggressively because they are consistently punished for such behavior. Thus apparent sex differences in behavior could be explained by environmental consequences rather than by individual or group characteristics.

In the previous chapter, we described four different ways of conceptualizing gender. Behaviorism's treatment of gender in some ways resembles both the socialization and the structural models of gender, because both emphasize the effects of the environment on individuals. The socialization perspective, however, relies far more on cognition than behaviorism does, and the structural perspective's conception of environment is far richer than behaviorism's. The social constructionist approach to gender is fundamentally incompatible with behaviorist theory because of its heavy reliance on cognition. The social constructionist approach argues that people behave in gendered ways because of their ideas about appropriate behavior and their perceptions of others' expectations; these factors are explicitly excluded from the behaviorist model. To the extent that behaviorism considers cognition, it sees cognition as a behavior resulting from external stimuli rather than as a stimulus for other behavior. To include cognition as a cause of gendered behavior, we must look to the two other variants of behaviorism, social learning and social exchange. Although these theories do not focus on cognition as directly as do other social psychological perspectives (e.g., social cognition and symbolic interactionism), they do recognize that cognition plays a mediating role in social behavior.

Social Learning Theory

Social learning theory retains the behaviorist emphasis on reward and punishment but expands and extends these principles in several important respects. First, it emphasizes the role of other people as the agents of reinforcement. When rewards or punishments are administered by influential others, they are likely to be more effective. Social learning theory has been particularly important in the field of developmental psychology, which studies how children develop psychologically and learn the norms and values of their society.

Second, social learning theory differs from behaviorism in its focus on modeling and imitation. According to Bandura and his colleagues, children observe the behavior of real-life (e.g., parents, teachers, or other children) and symbolic (e.g., television or literary) models and then reproduce this behavior themselves (Bandura and Walters 1963; Bandura 1977). The reproduced behavior need not be reinforced directly in order to become part of the child's repertoire; observation of the consequences of the model's behavior may be sufficient (Bandura, Ross, and Ross 1963). Thus children do not have to perform a behavior themselves to experience its consequences and learn from it. This is a significant departure from behaviorism, which suggests that learning of new behaviors occurs only through *successive approximation*—in other words, through trying out different versions of a behavior and being rewarded or punished for them.

Most important, social learning theory departs from behaviorism in its inclusion of cognitive processes as mediating factors between the environment and individual behavior.[1] Although reward and punishment remain important concepts, social learning theory focuses on the ways in which individuals think about their social experiences and how those thoughts affect their subsequent behaviors. Social learning theory thus introduces the realm of the symbolic: To learn from experience, people must retain experiences in memory (as images or verbal representations), integrate them with other knowledge, generalize them into rules for behavior, and apply these rules to new situations. Although social learning theory acknowledges these cognitive processes, it does not explore them in detail. That task is left to social cognition, the theory to which we turn in the next chapter.

Social Learning Theory's Treatment of Gender

Unlike behaviorism, social learning theory has been applied extensively to understanding gender, particularly the development of gender differences in behavior. The idea here is quite simple: Children observe the behavior of others, including other children, adults, and symbolic models, such as television actors. Children imitate the behavior of people of both sexes; however, the consequences of this imitation often vary depending on the sex of the child. Boys are rewarded more for performing typically masculine behaviors, and girls for performing typically feminine behaviors. Because only rewarded behaviors tend to be repeated, children develop gendered repertoires of behavior (Mischel 1966; Bandura 1969; Bussey and Bandura 1984), either through direct reinforcement or through observation of consequences experienced by others. The influence of behaviorism on this model of learning should be clear.

The importance of both of these processes—imitation and reinforcement—is illustrated by Bandura's research on aggression, which we discuss in more detail in Chapter 7. Bandura and his colleagues (Bandura et al. 1963; Bandura 1965; Bandura 1973) conducted a series of experiments that demonstrated that aggression can be learned from others. Children were shown films in which an adult hit and kicked an inflatable "Bobo doll." The children were then allowed to play with a similar doll. Those who had seen the aggressive behavior abused the doll in the same ways the adult had; children in a control condition, who had not seen the adult behaving aggressively, did not. The degree of reinforcement was also important: When the adult was rewarded for aggressive behavior, the children imitated the adult more. Overall, boys were more aggressive than girls; however, when the children were rewarded for aggressive behavior, the levels of aggression were equal. Both imitation and reinforcement are thus important in learning gendered behavior.

How does social learning theory map onto the four approaches to gender? Social learning theory is in fact the basis of the socialization approach to gender. Most social learning research focuses on the acquisition of gender-typed behaviors in childhood, implying that gender, once learned, becomes a relatively stable facet of one's personality. However, the theory does not address the question of why reinforcers are sex typed, and it does not challenge the conception of gender as an individual characteristic. In contrast, social learning theory is fundamentally incompatible with the essentialist perspective, because it views gender as learned, not innate. With some modifications, social learning theory could be compatible with the social constructionist and structural perspectives on gender, because it focuses on contextual influences on behavior.

Why has the theory not moved in these directions? There are several probable reasons. First, social learning theory grew out of behaviorism and has inherited some of its assumptions. Although behaviorism does conceptualize behavior as driven by the environment, the behaviorist's idea of environmental influences is limited to the immediate context and the reinforcement contingencies it presents. This is a very different conception of context from the sociologist's notion of social structure. As a result, social learning theory tends to ignore significant structural patterns, such as the fact that the organization of social institutions such as families, schools, or religions promotes the differential reinforcement of males and females for the same behaviors. Second, social learning theory has histori- cally focused on children, perhaps because the theory was first generated by developmental psychologists. The theory could, however, be equally applicable to adults—because, after all, adults are not immune to rewards and punishments. Applying the theory to adults would suggest that gendered behavior is con- stantly modeled and reinforced, even among adults—an idea that is much closer to the social constructionist approach to gender.

Social Exchange Theory

Like social learning theory, social exchange theory derives from behaviorism. We consider social exchange theory in greater depth than we have behaviorism or social learning, because it is quite influential in sociology and because the imagery of exchange theory (markets, transactions, and the like) resonates with hegemonic cultural ideas, making exchange processes salient in social interaction.

Like behaviorism and social learning theory, social exchange theory assumes that individuals pursue rewards and attempt to avoid punishments, and it considers an individual's past history of rewards and punishments to be impor- tant for predicting future behavior. However, social exchange diverges from behaviorism and social learning theory in several crucial ways.

First, the focus of exchange theory is not individual behavior but interaction between individuals. The exchange relationship—a series of transactions be- tween two or more actors occurring over time (Thibaut and Kelley 1959; Emerson 1972a, 1972b)—is the unit of analysis. The major question addressed by exchange theory is not "Why does an individual behave in a certain way?" but, instead, "Under what circumstances does a certain interaction (or exchange) take place?" Exchange theory contends that interaction takes place when it is mutually rewarding to the parties involved.

Second, as the preceding paragraph suggests, the model for exchange the- ory's view of interaction is the economic transaction. For example, when we go to the grocery store, we exchange money in return for food. Social exchange theory takes this economic model and applies it to other situations, such as choosing a job or a dating partner. In each of these situations, the actor exchanges her or his personal resources (work skills, status, attractiveness, conversational skills, and so on) for a desired benefit, such as employment or a date with a desirable partner. Thus the resources transferred in social exchanges need not be material; social approval, respect, and compliance are other valuable rewards (Blau 1964). However, as in market-based economic exchanges, actors in social exchanges are assumed to be seeking the best possible outcomes from interactions. When buying a loaf of bread, when accepting a job, or when choosing a dating partner, the actor considers whether the exchange in question is a "good deal" or whether he or she can find a better deal with a different exchange partner.

Like social learning theory, social exchange theory explicitly includes cognition in its model of interaction. When deciding on a course of action, actors are assumed to weigh the costs and benefits of the available options and choose rationally between them. Thus consideration of alternatives and choice are the principal forms of cognition in this theory. Of course, actors do not always know the actual consequences of their choices. What matters is perception: People choose the alternative they believe will be best, based on their assessment of the costs and benefits of the alternatives combined with their estimates of the probability of receiving these outcomes.

This is a very different kind of cognition than in social learning theory. Social learning theory's model of cognition envisions actors looking back toward the past, evaluating the results of similar choices (by oneself or others). In contrast, exchange theory's actors look toward the future as well as the past: What advantages, they ask, will different situations bring, and what is the likelihood that these situations will come to pass (Macy 1993)? Although decision making is clearly an important part of cognition, there is far more to thought than either social learning or exchange theory suggests. In social exchange, individuals are assumed to weigh the costs and benefits of particular outcomes. But we know from research on cognition (a topic we take up in greater depth in the next chapter) that other factors also influence decision making: beliefs, attitudes, and membership in and identification with certain groups (e.g., based on ethnicity, gender, or religion). Thus the richness of cognitive processes has not yet been incorporated into exchange theory's model of behavior.

A third way that social exchange theory differs from social learning theory and behaviorism is that exchange theory brings social structure into the model of interaction. Unlike behaviorism and social learning theory, which limit their conceptualization of environmental factors to reinforcement (and, in the case of social learning, modeling by other actors), social exchange theory considers individuals in a broader social context. According to exchange theory, interaction occurs because of individuals' interdependence—in other words, because each person depends on others for valued resources, both material and emotional, and because access to resources depends on structural locations. In addition, choices may be affected by an actor's position in a larger social network. For example, other exchanges occurring within a social group may affect what is considered to be a good deal: If a friend's new job pays $25,000 a year, you may expect to receive the same salary for a similar position. In turn, what is considered to be a good deal also varies by actors' structural locations; for example, a woman may consider $25,000 to be a better salary than does a man, given gender differences in pay. In addition, actors may join together to negotiate transactions with a more powerful party. For example, a group of workers may form a coalition to protest exploitive work conditions. (This, of course, is the principle behind labor unions.) Moreover, the position of an actor in a social network is also important: Actors who are more central (i.e., who mediate a large number of other relationships) may have more power and more alternatives available to them (Yamagishi, Gillmore, and Cook 1988). Thus exchange theory uses the structure of social relationships to explain behavior: "Rather than try to explain the nature of a relationship as a result of qualities within the actors, this research explains the qualities of the actors by exploring the nature of the relationship" (Cook, O'Brien, and Kollock 1990:162).

Social Exchange and Power

One of the most useful aspects of social exchange theory is its attention to power as a central mechanism of social interaction. *Power* is defined as an actor's ability to achieve a favorable outcome at the expense of another and is a quality of a *relationship*, not an *individual*. One's power over another person depends on the value of one's resources to that other person, together with the availability of those resources from alternate sources. Thus, to return to the example used in the first chapter, if a professor possesses information that is very important to a student and if there is no other source from which the student can obtain this information, then the professor holds a great deal of power over the student. However, the professor's power is due to the relationship with the student (and the underlying network of relationships between the student, the professor, and the university) rather than to the professor's personal qualities. In another relationship—for example, with a police officer who has stopped the professor for speeding—the professor's specialized knowledge will not be a valuable resource, and he will have little power over the police officer. The student, but not the police officer, is dependent on the professor; thus power and dependence vary together in exchange relationships.

This insight leads to what Homans (1974) called the "principle of least interest": The person who is least dependent on a relationship has the greatest power in it, because that person can more easily abandon the relationship. The professor presumably has many students, so the good regard of any one student is not particularly compelling. The student, however, has only one professor for any given class, and so that professor's behavior is very important to her. Later in the play from which we borrow this example, however, we see the power dynamics shift: The student has developed access to other resources and in fact gains partial control of the professor's access to tenure. This student's power over the professor thus increases dramatically. This change shows another strength of exchange theory: the acknowledgment that power is not a static quality of a person but a dynamic, shifting property of a relationship.

Critiques of Social Exchange Theory

Exchange theory has been tremendously influential in many of the social sciences, including sociology, economics, and anthropology, as well as social psychology. Perhaps because of that influence, it has also been subject to extensive critiques. For example, despite its recognition of power, exchange theory has generally been applied only to *voluntary* interaction. Coercive interaction—when one party forces the other to act through the use or threat of violence—is often seen as outside the scope of the theory. Although exchange theory could easily be used to understand coercive situations—one actor simply has very few resources and alternatives relative to the other—it has rarely been used in this way. Perhaps this is because of the association of exchange with choice; conceptualizing coercive interaction as involving *choice* is problematic. Some recent research has begun to include "punishment power" in studies of exchange (e.g., Molm 1988, 1989a, 1989b, 1990); however, this terrain remains largely unexplored by exchange researchers.

It is also curious that although the *theory* of social exchange is built around conceptions of power and social structure, very little of the *research* in this tradition explores power or stratification in any real-world sense. As we point out in the next section, exchange theory has rarely analyzed the way one's position in existing systems of social stratification—one's race, class, gender, age, and so on—affects one's resources, alternatives, and choices. (We discuss two exceptions in the second half of this chapter: research on power in long-term relationships and on equity and justice.) One reason for this inattention is clear: The experimental methodology used in much exchange research necessarily precludes investigation of these issues. Many exchange experiments (see Molm and Cook 1995) take the following form: Participants sit in separate rooms and interact only by typing messages over a computer network or by pushing buttons that illuminate lights on a panel in another room; they never see or hear each other. These arrangements have the advantage of reducing the effects of "extraneous" factors such as gender, race, or attractiveness. However, these situations also lack external validity; they are so unlike everyday interaction that the experimental results may not be generalizable to the real world. The factors that are "controlled" in the lab (gender, age, attractiveness, rewards, etc.) are central to social interaction and may influence the process of social exchange in unexamined ways. For example, people in different social groups may value different outcomes or have different perceptions about their alternatives in a given situation; these kinds of issues are rarely examined in exchange research.

Critics have also questioned the tasks frequently used in exchange research. For example, many studies involve pushing buttons to receive rewards, and many of these rewards are very small—a few cents or dollars. Money is used as the reward in these experiments because it is presumed to have relatively equal value for everyone. Class variation among research participants may make this assumption untrue, however. The small sums that are earned through participation may be important to a poorer participant, for example, but incidental (and therefore less compelling) to a wealthier participant. Indeed, the entire question of the value of various resources to exchange participants remains unaddressed. Thus, although social exchange is *theoretically* sophisticated, its *implementation* in research is much less so.

The limited focus of exchange research has also been subject to critique. The groups used in experimental research are usually composed of people who have never met and who are recruited specifically to serve as experimental volunteers. Although some everyday interaction does take place with strangers, most people spend the majority of their time interacting with people they already know—

family members, romantic partners, friends, coworkers, and so on—and with whom they have a long history of interaction and a great deal of prior knowledge. The theory of social exchange emphasizes the effect of this history on interaction. In fact, in Emerson's (1972a, 1972b) formulation, history *defines* the exchange relation, which is conceptualized as repeated interaction over time. In practice, however, history is often left out of exchange experiments or is represented by a series of transactions that occur a few minutes or, at most, a few hours before the experiment begins. Thus we know little about how real-world history affects exchange relations.

Finally, some feminists argue that exchange theory (and other theories rooted in neoclassical economics) is gender biased. England and Kilbourne (1990), for example, note that women and men tend to differ on the dimension of separation-connection. Because of their different life experiences, men tend to develop a "separative" self that emphasizes independence and autonomy, whereas women tend to develop a "connective" self that values empathy and caring. England and Kilbourne argue that social exchange-type theories are biased toward the separative model of self. For example, these theories often assume that actors are selfish and pursue only what will benefit themselves and that rationality, rather than emotion or empathy, guides behavior. Hartsock (1985) concludes that exchange theory's basis in men's experience "both justifies and obscures relations of gender domination" (p. 57). Others challenge these criticisms, arguing that they result from a misreading of exchange theory and that in fact such theories can help to explain gender inequality by showing how women and men make choices within different sets of social constraints (Friedman and Diem 1993). Although we agree with Friedman and Diem that exchange theory has the *potential* to address gender inequality, we must underscore the fact that such applications continue to be rare in practice.

Exchange Theory's Treatment of Gender

The exchange framework has been adopted by practitioners in a wide variety of disciplines, including social work, communications, and criminal justice, who have used the basic concepts of exchange theory to explain a broad range of social phenomena. Many of the topics to which these concepts have been applied are deeply gendered, such as the perception of and responses to sexual harassment (Jones and Remland 1992), the disclosure of intimate information in relationships (Cline and Musolf 1985), sex role attitudes (Morgan and Walker 1983), and even homicide (Rodriquez and Henderson 1995). However, these applications are far removed from the mainstream of social exchange research in social psychology, often using the concepts of social exchange (reward, costs, and alternative) without integrating the full richness of the theory.

In contrast, most research by social exchange theorists barely mentions gender, let alone race or social class. These studies offer no insights into the origins of persistence of gender inequality and provide no account for the similarities and differences in women's and men's experiences of social life. Many studies do include sex as an independent variable: Most use equal numbers of male and female participants, and a few report sex differences (or similarities) in behavior. However, as in many areas of social research, little work in the social exchange tradition has gone beyond the concept of sex differences to a more sophisticated conceptualization of gender.

Why has social exchange theory neglected gender? Again, the experimental paradigm that has become normative in social exchange research is partly responsible. When research participants never see or hear each other, the every-day social cues that constitute sex and gender—appearance, speech, and behavior patterns—are artificially removed from the situation, and their effects on exchange behavior go unanalyzed. However, other social psychological perspectives have been much more successful in integrating gender, race, and class into the experimental paradigm.

Another reason for the neglect of gender in exchange research is that exchange theory, like behaviorism, assumes that everyone's behavior is based on the same exchange principles. Regardless of race, gender, or class, every individual is believed to be guided by rewards and punishments, power and dependence. Although structural position and its effects on the availability of resources is a central part of the theory outlined by Emerson (1972a, 1972b), in practice, structure tends to be operationalized quite narrowly, as a set of relationships between a small number of individual actors. The connection to real-world social structures based on social class, race, or gender is rarely explored.

Two traditions of research in social exchange do pay more attention to gender than most: the exploration of power in long-term intimate relationships and research on perceptions of justice and equity. In the remainder of this chapter, we discuss these two research traditions and their evolving approach to gender.

Example 1: Power in Marriage and Other Long-Term Relationships. The earliest explorations of marital dynamics (e.g., Parsons 1955) did not focus on power at all. Families were believed to be locations of intimacy and communalism, places where individuals could escape the competition and impersonal attitudes that characterized the public sphere. Thus intimate relationships were presumed to be immune from power processes, and exchanges were assumed to be equal, even if the partners contributed different resources.

Later work, however, argued that these assumptions were naive and that in fact intimate relationships are no less likely than other relationships to be arenas for the exercise of power and control. The first researchers in this tradition focused on the exchange of money for other resources. Measuring power by factors such as influence over important decisions, researchers noted that husbands tended to have more power than wives, especially when wives were not employed outside the home (Blood and Wolfe 1960; Turk and Bell 1972). Theorists hypothesized that this power differential resulted from the traditional organization of families, in which men were responsible for earning money, whereas women were responsible for maintaining the home and rearing children. Marriage was thus conceptualized as an exchange: Women traded household service for financial support; men traded money and status for a comfortable home life. Men had more power because they contributed more of the more valuable resource: money.

Subsequent research has refined the rather crude equation of money and power. England and Farkas (1986), for example, argued that money is a key determinant of power not simply because it is a more valuable resource but because it (along with other resources, such as prestige and social status) is a more *transferable* resource—one that can be used in a variety of situations. If a man ends one marriage and begins another, his financial resources are equally useful in the new relationship. Thus it is relatively easy (financially speaking) for a man to change relationships. In traditional heterosexual relationships, however, women typically do not contribute transferable resources, such as money and status. Instead, they contribute household labor, child care, and social labor, such as maintaining relationships with friends and families—resources that are relatively nontransferable. For example, a homemaker's investments in learning what kinds of foods her husband likes or in maintaining bonds with his family are not easily transferred to a new husband; rather, she must start afresh in a new relationship. Thus, in this traditional situation, the wife has a much greater investment in the specific relationship than the husband does. According to the principle of least interest, then, the husband will have more power because he is less invested in the relationship.

This analysis represented an important advance in understanding marital power. Resources are indeed the key to power in relationships, they argued; however, the *type* of resources is also crucial. Money is not the only important resource in relationships, but its transferability makes it more powerful. Most important, England and Farkas noted that men and women tend to have different types of resources (because of the traditional division of labor and because of the fact that men continue to earn more than women); thus marital power is fundamentally gendered.

Brines (1993, 1994) offers a very different exchange approach to power in marriage. Brines takes issue with the assumption that the principles of exchange are gender neutral—that is, that men and women behave similarly in interaction, that they end up with different outcomes only because they have unequal resources, and that if they had equal resources, their outcomes would be the same. Brines examines a subset of marital decision making—how couples divide responsibility for housework—and asks why women tend to do over 70% of the cleaning, cooking, laundry, and child care, even when they also work outside the home (Bergen 1991; Shelton and John 1993; South and Spitze 1994). This difference has been found to occur across racial groups (Hossain and Roopnarine 1993) and classes (Wright et al. 1992) in the United States, as well as cross-nationally (Sanchez 1993).

Brines (1993, 1994) examines how the relative earnings of husband and wife affect the time each spends on housework. Her findings are fascinating. When the couple divides paid and unpaid work in traditional ways (i.e., the husband is the primary earner and his wife is dependent on him for financial support), housework is distributed according to the predictions of exchange theory: women do the majority of the housework, and men do very little. However, when the division of labor is nontraditional—when the woman is the primary breadwinner and the man is economically dependent on her—the man, on average, does *not* do the majority of the housework. In fact, these dependent men actually do *less* housework on average than many of their employed brothers—a finding that runs directly counter to exchange theory predictions.

How to explain these counterintuitive findings? Brines (1993) interprets these patterns as evidence of a "symbolic exchange" that operates along with the economic exchange predicted by exchange theory. She argues that marriage is an institution through which women and men can display masculinity and femininity—in other words, they can "do gender" in a socially expected and rewarded way. Despite changes in women's workforce participation over the past several decades, "gender accountability among married men remains tied to fulfillment of the provider role, and for wives to one's ability to manage adroitly the custodial and emotional needs of family members" (p. 331). In marriages in which the male earns more than the female, doing gender fits seamlessly with the exchange of resources: Men exchange their financial support for women's housework services, and both are able to fulfill gender expectations at the same time. When women outearn men, however, the situation becomes more complicated. The traditional exchange of money for housework would suggest that the men in these marriages should do the majority of the housework and that the women should do very little. However, doing so would run counter to norms of masculinity and femininity, seriously jeopardizing their ability to do gender.

Brines (1993, 1994) suggests that many of these couples solve this dilemma by distributing housework along traditional lines. In this way, they are able to bolster the gender differences that threaten to be undermined by the blurring of traditional economic roles. Both members of the couple are able to maintain the illusion that they are adhering to gender norms, despite their very nontraditional financial arrangements. Exchange is thus not gender neutral, Brines concludes: The gender of the participants does affect the processes of social exchange.

Interestingly, Brines's work (1994) suggests that doing gender may be more compelling for men than for women, at least when dividing household labor. She found that women's housework decreased steadily as their financial support for their husbands increased. However, men's housework patterns were not linear: Men did less housework when they were the main breadwinner *and* when they were dependent on their wives for support but more housework when financial contributions were relatively equal. Thus women's housework patterns conform better to a traditional exchange model. Why might this be so? Perhaps, Brines speculates, because masculinity is associated with higher status and power than femininity. As a result, crossing gender lines by failing to be the family's main breadwinner threatens to lower men's status significantly. To compensate for not meeting these cultural expectations, men shore up their threatened masculinity by avoiding "feminine" housework. Although crossing gender lines is not nearly as threatening for women as for men (because of the different valuations of masculinity and femininity), women nonetheless continue to do the bulk of the housework in these situations in order to bolster their femininity. Thus doing gender is so compelling that it leads husbands and wives to divide housework in extremely inequitable ways—directly counter to the predictions of exchange theory.

Brines's (1993, 1994) theory seems to work when applied to married couples. But what about people in other types of living situations? South and Spitze investigated this question in their 1994 study of the relationship between housework and marital status. Their findings support Brines's contention that doing gender plays an important role in the allocation of housework. In both married and cohabiting heterosexual couples, women did considerably more housework than men. Moreover, women and men in both types of couples differed in the *types* of work they did: Whereas women performed mostly "female-typed" tasks (cooking, dishwashing, housecleaning, clothes washing and ironing, and shopping), men performed mainly "male-typed" tasks (outdoor chores and car maintenance). In heterosexual couples, then, housework is tightly linked to gender in quality as well as quantity. However, the genderedness of tasks is more extreme in married couples: Married women do far more housework than cohabiting women, and married men do far fewer female-typed tasks than cohabiting men—despite the fact that the household configuration is the same for both types of couples.

Thus being married seems to make the gendered dynamics of household labor even more extreme. The total amount of housework performed in married households is considerably higher than in cohabitors' households; moreover, the allocation of work is more deeply gendered. One explanation for these differences is that marriage brings with it an established set of gendered roles and expectations for each partner. In cohabiting heterosexual relationships, roles are less predetermined, and many of these expectations are less rigid. Aspects of coupled life that are routinized in marriage are available for negotiation in unmarried cohabiting couples. Thus gender is invoked by cohabiting with someone of the opposite sex, but it is invoked even more by the institution of marriage.

If we limit our examination to heterosexual couples, however, we have no way of knowing whether the sex differences we see are the result of sex per se or the result of some other factor. For example, because men often have greater power than women in intimate relationships, it is impossible to tell whether the gendered division of housework is due to sex differences or to power differences. Examining same-sex couples allows us to disentangle these factors and look at gender and power independently. (Note that looking at gay and lesbian couples does not "control" or eliminate the effects of gender in these relationships. However, it does eliminate the sex *differences* present in heterosexual couples.)

As we have seen, heterosexual couples use gender to assign household tasks. Because same-sex couples do not have this built-in difference, they must use other criteria to allocate housework. Kurdek (1993) studied 300 gay, lesbian, and heterosexual married couples and found that the three types of couples have very different patterns of housework allocation. As described above, heterosexual couples tend to follow a pattern of segregation: One partner does the bulk of the household labor, whereas the other does much less, and the tasks of the two partners do not overlap. In contrast, gay male couples tend to follow a pattern of balance: As with married couples, each partner specializes in particular tasks, but unlike married couples, each partner is responsible for an equal number of those tasks. Finally, lesbians seem to follow a pattern of equality: All tasks are equally shared between the partners, either by doing them together or by alternating responsibility for each task. These differences suggest that housework is not an important arena of negotiation for all couples.

The question of why gay men and lesbians follow such different patterns is intriguing. Although we do not know of any research that directly investigates this question, we speculate that the answer may have something to do with the different tasks boys and girls learn to do in their parents' households. A number of studies have found that girls do more household chores than do boys, spending up to twice as much time doing housework during the teenage years (Timmer, Eccles, and O'Brien 1985). Moreover, these tasks are strongly gender stereotyped (Berk 1985). When two women begin living together, each brings experience and skill at a wide range of household tasks. However, when two men begin living together, neither has the same kind of skill at the range of household chores. Developing expertise in particular areas may be easier than increasing skill in all areas; thus specialization may be the more logical outcome. In addition, Blumstein and Schwartz (1983) suggest that lesbians may be especially sensitive to any hint of inequality in task allocation because they reject "a role that has been symbolic of women's low status" (p. 149). Thus lesbians may self-consciously avoid doing gender in the way that heterosexual couples do, because of a heightened sensitivity to power and inequity in relationships. Gay men, on the other hand, may not be as sensitized to these issues. It is interesting to note, however, that income seems to affect the division of household labor in the same way in all three types of couples—in each case, the partner with the higher income does less housework (Howard, Blumstein, and Schwartz 1986)—suggesting that power shapes exchange in same-sex as well as in cross-sex couples.

Finally, it is important to note that financial resources determine whether the allocation of housework within a relationship is even necessary. Those couples who have greater financial resources can simply pay someone else to do their housework for them, avoiding (or at least minimizing) the issue altogether. However, even this contingency is itself deeply influenced by gender. Because of the gendered distribution of jobs and wealth, those couples who are able to afford this option are likely to include one or two men. In other words, heterosexual and gay male couples are likely to have greater financial resources than lesbian couples. Moreover, regardless of the sexual orientation and sex of the employer(s), the person they hire to do their housework is likely to be a woman—and a person of color. Finally, if a heterosexual couple does pay someone else to do their housework, the hiring and supervision of that person is assumed to be the responsibility of the woman. A striking example of this assumption is the failed nominations of Zoe Baird and Kimba Wood to be Attorney General of the United States in 1993. Baird was President Clinton's first choice for the position; her nomination was withdrawn after it was disclosed that she had hired two undocumented workers from Peru as household help. Wood, Clinton's next choice, was forced to withdraw for similar reasons, even though her hiring of an undocumented worker from Trinidad to care for her children was not illegal at the time. Would this issue have been raised if the nominees had been men? Probably not. As Kathleen Brown, treasurer of the state of California, noted at the time,

For every man who has ever been confirmed to a Cabinet position, there has never been the notion of disclosure of his housekeeping arrangement, much less how much time he spent with his child. It has never been on anyone's mind. It just doesn't come up for male nominees to think about their pattern of child care as a matter for disclosure on an FBI search." (Manegold 1993:A6)

Thus the distribution of housework, even when it is performed by an employee, continues to be deeply influenced by gender, class, and race.

The various approaches to marital power described above suggest both the limitations and possibilities of social exchange theory. The theory itself is usually interpreted as gender neutral: Men and women are assumed to behave similarly in similar situations, and no mention is made of the fact that their situations are not usually similar. Some research, of course, does consider gender but usually in the form of sex differences. When such differences are found, there is usually little attempt to explain *why* they occur; interpretation is left open, implying that biological and social causes are equally plausible. This is the approach taken by early social exchange theory explanations of marital power. Men and women were assumed to exchange household labor for financial support; the fact that men are almost always the ones to contribute the income and women are almost always the ones to do the housework was not questioned.

In contrast, England and Farkas's work does take gender seriously. Socialization, ongoing social structural constraints, or both are understood to be sources of gender differences that influence the outcomes of exchange. Brines's work goes even further, incorporating symbolic exchange and gendered social expectations in her account of marital behavior. Some writers, however, have criticized Brines for not going far enough. Hartmann (1993), for example, although lauding Brines's attention to gender, questions her neglect of factors such as sexuality and coercion. She writes,

How does meeting sexual needs complicate the negotiations between women and men over housework? Nor does Brines's review mention domestic violence or wife-battering, rather widespread male behavior that must surely affect the domestic division of labor. Approximately half of women's emergency room admissions are thought to result from battering by men. Evidence suggests that battering often begins when women transgress gender norms. (p. 384)

Hartmann's critique suggests that exchange theorists must expand their idea of resources and pay more attention to power if they are to understand real-world behavior.

It is important to note, however, that Brines's (1993, 1994) study is not an orthodox use of social exchange theory. Brines is really borrowing ideas from another social psychological theory—symbolic interactionism, which we take up in more detail in Chapter 5—to fill in the gaps that exchange theory does not address. Traditional exchange theory is more concerned with concrete resources (whether material, such as money, or immaterial, such as status) and the way individuals use these resources to achieve their goals than with the larger symbolic meaning of those resources. As a result, social exchange theory cannot fully explain the distribution of housework in nontraditional heterosexual couples.

Example 2: Justice, Equity, and Social Exchange. We now turn to justice and equity as another example of a topic in social exchange that has grappled with the question of gender. As we were working on this chapter, a massive earthquake hit the city of Kobe, Japan. Entire sections of the city were destroyed; water, electricity, and other utilities were cut off; thousands of people were killed and many more left homeless. For several days, the city was virtually paralyzed, as frantic rescue efforts continued and the nation struggled to deal with the emergency.

During those first few days, basic resources such as food and water were scarce. Newspaper accounts in the United States described entire families subsisting on a few cups of rice or pieces of fruit. In situations like these, when food is scarce and everyone is hungry, how should food be distributed? What is a fair allocation of a limited resource? This question addresses notions of *justice*, or fairness, which is another major topic of study in social exchange. Issues of justice arise at all levels of social life, from the interpersonal (e.g., the allocation of food in a family, grades in a class, or salaries in an office) to the societal (e.g., the distribution of income or jobs among various groups in a nation, the use of affirmative action to counter past discrimination, or the use of the death penalty as punishment for the most heinous crimes). In each of these arenas, however, justice is an inherently subjective—and cognitive—concept: At issue are people's *perceptions* of fairness. There are many ways in which resources and punishments could be distributed, but not all of these are perceived to be fair. That is not to say that individuals' perceptions are idiosyncratic, however. Social norms strongly influence perceptions of justice. In general, people tend to feel that a situation is just when the actual distribution of rewards and punishments matches their expectations about what they deserve and what they are entitled to. However, these expectations vary depending on the situation, the individual actors involved, their social positions, and the social norms deemed relevant.

Distribution Rule Preferences. According to Eckhoff (1974), five "distribution rules" are commonly used to allocate resources among individuals or groups. First, resources can be divided *equally* among individuals. For example, the food in the Japanese situation described above could be divided into equal portions, and one portion distributed to each person. Second, resources can be allocated to individuals on the basis of *need* such that those who have the greatest need receive the most resources. Thus, after the earthquake, those people who were bigger, hungrier, injured, or otherwise more in need of sustenance would get the most food. Third, an assessment can be made of the contributions each person has made to the group, and resources allocated relative to those contributions, according to the principle of *equity*. For example, the person who has contributed the most—rescued the most earthquake survivors or carried the most water back to the group—would get the largest share of the food. Fourth, resources can be allocated according to *status* such that those with higher status (in this case, perhaps elders, men, or community leaders) receive a greater share of the scarce resources. Finally, fair procedures (such as drawing straws or participating in a contest) can be established such that each person has an *equal opportunity* to get the food, although the final distribution may not in fact be equal.

Which of these rules will apply in a given situation? Most studies of this question involve experiments in which participants are asked to allocate some reward (usually money) between themselves and another person based on their performance on some task. These experiments have found that a range of factors affect people's preferences for various distribution rules (Deutsch 1975; Mikula 1980). These experimental studies are reinforced by large-scale stratification surveys (e.g., Kluegel and Smith 1986) that investigate people's ideas about fairness and inequality.

First, characteristics of the relationship are important. When the relationship is one of friendship and intimacy, when there is a great deal of similarity between individuals, when there is a high expectation of future interaction, or when there is some combination of these, people prefer to use the equality rule (Leventhal, Karuza, and Fry 1980; Greenberg 1978). Equality rules are also preferred when performance is attributed to luck or other external factors beyond an individual's control rather than to individual effort (Wittig, Marks, and Jones 1981) and when preferences have to be stated publicly (Major and Adams 1983). However, when the welfare of individuals is the primary goal or when individuals are dependent on the group for essential needs (as in a family), the need rule is preferred. Notice that in all of these situations, individuals are interdependent—for friendship, support, or resources. In impersonal situations, in contrast—when the parties do not know each other and do not expect to interact in the future or when preferences are private—individuals tend to base their preferences on their own self-interest. In addition, those who perform well prefer equity rules, whereas whose who perform poorly prefer equality rules (Hegtvedt and Markovsky 1995).

Other kinds of contextual factors also affect distribution rule preferences. For example, a number of studies have found cultural differences in rule preferences. In particular, members of collectively oriented Asian cultures (e.g., China, Japan, or India) prefer equality or need-based rules; members of individually oriented Western cultures (e.g., Australia or the United States) prefer equity-based rules (Leung and Bond 1984; Kashima et al. 1988; Murphy-Berman et al. 1984). This preference extends across both interpersonal and macrolevel situations; for example, individuals in the United States also tend to believe that unequal distributions of economic wealth (i.e., distributions believed to be based on equity) are fair because the economic system allows individuals ample opportunity to improve their position through hard work (e.g., Kluegel and Smith 1986).

Not all U.S. citizens believe equally strongly in this "dominant ideology" of economic opportunity, however. An individual's position in various stratification hierarchies has also been found to affect preferences for particular distribution rules. In exchange experiments, people in advantaged or powerful positions are likely to perceive an unequal distribution as just, whereas those in disadvantaged positions are likely to feel it is unjust (Cook and Hegtvedt 1986; Stolte 1987). These experimental findings are echoed by studies of perceptions of fairness outside the laboratory. For example, people in lower social classes are less likely to perceive inequality to be fair (e.g., Robinson and Bell 1978) and more likely to prefer an economic distribution based on need than are people in upper classes (Form and Hanson 1985; Kluegel and Smith 1986). People in lower socioeconomic groups are also less likely to believe that people in general, and themselves in particular, have a fair opportunity to get ahead (Kluegel and Smith 1986). Race and gender have also been found to affect perceptions of inequality and fairness. Kluegel and Smith (1986) report that blacks are far more likely than whites to express doubts about the fairness of the American stratification system. Their study also found similar, although smaller, differences between women and men: In general, women believed the economic system to be less fair than did men. In addition, race, sex, and class interact to produce variation in belief among groups. For example, wealthier whites (and, to a lesser extent, wealthier blacks) had more faith in the economic system than did poorer whites (and blacks). Black men perceived more opportunities for blacks and the poor than did black women. Despite these differences, however, faith in the existing system of economic distribution is surprisingly high. In every social group, most people do not question the dominant ideology that economic inequality is necessary and fair and that individuals are responsible for their economic position. Although they may question the fairness of the economic system for specific groups (e.g., people of color, women, or the poor) or for themselves as individuals, "Most Americans believe that economic inequality is just in principle, and correspondingly, endorse individual and societal equity as just criteria for the distribution of income" (Kluegel and Smith 1986:141).

We must note, however, that much of this research on group differences in stratification beliefs has been conducted outside the mainstream of social psychology. In particular, sociologists have been much more actively interested in these questions than have psychologists. Within social psychology, most of the research on group differences has focused on gender, perhaps because researchers have fewer qualms about exposing power differences between men and women than between racial categories and are more comfortable attributing these differences to "innate" qualities of women and men. Many studies (Kahn, Nelson, and Gaeddert 1980; Major and Deaux 1982) find gender differences in rule preferences:

> When asked to split rewards between themselves and a partner with performance inferior to theirs, men tend to allocate the rewards equitably (i.e., in proportion to inputs or performance) whereas women tend to allocate the rewards equally. When the partner's performance is superior to theirs, both men and women tend to divide rewards equitably, but women generally take less for themselves than men do. Even when the allocator's and partner's performances are equal . . . women tend to take less reward for themselves and give more to their partners than men do. (Major 1987:126)

In short, women seem to engage in "hyperpoliteness," always allocating less to themselves than men.

How can these differences in allocation be explained? Kahn and Gaeddert's (1985) review concludes that there are at least four explanations. The first proposes that both men and women use the equity rule when allocating resources, but each sex (for unspecified reasons) considers different factors to be relevant when calculating investments. For example, men may consider skill to be more relevant, whereas women may consider participation or effort to be more relevant.

A second approach (e.g., Deaux 1976; Kahn et al. 1980; Sampson 1975) takes at face value the claim that women and men prefer different distribution rules and focuses instead on the causes for this difference. Males and females, according to this approach, have different desires, goals, and motivations (as a result of biology or socialization). For example, a great deal of research has suggested that men tend to be *agentic;* in other words, their motives center around achievement and success. Women, in contrast, tend to be more *communal,* having motives that focus on interpersonal relationships, intimacy, and attachment (Carlson 1971). These different motives lead to different allocation strategies: Agentic goals are best met through equity, and communal goals through equality.

As we have noted throughout this book, however, an observation of gender differences does not mean that *sex* itself is the causal variable. A more sophisticated approach to gender takes a correlation between sex and other variables as something to be explained rather than as an explanation in itself. For example, Watts, Messe, and Vallacher (1982) tried to disentangle the relationship between sex, motivation, and the distribution of resources. They found that agentic individuals, regardless of their sex, distributed rewards more competitively. In contrast, those who had a communal orientation distributed rewards more equally. The researchers concluded that although men and women tended to allocate rewards differently, the cause was not sex per se but sex-related differences in agentic or communal motives.

A third perspective suggests that other researchers have overlooked an important confounding variable in allocation research: the sex of the stimulus person (i.e., the person with whom the participant is interacting in an experiment). Most allocation research has been based on same-sex dyads: Men are asked to interact with other men and women with other women. This perspective suggests that the sex differences in allocation found in these experiments are due not to the sex of the *research participant* but to the sex of the *stimulus person* (Hansen and O'Leary 1983). In other words, the differences observed between male and female allocators are due not to some internal difference between males and females but to social expectations about how people (of either sex) should interact with males and females. As Kahn and Gaeddert (1985) summarize this hypothesis, "Women and men do not necessarily have different conceptions of how to solve the distribution problem, but all people solve the problem differently when they interact with women than when they interact with men" (p. 133).

Finally, the fourth perspective argues that power and status are the real confounding variables in studies of justice (Unger 1976, 1978; Meeker and Weitzel-O'Neill 1977). As noted earlier, those in advantaged positions in a stratification system tend to prefer distribution rules based on equity, whereas those in less advantaged positions tend to prefer equality or need-based rules. Because gender and power are correlated, we see a similar difference in preference for distribution rules. Thus again, gender differences are not the result of sex per se but of the fact that men tend to be more powerful than women.

In summary, distribution rule preferences seem to vary depending on the characteristics and relationship of the persons involved, the goals of the distribution, and the social context. The observation of gender differences in these experiments has stimulated extensive research; however, exploring these differences further has demonstrated that exchanges are far from gender neutral. The same conclusion can be drawn from research on perceptions of fairness, to which we now turn.

The Equity of Exchange. Matching a given distribution rule does not ensure that a situation will be perceived as fair. As we have noted, many objectively equal situations are perceived as unfair, and many unequal situations are widely perceived to be just. In other cases, it is difficult to assess what factors should be considered in determining fairness. How are perceptions of fairness developed?

The distribution of housework is an example of a seemingly unfair exchange. As discussed earlier, research on heterosexual couples consistently shows that women perform far more housework than men do, regardless of the amount of paid work either partner does outside the home. Is this situation fair? If we use a principle of equality to evaluate this situation, it is clearly not fair; housework is rarely distributed equally. Nor is housework distributed according to need or equal opportunity. If we examine traditional couples, where the man works for pay outside the home and the woman works inside the home, it can appear that housework is distributed according to a principle of equity: The person who contributes more economic support to the household is rewarded by being relieved of household chores. However, if we look at dual-earner couples, the principle of equity breaks down. Even when both partners work an equal number of hours outside the home, wives do the majority of the housework. And as Brines (1993, 1994) found, when wives are the main breadwinners for the family, their husbands do even less housework than other married men. The distribution of housework, then, does not seem to follow any rule of just distribution.

However, as we noted above, justice is based on subjective perceptions of fairness rather than on objective distributions of time or money. Thus it is appropriate to ask whether women (or men) feel that this skewed distribution of labor is unfair. Interestingly, the answer to this question appears to be no. On average, both women and men report that they are generally satisfied with the existing distribution of housework in their families, even though they recognize that it may be inequitable (Spitze 1988; Thompson 1991; Major 1993). In fact, a similar statement can be made about women's pay in the work world: Although women consistently earn less than men for comparable jobs, they report very little sense of injustice (Crosby 1982; Major 1987, 1989).

How can this be? How can a situation that appears unfair according to every rule of justice discussed above be considered fair by the people involved? The traditional explanation for this phenomenon attributes this sense of fairness to sex differences: Men and women are simply different and want different things from their work and family relationships. In other words, women simply enjoy housework or are more concerned with the communal good or wish to maximize the interpersonal harmony of their relationships; men, in contrast, like housework less, are less competent at it, are more concerned with agentic goals, and wish to maximize material rewards.

Major (1987, 1993; see also Thompson 1991) proposes a different explanation. She suggests that evaluations of fairness do not simply take into account the distribution of rewards within a particular relationship but also include comparisons to other relationships and existing social norms, as well as an assessment of the fairness of the procedures used to allocate labor. Major (1987) proposes "that women and men use different comparative referents when they evaluate their existing outcomes or when they estimate what they deserve or are entitled to receive" (p. 125). Specifically, they use different *social comparisons:* They compare their contribution to housework not with their spouses but with others of the same sex:

> To the extent that wives compare their family work load with that of other women, rather than that of their husbands, or other men, they may feel that they are doing the amount of work that they should. Similarly, to the extent that wives compare their husbands' family work with the amount of work done by other husbands, rather than with the amount of work done by themselves, they may feel that their husband is doing no less than he should. (Major 1993: 148-9)

Normative comparisons also come into play when evaluating the household division of labor. According to this view, "awareness of what is a socially acceptable or appropriate distribution creates the expectation that this is the level of distribution one is entitled to" (Major 1993:150). Despite changes in gender expectations over the last several decades, research shows that both women and men still consider housework to be "women's work" (Thompson and Walker 1989). Thus women may feel that an unequal distribution of labor is fair because it accords with prevailing norms about gender roles.

Third, *feasibility comparisons* play a role in perceptions of fairness. Exchange theorists argue that the availability of attractive alternatives is important when evaluating a situation. Wives, in particular, may evaluate unequal distributions of labor as fair relative to the possible alternatives—which may involve giving up paid employment (Spitze 1988), dealing with increased marital conflict (Thompson and Walker 1989), or even divorce.

Finally, *self-comparisons*, or comparisons of current outcomes with outcomes received in the past, are also relevant. Research shows that gender differences in housework exist even for boys and girls living in their parents' homes (South and Spitze 1994); thus women's greater contribution may be proportional to their contributions in other settings. Because women's housework level decreases when they are employed (although men's does not increase to compensate), women who work outside the home may feel that their contribution to housework is fair because they have done more in the past.

Major also believes that notions of fairness are affected by the perceived legitimacy of allocation procedures. For example, if women believe they had a "voice" in the decision-making process that led to the existing distribution or if they believe some goal other than fairness is served by the distribution (e.g., communal welfare, closeness, or caring), they may believe an objectively unjust distribution to be fair. Moreover, Ferree (1991) notes that the meaning attributed to work inside and outside of the home is important. In households where wives work outside the home, their income is frequently considered "supplementary," even if it is crucial to the family's economic survival. Men are still considered to have primary responsibility for breadwinning, regardless of the wife's income. These conceptions of responsibility may legitimize the uneven division of labor.

Thus attempting to understand the gendered dynamics of housework exposes some of the weaknesses of social exchange theory. To explain differences in perceptions of just distributions of housework, scholars have been forced to go far afield from the tenets of exchange theory. Specifically, understanding perceptions of justice necessitates understanding how people think about what is fair. The types of cognition included in explanations for justice preferences go far beyond consideration and choice, the cognitive processes usually included in exchange theory models. Thus the example of justice, like the example of the household division of labor, suggests that a synthesis of multiple theories may be more powerful than any single theory alone.

Conclusion

Although social exchange theory is based on principles assumed to be gender neutral, researchers have found that human behavior does not always conform to these principles. Gender frequently throws a wrench into the workings of the theory, and explaining sex differences in behavior may require bringing in other theories, such as social cognition and symbolic interactionism. We explore these theories further in the following chapters.

Social exchange theory could be combined with any of the perspectives on gender discussed in Chapter 2. Women and men might behave differently because they are innately different or because they have been socialized differently or because they find themselves in different structural positions. Indeed, social exchange theory is strongest in its conceptualization of social structure as a primary determinant of human behavior. Social exchange theory also could be compatible with social constructionist approaches to gender if it were combined with other theories that attend to the symbolic realm. Brines (1993, 1994) for example, integrates exchange theory with symbolic interactionism, arguing that men and women behave differently because they are negotiating not only economic resources but also gender expectations and performances.

A number of other theorists have seen the same potential for combining social exchange theory and symbolic interactionism. Triandis (1976), for example, questions exchange theory's neglect of the question of value. What do people find rewarding? How can we account for differences and similarities between people in their perceptions of rewards and costs? Triandis argues that to answer these questions, we must look beyond social exchange theory and explore the *meaning* of particular resources, a task for which symbolic interactionism is well suited, as we discuss further in Chapter 5. Kollock and O'Brien (1992) note the ways in which social exchanges are themselves socially constructed. "Minds are private and reliable information is a costly commodity. For these reasons information asymmetries often exist between exchange partners" (p. 89). As a result, exchange partners must constantly gather information abut the resources of their exchange partners and at the same time control the information they provide to others about their own resources. Thus the management of information and impressions becomes crucial to the process of exchange. This kind of impression management is the realm of symbolic interactionism, not of exchange theory. Thus Kollock and O'Brien suggest that a combination of the two theories is more powerful than social exchange theory alone.

With its emphasis on relationships, structure, interdependence, and power, social exchange theory has the potential to add a great deal to our understanding of gender. However, social exchange *research* has not yet explored this potential. For example, although some versions of the theory focus on power as a central determinant of social behavior, in practice, researchers have ignored the social statuses—such as gender, race, and class—that are central to power in the world outside the experimental laboratory. Indeed, Turner (1982) notes that Marx's theory of class conflict is "a variety of exchange theory" (p. 231), yet social exchange theorists have rarely examined social class in any real-world sense.

Why is there such a disjuncture between social exchange theory and research? We have discussed one reason earlier: a dominant research paradigm that emphasizes tightly controlled research procedures and discrete, easily measurable variables. Although the theory focuses on relationships between people, the experimental procedures typically sanitize interaction to such an extent that the participants may never see, hear, or talk to each other. As a result, the *process* of interaction—which might be described as the process of "doing exchange"—disappears. In addition, exchange researchers tend to focus on individual-level manifestations of supposedly multilevel processes and limit their analysis to dyadic or small-group interaction rather than examining social groups, organizations, and institutions. Furthermore, we speculate that social exchange theory (like other contemporary scholarship) is influenced by its location within a capitalist market economy. The assumptions inherent in this kind of economic system tend to shift researchers' attention toward marketlike transactions between individuals and away from potential unfairness and inequality.

Finally, exchange theory performs best when analyzing the exchange of quantifiable factors, such as dollars of income or hours of housework. As we have seen, the theory proves more problematic when symbolic factors, such as the value of doing gender (or race or class) appropriately, are considered. This is not to imply that gender, race, and class are *only* symbolic markers. Each has very real material consequences, for both individuals and social groups. Nonetheless, although it is relatively easy to include rudimentary measures of gender, race, and class in exchange studies (by measuring the participant's sex, racial category, and dollars of income or occupation), capturing the full symbolic import of these categories is far more difficult. Factors such as gender identity or race-based prejudice do not fit easily into exchange theory equations, and thus the symbolic meanings of group membership are often neglected.

Social exchange theory does not address any of these social positions in great depth, but race has been particularly invisible. For example, the most recent review of exchange theory and research (Molm and Cook 1995) includes no mention of race or ethnicity in the 26-page chapter.[2] This gap seems curious, particularly given exchange theory's focus on social structure and power. We suggest two explanations for the invisibility of race in social exchange theory.

First, exchange theory is especially ill equipped to deal with race because of the theory's conceptualization of social actors. Individuals, according to exchange theory, come to the marketplace of interaction essentially as equals. They may have different amounts or types of resources or different structural positions, but they are otherwise interchangeable. The theory implies that these resources and positions are not permanently attached to individuals; they are malleable and transferable. The meaning of these resources, and the other personal or group characteristics of individuals, are not central. This allows the exchange theorist to ignore the more insidious consequences of social positions. According to exchange theory, women and men, whites and people of color, people from the working class and people from the upper class, appear different only insofar as they hold different resources. This approach fits neatly with what Frankenberg (1993) has called "color evasion." She writes, "For many people in the United States . . . 'color-blindness'—a mode of thinking about race organized around an effort not to 'see,' or at any rate not to acknowledge, race differences—continues to be the 'polite' language of race" (p. 142). More than any other social psychological theory, the assumptions of exchange theory mirror this practice of color evasion; race becomes essentially invisible and unexamined.

Second, the neglect of race (and class) in social exchange research parallels their neglect throughout social psychology and academia more generally. As we noted in Chapter 2, this pattern is due in part to the composition of the academy: Although the proportion of women faculty and students has increased dramatically in recent years, the proportion of people of color and members of the poor and working classes working as professional academics and researchers remains shockingly low. Although Marxist academics have always believed social class to be central to understanding social life, their influence on other scholars has been relatively limited. Thus although individual researchers have studied race and class, there is still relatively little pressure on the mainstream of academia to take these issues seriously.

As we have noted, social exchange theory has a number of significant problems, as well as a number of potential strengths. Nonetheless, it remains one of the most influential theories in social psychology and the social sciences more generally. On the basis of our discussion above, we suggest that the most fruitful direction for social exchange theory may involve integration with other social psychological theories. We now turn to one such theory: social cognition.

Notes

1. In fact, Bandura (1986) has renamed his theory "social cognitive theory" to more precisely reflect its model of behavior.

2. This gap mirrors the tendency to neglect race and ethnicity in social psychology more generally. In their introduction to the book in which this review is located, a volume that represents the state of the discipline of sociological social psychology, the editors note that their "biggest disappointment in the volume was [their] inability, despite prolonged efforts, to obtain a chapter on 'Race, Ethnic, and Intergroup Relations' " (Cook, Fine, and House 1995:ix).

CHAPTER 4

Social Cognition

In the spring of 1994, a renowned athlete and public figure captured the attention of virtually the entire U.S. population. O. J. Simpson was accused of murdering his ex-wife, Nicole Brown Simpson, and her friend, Ron Goldman. TV cameras broadcast a bizarre slow-motion chase scene on the Los Angeles freeways. Millions of people speculated about his guilt or innocence. Some focused on the fact that throughout their relationship Simpson had been accused of physically abusing his wife. Others analyzed the debacle in terms of the racial dynamics: What did it mean that Simpson is black, his former wife, white? During jury selection, both defense and prosecution cynically observed that they thought most of the prospective jurors were lying. By the time the trial was concluded in October 1995, all involved—and millions of others—agreed that the media played far too influential a role in framing public debate about the incident. This tragedy sank to the depths of public spectacle.

Definition

However one views it, this incident illustrates many of the features of social cognition, the perspective we present in this chapter. In reacting to this event, the actors involved, the jurors, and the general public drew on cognitive schemas about gender, race, and class to form particular judgments—evaluations of the character of Simpson and possibly of his ex-wife, assessments of the competence of those brought in to testify and of the attorneys for both sides, attributions about the cause of the murders, and judgments of responsibility about and appropriate punishments for these crimes. Cognitive schemas, cognitive judgments, and the processes through which we form those judgments—these are the components of social cognition. *Social cognition* is a theory of how we process information; the term refers both to the name of the theory and to the process itself.

Traditionally, social cognition has emphasized psychological, intraindividual aspects of human thought. Thus psychologists Fiske and Taylor (1991) define social cognition as "the study of how people make sense of other people and themselves" (p. 1). Social cognition describes the elements of thought and how those elements come into play as people process the rich array of social information they encounter daily. Social cognition theorists have begun to pay more attention to the social contexts in which people think. As we present the key principles of this perspective, we pay special attention to these *social* aspects of thought. We consider not only the elements and organization of human thought but also how knowledge is created, shared, affirmed, and changed. We address not only the major steps in processing information but also how social forces shape these processes. We emphasize how individual cognitive processes shape social action. We weave into our discussion examples that illustrate the treatment of gender, in its particular intersections with race, class, and sexuality, in social cognition.

Working Assumptions of Social Cognition

In the previous chapter, we noted that behaviorism does not attend to cognition; the effect of the environment on behavior is assumed to be unmediated by thought. In contrast, social cognition assumes that how we think about the world around us shapes how we feel and how we behave. One interpretation of *Oleanna*, for example, suggests that the student does not automatically perceive the professor's embrace as inappropriate; it is only after she thinks about it, and thinks about it within particular cognitive frameworks provided to her by her friends, that she decides she has been sexually harassed.

If behavior depends on human thought, our minds must be continually active. Human cognitive capacities are limited, however. We cannot possibly attend to or remember all the information to which we are exposed in the course of daily life. Were we to try, we would experience "cognitive overload." Anyone who has ever crammed for an exam or tried to coordinate too many professional and family commitments has experienced this state. Thus a second assumption of social cognition is that we often behave as "cognitive misers," streamlining information to manage the demands of everyday interaction. As we shall see, the metaphor of the human being as cognitive miser underlies many of the principles of social cognition.

One of the ways we manage this need for cognitive efficiency is by categorizing information. We categorize information about people, objects, and situations before we store it in memory, retrieve it from memory, or use this information in forming judgments. Categories allow us to organize, store, and retrieve information considerably more efficiently. Without categorization, we would experience cognitive overload. There are, of course, costs to categorization. The very act of categorizing people means defining them in terms of a subset of their characteristics, whether it be their hair color, that they have children, or their racial identities. To categorize is usually to reduce; potentially valuable information is lost in such summaries. Moreover, to categorize is also often to evaluate. Categorization is almost always accompanied by evaluations of some categories as better or worse than others, particularly when they refer to human groups. The differential evaluation of social categories may well reflect prevailing political values; we do not maintain that this is inherent to the process of categorization. Nonetheless, the two almost always go together. Because categorization may be cognitively unavoidable, it may be more fruitful to explore how the principles of categorization could be used to undermine systematic devaluation of certain groups than to try to eliminate this process.

Thus social cognition rests on three assumptions: first, that the influence of the social environment on human behavior is mediated by thought; second, that the limits of human cognitive capacities lead us to behave as cognitive misers; and third, that this need for cognitive efficiency leads to a fundamental reliance on categorization. In the next section, we describe the basic building blocks of human thought—cognitive structures. These structures provide the bases for categorization.

The Organization of Thought

Early approaches to social cognition identified beliefs, attitudes, and values as the major elements of thought (Bem 1970). These constructs emphasize the content and evaluation rather than the organization of thought. Contemporary social cognition emphasizes instead the organization of thought in cognitive structures; social schemas are the primary forms of cognitive structure. Gender has been an important theme in both approaches. We begin by discussing attitudes, emphasizing attitudes about significant social categories, and then turn to an extended discussion of social schemas.

Attitudes

Attitudes are evaluations of a specific object or concept. Social psychologists posit that attitudes conform to a principle of consistency: Social actors are motivated to seek consistency among our attitudes, feelings, and behaviors (Festinger 1957). Attitudes, therefore, should shape human behavior. If a prospective juror for a trial such as the Simpson case expressed a strong positive attitude toward blacks, coupled with the belief that blacks tend to be treated unjustly by the criminal justice system, for example, the prosecutor would be likely to assume that the juror's attitudes would shape her vote in the jury room and therefore dismiss her. Research results, however, have never fully supported the prediction of attitude-behavior consistency. In an early review of research in this area, Wicker (1969) reported that attitudes explained only 10% of the variability in behavior. Although social psychologists are considerably better able to predict behavior from attitudes in the 1990s than they were in the 1960s (due primarily to more adequate measurement procedures), it is clear that knowledge of attitudes and other cognitions may be necessary, but not sufficient, to predict behavior. The immediacy of situations and factors such as the opinions of others also shape human behavior, as examples in the next section illustrate, sometimes overriding the effects of individual attitudes.

Social psychologists have developed measures of attitudes toward members of particular social categories. Attitudes toward both women and blacks began to receive attention in the 1970s, in response to the civil rights and women's movements. Measures such as the Attitudes Toward Women Scale, or ATW (Spence and Helmreich 1972), are among the most widely used of the thousands of social psychological scales.

Attitudes toward women have been assessed in terms of the endorsement of gender-prescribed roles. Take, for example, an item from the ATW scale: "Women should be concerned with their duties of childbearing and house tending, rather than with desires for professional and business careers." Women tend to have less traditional attitudes than do men on such scales. Interestingly, attitudes toward blacks have focused not on role-based prescriptions of behavior but, rather, on general evaluations. One prong of this research has focused on attitudes of members of different racial minority groups toward their own and other racial groups. A literature on racial attitudes of children (Stephan and Rosenfield 1982) shows that both white and black children attribute positive traits (e.g., clean, nice, smart) more often to whites than they do to blacks; this pattern is stronger among white children than among black children, however, and blacks' tendency to follow this pattern declines with age. These patterns have been interpreted as signs of black self-rejection, but this interpretation seems simplistic. Many studies have shown that black adults have self-esteem (a self-attitude) equal to or greater than that of whites (see Hughes and Demo 1989).

A second prong of work on racial attitudes addresses the changing nature of racism. Focusing on relations between blacks and whites, Sears (1988), for example, is one of many who have suggested that "symbolic racism" (antiblack sentiment and beliefs that blacks violate American values of self-reliance, a work ethic, and discipline) is replacing "old-fashioned racism," or open bigotry. Thus research on attitudes toward blacks is oriented to real-world social conflicts; research on attitudes toward women, in contrast, emphasizes accommodation to social roles. Note that both literatures, however, focus on attitudes toward those in the less powerful position of a social category—women in a gender system, blacks in a racial system. Attitudes about men and about whites have received considerably less attention.

Social Schemas

Attitudes emphasize the content of thought and the evaluation of that content. *Cognitive schemas*, in contrast, emphasize the organization of social information. Schemas store and organize information about a particular object or concept. A schema for one's mother, for example, includes what one perceives as her typical attributes, ways of behaving, common emotions, interactional styles, and the relationships between these. Schemas are abstract. They serve as theories, as preconceptions that drive cognitive processes. The construction of social schemas is precisely what allows us to think as cognitive misers. Through schemas, people simplify reality, interpreting specific instances in light of a general category. We create schemas for other persons, for ourselves, for social groups, and for social situations.

Schemas are vital for processing information. Schemas influence what information we attend to and what information we do not "see" in social situations. Schemas shape the storage and retrieval of information from memory; we store new information in categories determined by our existing schemas, and we retrieve already stored information from schemas relevant to the situation.

Cognitive schemas about the professor-student relationship, for example, may guide some viewers of *Oleanna* to almost not notice the short embrace in Scene 1. To those who view professors primarily as mentors, this gesture appears to be a supportive hug. Viewers whose schemas about the professor-student relationship emphasize the potential abuse of power differences may perceive this gesture as a sexual advance. What each viewer perceives will dictate how she or he responds later in the play. As we combine new and existing information to make inferences, schemas guide what information we select and how we form judgments. Those who have a well-developed cognitive schema for wife abuse, for example, are likely to have formed their opinions about the Simpson trial on the evidence of abuse in the Simpsons' marriage; at the same time, such onlookers may have ignored other information emphasized by the defense—for example, evidence of racial prejudice on the part of key police officials.

Thus we rely heavily on preexisting schemas both when we encounter new information and when we interact in familiar situations. One consequence of this reliance is what Ellen Langer (1989) calls "mindlessness." When we process information through schemas, we pay less careful attention to the details of the situation. We behave in accord with what our schemas lead us to expect (Langer, Blank, and Chanowitz 1978). When someone replies to our absent-minded "how are you?" with an honest "not so well," often we respond with an equally absent-minded, and inappropriate, "good." The implications of this default inattention are not trivial. When we process information mindlessly, we are less likely to notice or retain disconfirming information, such as the "not so well" in this hypothetical encounter.

It is important to note that social schemas are more likely to shape cognitive judgments when some degree of interpretation is required. When situational information is extremely clear, people usually rely on that information in forming their judgments. When the situation is ambiguous (probably the more typical pattern), schemas are one important basis on which ambiguity is resolved (Baron, Albright, and Malloy 1995).

Cognitive schemas thus contribute to the perpetuation of social expectations. When we process information in terms of preexisting schemas, we are likely to see and remember information that is consistent with those schemas. When we make judgments on the basis of schemas, we are likely to make judgments that confirm those schemas. Schematic information processing is a highly reproductive cognitive system. Through the influence of social schemas, we perpetuate both our individual and societal expectations about others. This is one consequence of the need for cognitive efficiency. If schemas did not reduce the dense array of social information into a more streamlined package, if schemas were not resilient and highly resistant to change, they would not serve the needs of the cognitive miser. As we elaborate below, these cognitive tendencies are the cognitive underpinnings of social stratification.

Self-Schemas. The social cognitive perspective on gender and other social categories is reflected in two types of schemas—schemas about ourselves and schemas about social groups. *Self-schemas* include organized knowledge about the self. From the social cognitive perspective, self-schemas represent identity, our answers to the question, Who am I? (The term *identity* is used in various ways by different social psychologies; we revisit this term in Chapter 5.) In contrast to social exchange theory, which lacks a theory of self and identity, social cognition has devoted a great deal of attention to elaborating the nature of self and identity. Self-schemas include the characteristics, preferences, goals, and behavior patterns we come to associate with ourselves.

Gender Self-Schemas. Development of a self-schema based on gender means that gender is a central system of classification in one's self-concept. (Gender can also be the basis for a group schema; in this case, one classifies other people, behaviors, and situations on the basis of polarized conceptions of masculinity and femininity. We return to this broader conception below.)

Developing measures of constructs such as personality, identity, attitude, or schema presents a formidable methodological challenge. Cognitions are inherently unobservable. Unlike behavior, thought cannot be seen. Therefore, it is necessary to look for indirect traces of these hypothesized constructs. The first test of gendered personality, the M-F test developed by Terman and Miles (1936), demonstrates several of the problems that arise in measuring unobservable constructs. Virtually all of the items on this test are easily identifiable as more typical either of males or of females. For example, femininity points can be acquired by saying one is afraid of the dark or careful about how one dresses. Masculinity points are earned by saying one is able to stand pain or was disobedient as a child. If respondents are well versed in the norms and expectations of Western culture, they know which responses are appropriate for their sex. Hence responses may reflect the pressures of social norms rather than respondents' underlying personalities. Moreover, the method of scoring represents masculinity and femininity as opposite ends of a single dimension. One can be either feminine or masculine but never both or neither. Thus the design of this instrument necessarily produces the appearance of significant personality differences between women and men.

The Bem Sex-Role Inventory (BSRI), one of the most important developments in measures of gender identity, challenged each of these assumptions. As we noted in Chapter 2, the BSRI was developed by Sandra Bem (1974) to assess psychological androgyny, a self-concept that incorporates both masculinity and femininity. Responses can range from high to low on both dimensions, thus challenging the idea that gender is a single dimension. That individuals may have little of either femininity or masculinity marks the first recognition that not all people form self-schemas on the dimension of gender. In other words, for some people, gender is a central part of who they are, and for others, it is less so. Although the concept of androgyny has been severely criticized, as we discussed in Chapter 2, this was an important step in the conceptualization of gender identity.

Hazel Markus (Markus et al. 1982) was one of the first to conduct empirical studies explicitly addressing self-schemas about gender. Markus assessed the extent to which individuals develop self-schemas about their gender and how these schemas influence subsequent information processing. Markus used the BSRI to assess gender schemas, then used gender schemas to predict various consequences of cognitive processing. Such consequences include the ability to supply behavioral examples of one's gender self-schema—for example, instances of one's nurturance or how well one remembers information consistent or inconsistent with one's gender self-schema.

The potential utility of the concept of gender schemas has only begun to be realized. In analyzing variations in the strength of people's gender self-schemas, we could begin to trace how gender is culturally constructed. In contemporary Western society, for example, it is virtually impossible to avoid the labeling of many experiences in terms of gender: The way people drive, the way we throw a ball, the way we talk, all are accountable in terms of gendered expectations. Identification of those environments that might promote or minimize the significance of gender as a central way of defining the self would be an extremely important contribution to a theory of gender (although we know of no such research at present).

We should acknowledge that such questions are being asked only at the frontier of social cognition. Reflecting the deeply essentialist legacy of modern conceptions of gender (as well as of identity), gender self-schemas have been treated as if they are static and transcend situations. In reality, the salience of gender varies across situations as well as across individuals. Being charged with sexual harassment is likely to heighten the salience of gender for any man; in contrast, one's gender is likely not to be salient when one is stuck in a traffic jam. Self-schemas, of course, can shape what situations we put ourselves in; Bem and Lenney (1976) demonstrated that women and men with strong gender self-schemas actually avoid even minor activities that contradict those schemas—for example, for women, oiling a squeaky hinge. The salience of gender schemas also varies across the life span; research suggests that gender is less salient for all individuals when they are very young and very old. One likely explanation is that the meaning of gender is closely related to the social significance of reproduction; reproductive potential is inactive during the early and later years of the typical life span.

Racial Self-Schemas. As we have noted above and in Chapter 2, the social psychological literature has tended to treat gender as a neutral and functional difference. In contrast, this literature has theorized racial difference more often in terms of structural and interactional inequalities. Accordingly, no research on racial self-schemas directly parallels the concept of gender self-schemas. Scales that measure attributes of self in terms of racial polarities, for example, do not exist. This is due in part to the assumption that gender is dichotomous, whereas there are multiple racial and ethnic groups. More important, a structural approach to racial identity points away from a sense of racial identity as essential and natural and toward a focus on contextual influences.

Some research explores situational variations in the salience of one's race and the extent to which race is encoded into one's sense of self. McGuire et al. (1978) reported that only 1% of the Anglo students at a predominantly Anglo high school spontaneously mentioned their race in describing themselves. In contrast, 17% of the blacks and 14% of the Latinos mentioned their racial or ethnic background. (Similarly, men are more likely to mention being male when they come from predominantly female families.) In other words, social contexts shape the salience of social identities. A number of studies attest to the influence of context on racial and ethnic identity (see Phinney 1990).

Some recent studies address the effects of sustained historical and material circumstances on the development of racial identities. Hurtado, Gurin, and Peng (1994) explore the development of identities among persons of Mexican origin living in the United States. Chicana/os (longer-term residents who are U.S. citizens) make more numerous social categorizations of themselves and others (e.g., in terms of skin color, family roles, citizenship, language fluency, occupation, and so forth) than do first-generation immigrants. Hurtado et al. attribute these patterns to the different structural and historical conditions of these groups. Chicana/os are more competent in English, are more dispersed geographically, and work in a wider range of occupations; in short, they are located in more variable social structures than are first-generation immigrants, who tend to have much more limited intergroup contact.

One of the most prominent research questions concerns racial patterns of self-esteem or the valence of one's attitudes toward one's self. (Interestingly, this is a question rarely asked about gender.) Although early studies assumed that identifying with a low-status group would result in low self-regard, most of the empirical research suggests that those who identify more strongly with their racial and ethnic minority groups have higher self-esteem (Crocker and Major 1989; and see Phinney 1990).

There has been virtually no research on the intersections of racial and gender identities. The few exceptions to this pattern suggest that women may be more actively involved than men in sustaining ethnic identities; women, that is, may be the carriers of ethnic traditions (see Phinney 1990). Moreover, there has been no research on self-schemas about social class positions or about sexual identity.

Schemas of Social Groups. *Group schemas* are a second type of social schema; these include organized information about social roles, such as parent or teacher, and stratification statuses, such as gender, race, age, and class position. These are more often referred to as role schemas. Because *role* implies that these categories serve societal functions, however, we refer to them instead as group schemas. Stereotypes, probably the most widely recognized cognitive construct, are roughly equivalent to group schemas. The processes of categorization and differential evaluation are particularly important to the operation of group schemas and stereotypes.

Categorization. *Categorization* seems to be a pervasive human tendency, as we noted earlier in this chapter. In a series of studies by Henri Tajfel (1981), people consistently formed cognitive groupings on the basis of virtually any characteristic. Whether we think we differ from others in significant social characteristics, such as race or class, or in meaningless capacities, such as our skill at estimating numbers of dots in an ambiguous visual field or in preferences for particular artists, we form in-groups and out-groups. What characteristics are most likely to become the basis of group categorization? The need for cognitive efficiency suggests that we categorize on the basis of readily available information. Gender, race, and age are usually visually evident, hence readily available, characteristics. Prevailing norms of dress, hairstyle, stance, and so forth contribute to the visual prominence of gender and race, and perhaps also of age, class, or sexual orientation. The tweed jacket, jeans, and deck shoes of the professor in *Oleanna* convey a very particular, age-specific, class-specific type of masculinity, for example. Although cognitive efficiency is not the sole basis for gender, racial, age, or class differentiation, it is the cognitive underpinnings of these bases of social stratification.

Categorization can produce cognitive errors. When people encode information on the basis of group characteristics, individual differences are lost. In several studies by Taylor et al. (1978), people listened to a conversation among three black and three white speakers (or among three women and three men). Respondents were likely to make mistakes in remembering which black speaker and which white speaker (or which woman and which man) said what, but they made very few errors in identifying the race (or gender) of the speaker. Group membership also has consistent effects on cognitions, emotions, and behaviors. People show marked preferences for members of their own in-groups and marked biases against members of out-groups in allocating money and other valued goods, in evaluating the abilities and characteristics of others, and in assumptions about what beliefs they might have in common. Categorization even affects how we gather information: We are less likely to seek information about out-group members and therefore tend to have much less complex conceptions of out-groups than of in-groups.

Gender Group Schemas. As we noted in Chapter 2, the earliest research on gender group schemas focused on personality attributes, reporting that men are generally rated high on instrumental attributes such as objectivity or competitiveness, whereas women are rated high on expressive attributes such as tact and being aware of feelings of others (Broverman et al. 1972). More recent studies continue to show widespread support for these patterns across a wide variety of populations. Traits are not the only component of gender group schemas. Deaux and Lewis (1984) report that such schemas include role behaviors (financial provider, child care provider), physical characteristics (sturdiness, grace) and occupation, in addition to personality traits.

Beliefs about gender are also represented at different levels of specificity (Deaux 1995); people develop subtypes of both female and male group schemas. The number of recognizable subtypes is considerable; in one series of studies, Ashmore and Del Boca (1986) identified 120 male and 115 female types. The number we commonly use is much smaller: There appear to be at least three common subtypes of women: "the housewife (traditional woman), the professional woman (independent, ambitious, self-confident), and the Playboy bunny (sex object)" (Basow 1992:6). Gender subtypes recognize variation within the schema, yet at the same time reinforce the overall picture of gender as dichoto-mous. Indeed, one might argue that some schemas are so embedded in cultural beliefs that they cannot be challenged, thereby forcing the development of subtypes.

Subtypes are also developed through the intersections of gender with other significant social statuses. Schemas about gender interact with conceptions of race, ethnicity, social class, and age (as we noted in Chapter 2). Stangor et al. (1992), for example, report that people are more likely to categorize others in terms of their race and gender together rather than race or gender alone. Brewer, Dull, and Lui (1981) demonstrated that there are gender subtypes within the general category of age. Respondents identified at least three variations within the general category of elderly person, for example: grandmotherly type, senior citizen, and elder statesman. Brewer et al. found that age-gender subcategories better characterized how respondents conceived of these groups than did age categories alone. Moreover, when pictures were categorized into meaningful groups (all grandmothers, for example) as opposed to being mixed up, respon-dents attributed many more traits to each set of pictures. Brewer et al. (1987) also suggest that the purpose for categorization shapes the nature of such intersec-tions: When desired intimacy of interaction was at issue, gender categorization was more prominent than ethnic categorizations; when perceived similarity to self was at issue, ethnic categorizations were more prominent than gender categorizations.

Racial Group Schemas. Echoing research on gender, personality traits have been the most common indicator of the attributes of racial group schemas, from the earliest studies through contemporary research. For example, in 1933 Katz and Braly assessed white male Princeton students' conceptions of 10 racial, ethnic, and national groups. The students were given a list of 84 traits and asked to indicate the 5 traits that were most typical of each group. (Note that this meas-urement technique forced respondents to endorse some characteristics for each group.) Some examples: Blacks (termed *Negroes* in this study) were believed to be superstitious, lazy, happy-go-lucky, ignorant, and musical; Jews to be shrewd, mercenary, industrious, grasping, and intelligent; and Chinese to be supersti-tious, sly, conservative, tradition loving, and loyal to family ties. "Americans" were described as industrious, intelligent, materialistic, progressive, and aggres-sive; "white" was not used as a category.

These scales were administered to Princeton students again in 1951 and 1967, allowing a rare examination of historical changes in group schemas (Karlins, Coffman, and Walters 1969). Some aspects of these schemas changed a great deal: The proportion describing Jews as shrewd, for example, dropped from 79% in 1933 to 30% in 1967, after World War II. The proportion describing Americans as materialistic increased from 33% in 1933 to 67% in 1967. Other aspects of these group schemas changed barely at all: Chinese were described as equally tradition loving, blacks as equally happy-go-lucky, and Japanese as equally industrious. Overall, however, many researchers have interpreted these data as suggesting that racial stereotypes in the United States have faded over the years. Devine and

Elliot (1995) contest this interpretation. Focusing on stereotypes about blacks, they used the same scales as Katz and Braly (1933) but added more contemporary terms (e.g., *hostile, criminal, athletic, poor*), provided clearer instructions, distinguished explicitly between stereotypes (defined as a "well-learned set of associations that link a set of characteristics with a group label") and personal beliefs ("propositions that are endorsed and accepted as true"), and assessed white undergraduate respondents' levels of prejudice. Devine and Elliott maintain that rejection of a stereotype does not eradicate it from people's cognitive schemas. Thus it is possible to categorize on the basis of a stereotype, while at the same time denying its truth. They conclude that these students have a clear, consistent, highly negative group schema of blacks but also an equally consistent and positive set of personal beliefs about blacks.

Another recent study focused on the intersection of race and gender stereotypes. Weitz and Gordon (1993) used a modified version of the Katz and Braly scales to assess white students' images of black women, compared to perceptions of "American women in general." The most frequent descriptors of American women in general were intelligent, materialistic, sensitive, attractive, and sophisticated; the most frequent descriptors of black women were loud, talkative, aggressive, intelligent, and straightforward. Further analyses suggested the presence of three subtypes among the black female stereotype: a "threatening" type (loud, dishonest, argumentative), a "good mother/wife/daughter" type (intelligent, family-oriented, loyal to family), and a "welfare mother" type (too many children, fat, lazy). These data show that gender images do not hold across racial categories. Given that this study was conducted in 1991, when respondents were highly likely to have recognized that negative images of members of racial minority groups are not socially desirable, the negativity of some of these responses is striking. This supports Devine and Elliot's (1995) position that racial stereotypes have not died out.

Respondents in these studies are asked to evaluate a given group, not to compare racial groups to each other. (In contrast, conceptions of gender have routinely been assessed through comparisons, presumably because gender is conceived as bipolar.) This is not to say that respondents do not use a comparative framework to analyze such responses. Indeed, some of the same behaviors might be viewed in very different ways by different perceivers. This possibility was supported explicitly in a study by Campbell (1967): What Americans saw in themselves as friendly and outgoing, the British saw as intrusive and forward (and see Stephan and Rosenfield 1982). Note that these measures ask respondents to adopt an "all or none" framework: They are asked to judge whether these attributes are or are not typical of the target group, not to assess the degree to which an attribute might be characteristic. Recent studies have made improvements in the measures of group schemas: In some studies, respondents are now asked to indicate the percentage of the group that possesses each trait or the extent to which a given group is perceived to differ from other groups on a trait.

Beliefs about race, like beliefs about gender, are organized at varying levels of specificity. Devine and Baker (1991) show that "streetwise," "athlete," "welfare," and "businessman" are recognizable subtypes of the global category

"Black." It is important to note that this study is based on the responses of white students; assessment of the responses of blacks and of others who do not identify as white is necessary to establish the generality of these subtypes.

Social Class Group Schemas. So far, we have said little about representations of social class. Social psychologists have asked different, and fewer, questions about class than about gender or race. Some have argued that social class is an "unspeakable" topic in the United States. As one instance, we cite a story shared with us by a colleague, concerning her research on the perceptions held by high school students of their race and class positions. New York City school officials told her she could not ask students questions about their income or finances. Why? Because this would "remind them of their poverty." This incident suggests that it is *talk* about class that is unacceptable; class variation itself obviously exists. This "unspeakability" inhibits the social psychological study of social class.

We know of no studies that have assessed the content of group schemas about class position. Several older studies do assess perceived traits of combinations of race and class position, however; these show that class influences these schemas more than does race (Bayton, McAlister, and Hamer 1956). Both blacks and whites describe members of upper-class groups, across racial categories, as intelligent, ambitious, industrious, and progressive. Lower-class groups were described as ignorant, lazy, loud, and dirty. In contrast, there were no traits that the sample as a whole attributed to blacks of both classes or to whites of both classes. Showing the force of history, a similar study 20 years later reported the same pattern for white respondents but dramatically increased salience of race for black respondents (Smedley and Bayton 1978).

Several studies have attempted to manipulate perceptions of the social class background of actors in vignettes shown to research participants. To the extent that these portraits successfully shape perceptions of class positions, they are at least indirect indicators of schemas of social class. Howard and Pike (1986) varied the number of children in a household, the type of car one drives, the type of church one attends, and the degree of one's community participation, as well as more obvious financial information, such as having a savings account, income, receipt of social welfare payments, and occupation. Baron et al. (1995) varied the size of home, type of neighborhood, and quality of school playground and buildings. In each study, participants did successfully perceive the intended social class of the actors.

Social cognitive research has addressed two topics related to social class: (a) descriptive studies of how people conceptualize the class structure and their locations in it and (b) attributional studies of how people explain class positions. Kelley and Evans (1995) show that people's images of class are based on strong perceptions of equality and consensus among family, friends, and coworkers. These relationships foster consensual rather than conflictual views of class relations and contribute to the fact that most U.S. citizens describe themselves as middle class (although fewer do so if working class is included as an option [Evans, Kelley, and Kolosi 1992]).

Turning to explanations for social class position, the majority of respondents in several large national surveys attribute people's economic situations to their own individual skills, abilities, and motivations (Evans et al. 1992). At the same time, most surveys show that people think the gap between the incomes of the rich and poor is too large. Reflecting the deep individualism of Western societies, people generally evaluate both their own and others' economic situations as legitimate and just (see related discussion of justice in Chapter 3). In one of the few comparative studies of the effects of lower-status positions in systems of class, race, gender, and age on political perceptions and judgments, Gurin, Miller, and Gurin (1980) show that identification with these statuses is crucial to generating discontent with prevailing power structures. In the language of social cognition, those who have self-schemas about these positions are more likely to process their social experiences in terms of these schemas and to question the lack of political power associated with being black, a woman, or elderly, for example. Class is a striking exception. Even those who identify closely with lower economic strata do not question the legitimacy of economic differentials (Kluegel and Smith 1986). The working-class respondents in Gurin et al.'s (1980) survey accepted the legitimacy of poverty, attributing the disadvantages of some and the advantages of others to their personal characteristics.

We have observed that studies of personality traits associated with social class are less common than studies of attributes associated with gender and race. Studies of how people explain class position are much more common; explanations of the "achievement" of gender and race do not exist. The different questions asked about class on the one hand, and about gender and race on the other hand, reflect the beliefs that class is an achieved status and gender and race statuses are ascribed at birth. Questions of how people "obtain" their gender or race seem nonsensical. As we suggest in our discussion of the social constructionist approach, however, both gender and race have achieved as well as ascribed elements, whereas class clearly has ascriptive elements.

Connections Among Group Schemas. Researchers have only begun to explore the potential complexities of the intersections among these statuses. The human need for cognitive efficiency works against too much complexity; in some situations, therefore, we may privilege one system of categorization over another. Thus we might respond to the play *Oleanna* primarily in terms of our schemas about gender. Other social situations may encourage the activation of multiple and simultaneous categorizations; many analyses of the O. J. Simpson trial, for example, focused on both race and gender.

Social psychologists are also exploring how people balance the tendency to rely on social categories with the situational need for information about particular individuals (Brewer 1988; Fiske and Neuberg 1990). Reliance on social categories does have priority in how we form impressions of others. As we noted above, there is a good deal of evidence that people often pay less than complete attention to their social environments; social behavior is not always under conscious control. This suggests that cognitive schemas may have undue influence on our behavior. Conscious attempts to override these schemas can be successful, however. Devine (1989), for example, shows that most members of majority groups of a given culture are familiar with cultural stereotypes about minority groups and that these preconceptions can lead to prejudicial behavior toward members of these groups. When situational factors lead people to attend more directly to their own behavior, however, those who have less prejudicial attitudes are capable of inhibiting the stereotypes and behaving in ways consistent with their attitudes.

Most (although not all) of the studies discussed here have been conducted in the United States. Citizens of the United States appear to believe that equality of opportunity is a reality in this country. Taken together with the general tendency of Westerners to attribute events to people rather than to environmental circumstances (discussed below), the conviction that we all have equal opportunities leads to a pattern of causal reasoning that argues that if some people have not achieved social and economic advantages, this must be due to their own individual failings. Della Fave (1980) traces this pattern in his analysis of how cognitive processes of self-evaluation and attribution contribute to the legitimation of social stratification. Jost and Banaji (1994) take this analysis one step further. They focus on two aspects of stereotypes (schemas about social groups): one, that disadvantaged individuals and groups often endorse negative stereotypes about themselves and, two, that stereotypic beliefs are highly consensual. To make sense of these patterns, they maintain that stereotypes justify and thus contribute to the preservation of existing social inequalities. Hoffman and Hurst (1990) provide experimental support for this reasoning; they show that gender stereotypes can arise solely to rationalize the distribution of the sexes into social roles, in this case, "child raisers" as opposed to "city workers."

Event Schemas. Both self and group schemas refer to preconceptions about human actors. Another type of schema refers to information about situations, the social environments in which humans act. *Event schemas* include preconceptions about the kinds of actions likely to happen, the sequence in which these actions evolve, and the props necessary to perform these actions. These situations may vary from the particular, such as a class one is taking in a specific semester, to the general, such as going to a movie. The essential element is that the event be habitual so that it is possible for the individual who experiences it regularly to form a schema. As we noted earlier, reliance on event schemas encourages a state of mindlessness in which we pay less careful attention to the details of the situation, attending instead only to those details consistent with our expectations.

Some event schemas are shared within a group or within a culture; gender, race, and other social positions are important bases for such schemas. In a sense, these schemas combine expectations about social groups with expectations about particular situations. Assumptions about what women and men do in the kitchen, for example, reflect both event schemas and gender schemas. When event schemas carry expectations about the gender of the actors involved, we may describe these situations as gendered. The reason gender was relevant to the O. J. Simpson trial, for example, was not only because of the genders of the accused and of his former wife but also because domestic abuse is a highly gendered situation. Although some women do abuse some men, the much more prevalent profile (both statistically and cognitively) is that of a man abusing his female partner;

most studies suggest that women are between 90% and 95% of the victims in domestic assaults reported to the criminal justice system (Dobash et al. 1992). Thus, when a case of domestic abuse comes under public scrutiny, the full panoply of expectations based on gender is brought to bear in the investigation and judgments that follow.

Schemas of Cognitive Social Psychologists. Social schemas shape the research agendas of social psychologists and thus have influenced the very research we have summarized in this chapter. We illustrate with just a single study but invite the reader to consider other studies in this light. Langer et al. (1976) examined whether the salience of people who are physically different might explain why they are avoided. In the first part of this study, respondents viewed photographs of a "physically normal" woman, a pregnant woman, and a woman wearing an intricate leg brace that suggested she was handicapped. Women directed more visual attention to the more novel pictures, whereas men looked at the three pictures roughly similar amounts of time. Langer et al. speculated that "male subjects' desire to stare at an attractive normal female may have been as great as their desire to stare at novel stimuli" (p. 455). In the second part of the study, male respondents viewed pictures of two other males, one of whom was "physically normal," whereas the other had a hunchback. When they were unobserved, male respondents directed more visual attention to the picture of the hunchbacked man than to the other man. The authors concluded that when there are no norms against doing so, people direct more attention to novel, salient stimuli.

This study illustrates several intriguing assumptions. First, the researchers treat pregnancy as a form of physical handicap (a label echoed in laws that treat pregnancy as a disability). They note that people may have some degree of fear and discomfort around pregnant women because of a desire to stare at these presumably novel stimuli. If one assumes that men might find a pregnant woman more unusual than would women, this assumption suggests a male viewpoint on pregnancy (that three of the four authors of this study are women notwithstanding). Second, the account provided for the failure of men to conform to predictions in the first round of the study assumes their heterosexuality. Men (and not women) are assumed to have a "natural" desire to look at an "attractive normal female." The design of the second version indicates that men are assumed not to have such a desire to look at other men. Note also that this second round did not use female respondents, a design element that would have allowed the researchers to evaluate the generality of their explanation of the gender difference in the first round.

This study is now 20 years old. It may well be that if the same researchers were conducting a follow-up today, they might use different stimuli. We suggest, however, that those stimuli would likely continue to reflect prevailing contemporary assumptions about gender, sexuality, race, or other social systems. Our point is that social schemas influence researchers as strongly as they do others; some phenomena are so taken for granted that scientific substantiation is thought to be unnecessary.

Thinking: Processing Information

We form cognitive categories on the basis of self-perceptions, perceptions of others, and membership in significant social groups. These categories direct the several systems of information processing: attention, memory, and social inference.

Attention

The first step in thinking is *attention*. What we attend to is determined in large part by the salience of various features of a given situation, that is, the extent to which they stand out. Novelty, physical features such as brightness or mobility, violation of prior expectations, and social characteristics all shape what is salient. Thus a sole woman in a group of men, a white in a group of blacks, or an older person in a group of teenagers, is likely to be salient. The schemas we hold for each of these systems of social categories also shape salience: Violation of schema-based expectations increases salience and therefore heightens attention. Any characteristic or behavior that is unusual for a given person, for a person's social categories, or for a given situation, will be salient.

One of the reasons for the widespread attention to the discharge of Colonel Grethe Cammermeyer from the U.S. Army in 1992 when she disclosed that she is a lesbian, for example, is that homosexuality is inconsistent with cultural schemas for the military. Cammermeyer's gender also heightened the salience of the case; despite the consistent participation of women in the U.S. armed services, the schematic expectation is that military personnel, particularly high-ranking officers, are male. Similarly, one of the reasons for the dramatic intensity of *Oleanna* is the extreme disjuncture between the event schemas in the two parts of the play. The first scene appears to concern a faculty-student mentoring relationship. The last scene, which focuses on a violent confrontation between the professor and the student, entails an adversarial relationship between a harasser and a victim. The later violation of expectations generated at the outset of the play leads the viewer to pay attention.

Variation in salience and consequent variation in attention shape subsequent stages of information processing. McArthur and Solomon (1978) showed that actors who are more visually salient are assumed by observers to exert more control over social interactions. In this study, research participants watched a videotaped interaction between two women arguing about a bridge hand. One of the two women was verbally aggressive toward the other. In one version of this encounter the "victim" of this aggression wore a leg brace, making her particularly salient; in another version she did not wear the brace. Observers attributed more blame for this encounter to the woman wearing the brace than the woman without the brace—that is, to the salient victim. This finding suggests that victims who are salient are more likely than nonsalient victims to be attributed some blame for the situations in which they are victimized.

Memory

Having attended to information, we then may encode it into *memory*. At a later point, we may retrieve that information for use in a current situation. Social schemas shape both encoding into memory and retrieval from memory. As preexisting organizations of information, schemas provide the frameworks into which new information can be encoded. In most situations, information that fits easily into existing schemas is more likely to be retained in memory than information for which we do not already have relevant schemas. Similarly, because we retain information by organizing it into schemas, retrieval also necessarily relies on social schemas.

Our group memberships and their associated social schemas thus strongly affect memory. People recall more information about in-group than out-group members and are more likely to recall negative details about members of disliked out-groups. They also tend to recall how out-groups differ from in-groups, rather than how they are similar. These effects of categorization and social schemas on memory thus perpetuate our stereotypes and preconceptions.

Snyder and Uranowitz (1978) offer a remarkable demonstration of these processes. Participants first read an extensive case history of a woman named Betty K. After reading this narrative, some participants were told Betty was now a lesbian. Others were told she was now heterosexual. (The case history had included no information about sexual orientation.) All were later asked to remember a variety of details concerning, for example, her attitudes about women and men, her social patterns in high school, and her relationship with her parents. Those who believed that Betty was now a lesbian remembered the events of her life as consistent with stereotyped beliefs about lesbians (e.g., she never went out with men) to a greater extent than did those who believed she was heterosexual. Interestingly, this pattern did not occur for a third group who were told only that Betty was a lesbian and were asked to guess at her background. It was only those who were given specific information about her past who reconstructed a life history for a lesbian that differed significantly from that reconstructed for a heterosexual woman. This subtle study reveals that stereotypes and preconceptions interact with memory; stereotypes shape selective, rather than unbiased, memory.

Another classic study demonstrates the active, constructive nature of human memory. Cohen (1981) created a short videotape that showed a man and woman having a birthday dinner. Participants were told before viewing the tape either that the woman was a librarian or a waitress. They were then asked a series of questions about the tape; participants were much more likely to remember having seen schema-consistent details. Those who thought they were viewing a waitress remembered her drinking beer, owning a TV, having a hamburger and chocolate cake for dinner, and liking to bowl. Those who thought they were viewing a librarian remembered her wearing glasses, owning classical records, having roast beef and champagne for dinner, and having fresh flowers on the table. In some cases, these details were not a part of the videotape. Participants constructed situational details that were not present but that were consistent with their prior expectations. In other words, preexisting social schemas shaped retrieval so completely that participants "remembered" details on the basis of these schemas rather than the actual videotape. This is the essence of the social construction of memory.

It is worth considering precisely what schemas are at work here. Cohen (1981) presents these as occupational schemas—that is, preconceptions about characteristics of waitresses and librarians. However, both are highly gender-typed occupations and both are typed as female. Indeed, *waitress* is an explicitly gendered term (in contrast to the neutral *server*). The different details manipulated in the study also suggest that these occupations are distinguished by their class; waitresses are ranked lower in the class hierarchy than are librarians. Thus these occupational schemas also rely on schemas about gender and social class. These studies illustrate precisely how we can seem to see gender differences that are not really present; our reliance on schemas about gender leads us to remember those details that are consistent with our expectations and, importantly, not to notice, and not to encode in memory, details that are not consistent with our expectations.

Social Inference

In the next stage of cognitive processing, we draw on memory, immediate situations, or both, to make a variety of types of judgments, from predictions to decisions to causal attributions. Guided by the need for cognitive efficiency, we often use cognitive shortcuts or *heuristics* in making inferences. Social schemas are no less influential in the formation of such social inferences than in attention or memory. In judging what groups people belong to, we often rely on preexisting group schemas—witness the hapless academic who mistakenly assumes that the new assistant professor sitting in the department office is the secretary. (And witness the reader's possible assumption that the secretary is a woman and the academic is a man!)

Estimates of probability rely on the cognitive availability of information—instances or associations that easily come to mind influence perceived probabilities. This availability heuristic underlies significant social patterns: High-status people exaggerate the size of upper classes, envisioning a relatively egalitarian society, for example, whereas low-status people exaggerate the size of the lower classes, envisioning an elitist society (Evans et al. 1992). In making decisions or evaluating past events, we may engage in cognitive simulations, imagining what might have been or what might come to pass, on the basis of cognitive schemas. Such simulations can affect other inferences; for example, Howard (1984a) reports that both women and men held female victims more accountable than male victims for being assaulted when they were hitchhiking. Presumably, cognitive simulations of what might happen when one is hitchhiking lead respondents to assess higher probabilities of assault to women than to men and in turn to attribute more blame to women who hitchhike.

Some of the most compelling examples of the effects of schemas on social inferences illustrate how group schemas affect attribution, the process through which we explain events. One study conducted in India examined the effects of intensely held group schemas, the beliefs held by Hindus about themselves and about Muslims, who are for Hindus a hated out-group (Taylor and Jaggi 1974). Hindu respondents were asked to describe the traits characteristic of Hindus and of Muslims. Then they were asked to read a set of paragraphs, each of which described either a Hindu or a Muslim performing a behavior that was either clearly good or clearly bad. These Hindu respondents attributed the good behavior of Hindus to internal factors such as their own abilities or strong morals, and the bad behavior of Hindus to external factors such as the influence of other people. In contrast, they attributed the good behavior of Muslims to external factors and the bad behavior of Muslims to internal factors. Thus, on the basis of their preconceptions about these groups, they showed attributional patterns of in-group favoritism and defensiveness and out-group derogation.

The effects of group schemas on cognitive judgments are not always so straightforward. Howard (1984a) explored how attitudes toward women and men shape both attributions and evaluations. Research participants watched a videotaped interview between a police detective and a male or female victim of a rape or a robbery. Both women and men attributed more blame to female than to male victims and, interestingly, both female and male participants attributed more blame to the character of female victims and to the behaviors of male victims. Women were blamed for stable, internal, uncontrollable characteristics—for example, their "trusting nature." Men were blamed for unstable, more controllable behaviors—for example, "not fighting back." These patterns are consistent with gender schemas that characterize women as passive and lacking control and men as active, powerful, and exerting control. Evaluations of these victims were also gendered. Some patterns were consistent with gender schemas; female victims, for example, were rated as more foolish than males. Male victims, on the other hand, were rated as less forceful than female victims, directly contradicting male stereotypes (Howard 1984b). Victimization may be so deeply "female" an experience that a man who is victimized is literally "feminized" in respondents' cognitive evaluations. This gendered situation is another example of the connection between group and event schemas.

As is evident from this discussion, social inferences are not always "rational." When we rely on these cognitive heuristics to form inferences, we use only a subset of the relevant information. The attribution process is also vulnerable to a host of social and cognitive factors that lead us to emphasize some types of information at the expense of others. The "fundamental" attribution error, for example, is a tendency to attribute blame more to people than to situations (a tendency limited to Western societies [Miller 1984]). This bias is exacerbated when observers make attributions about the behavior of others and muted when people make attributions about their own behavior (the "actor-observer bias").

These biases, produced by both cognitive and motivational processes, underlie significant societal patterns. As we have noted above, members of groups with more social advantages generally attribute the disadvantaged positions of others to their personal inadequacies (Gurin et al. 1980), as self-interest would predict. These and other studies (Coleman, Rainwater, and McClelland 1978; Kerbo 1976) have shown that members of lower economic classes often legitimize not only the social positions of those with more economic advantages but also their own social positions. Attribution biases contribute to these perceptions. The fundamental attribution error encourages members of subordinate social positions to accept responsibility for their own disadvantages, and the actor-observer bias encourages members of advantaged social groups to view their own advantages as situational and others' disadvantages as self-produced (Gurin et al. 1980).

Constructing Gender: Behavior and Cognition

Recent work in social cognition has stressed the behavioral confirmation of cognitive expectancies, a process whereby we essentially elicit from others the behavior we expect from them. This research falls at the intersection of social cognition and symbolic interaction, the theory we take up in the next chapter. The prolific research of Mark Snyder offers many examples of behavioral confirmation. In one study, for example, pairs of previously unacquainted college women and men became acquainted in phone conversations (Snyder, Tanke, and Berscheid 1977). The men were given pictures ostensibly of the woman they would be talking to. In reality, these pictures were either of a "very attractive" or a "very unattractive" woman, not of the person with whom they would be talking. The conversational styles of these men were clearly guided by the expectations they formed on the basis of the pictures: Those who expected an attractive partner were warm, friendly, humorous, and animated. Those who expected an unattractive partner were distant and reserved. The women with whom they spoke responded to these conversational styles as one might expect: Those treated warmly responded warmly; those treated coldly responded coldly. Expectations based on gender schemas shaped these men's behavior so that their conversational partners confirmed the men's schemas. Snyder's research on behavioral confirmation illustrates powerfully how cognitive expectancies guide the construction of social systems such as gender. (See Snyder [1984] for other examples.)

This study also provides another example of how cognitive schemas shape the research of social psychologists themselves. Note the gendered expectations embedded in the design of this study: Men are assigned the position of initiators of conversation, and it is men's opinions of women that are sought. Would the same effects have been obtained if women had been asked to initiate conversations with men whose pictures they had been given? Anderson and Bem (1981) replicated this study but reversed the sexes; they found that women also lead men to confirm beliefs about their personalities but add the important caveat that highly gender-typed individuals are most likely to initiate this behavioral confirmation process.

Conclusion: Social Cognition on Gender

In contrast to social exchange theory, social cognition offers an explicit account of the microlevel aspects of systems through which gender, and gender inequity, are created, sustained, and changed. Gender has been treated as an important category in social cognition, from early research on attitudes about gender through more recent research on gender schemas and gender identity.

The effect of gender on cognitive processes has been addressed in research on attention, memory, and social inference.

The social cognitive account of gender draws from both the socialization and the social constructionist approaches. Some of the earlier research, particularly that on personality and androgyny, adopts a relatively static conception of gender as a set of characteristics acquired early in life that remains relatively stable throughout the life span. Later work emphasizes the informational basis of the social dynamics of gender, race, and other social systems. The social cognitive emphasis has been on the stability of such systems, due primarily to the human need for cognitive efficiency. Our reliance on preexisting cognitive expectations tends to perpetuate those expectations. Recent research on behavioral confirmation processes shows how cognitions shape behavior so as to reproduce those cognitive expectations. This approach also addresses how expectations can change, as we discuss in Chapter 5; those toward whom behavior is directed may explicitly counteract the expectations, and those who hold certain expectations can explicitly try to elicit contradictory behavior. These recent syntheses of cognitive approaches with models of social interaction bring us closer to a social constructionist model of gender and other social systems.

As one example, research has treated memory as one of the most individualistic and cognitive of the cognitive processes. What could be more cognitive, after all, than human memory? Wegner (1986) challenges this conception of memory, observing that many people store information in places such as file cabinets, computer disks, and address books. More significant, we also allocate to other people responsibility for memory of particular categories of information. Is there a U.S. household, for example, that does not look to some members to know what food (if any) is in the refrigerator, to another to know what tax-deductible expenses the household has incurred over the year (if relevant), and to others to know how to reach family friends? Wegner's point is that even memory is a social process. In that the reader can make educated guesses about which genders are likely held responsible for remembering particular categories of information, we can speculate that gender shapes social memory and social memory shapes gender.

Despite the fact that the study of social cognition is increasingly social, what is often absent in the social cognitive analysis of gender and sexuality, and to some extent of race and class as well, is explicit recognition of the power associated with membership in particular social categories. Social cognition has been relatively silent about power; categories are often treated as neutral. Difference is a fundamental principle of social cognition, but inequity has received a good deal less attention. Consider prevailing models of social identity (Tajfel 1982). Social identity theory holds that members of in-groups tend to process information so as to bolster their own self-esteem through derogating members of out-groups and ennobling members of their own in-groups. In a society in which in-groups and out-groups do not have equal power, however, are these processes likely to hold for all groups? Argyle (1994) summarizes recent thinking on this question with the observation that out-groups are not always rejected; minority and lower-status groups may believe that high-status out-groups are superior. That significant proportions of lower-status groups report that they accept the class system as just and legitimate and believe that middle-class people are superior in intelligence and leadership are striking reminders that social cognitive processes are not neutral but are shaped by the structural positions of individuals.

Accordingly, scholars have begun to critique measures of cognitive constructs that fail to consider existing relations of power. In one such critique, Howard (1988) reconsiders Hendrick et al.'s (1985) conclusion that gender differences in sexual attitudes reflect women's greater sexual conservatism. Hendricks et al. report, for example, that women are likely to disagree, and men to agree, that "I do not need to be committed to a person to have sex with him/her." Women are more likely than men to disagree that "sex is more fun with someone you don't love" and "it is all right to pressure someone into having sex." Howard argues that failure to consider the societal context in which sexual attitudes are formed invalidates Hendrick et al.'s attribution of these patterns to women's greater sexual conservatism. Power differences, not sexual conservativism, underlie these gender differences in attitudes toward sexual behaviors.

Social cognition historically has paid much less attention to behavior than to cognition. Although the rationale for the importance of cognition is that, ultimately, it affects behavior, both theory and research have underemphasized the cognitive contribution to behavior. Contemporary research has been increasingly likely to place cognition in interactive situations. We anticipate that the next decade will see increasing interchange between social cognition and the theory to which we now turn, symbolic interaction.

CHAPTER 5

Symbolic Interactionism

Readers of Louisa May Alcott's classic *Little Women* may remember a series of episodes centering around a lost glove. The four March sisters (Meg, Jo, Beth, and Amy) go on a picnic outing with their neighbor Laurie and his tutor, John Brooke. When they return, Meg realizes that she has lost a pair of gloves. Later, one of the pair is returned to her via the "office," a mailbox in the hedge between the neighboring properties:

> "Miss Meg March, one letter and a glove," continued Beth, delivering the articles to her sister, who sat near her mother, stitching wristbands.
>
> "Why, I left a pair over there, and here is only one," said Meg, looking at the grey cotton glove.
>
> "Didn't you drop the other one in the garden?"
>
> "No, I'm sure I didn't; for there was only one in the office."
>
> "I hate to have odd gloves! Never mind, the other may be found. My letter is only a translation of the German song I wanted; I think Mr. Brooke did it, for this isn't Laurie's writing." (Alcott 1924:161)

The disappearance of Meg's glove is odd, but none of the sisters takes much notice. Some time later, however, Jo and her friend Laurie (a young man whom she calls "Teddy") make a playful agreement to exchange secrets. Jo confides that one of her stories has been accepted for publication in a local newspaper; then she demands that Laurie reciprocate by sharing his secret:

> "Where's *your* secret? Play fair, Teddy, or I'll never believe you again," [Jo] said.
>
> "I may get into a scrape for telling; but I didn't promise not to, so I will, for I never feel easy in my mind till I've told you any plummy bit of news I get. I know where Meg's glove is."
>
> "Is that all?" said Jo, looking disappointed, as Laurie nodded and twinkled, with a face full of mysterious intelligence.
>
> "It's quite enough for the present, as you'll agree when I tell you where it is."
>
> "Tell, then."
>
> Laurie bent, and whispered three words in Jo's ear, which produced a comical change. She stood and stared at him for a minute, looking both

surprised and displeased, then walked on, saying sharply, "How do you know?"

"Saw it."

"Where?"

"Pocket."

"All this time?"

"Yes, isn't that romantic?"

"No, it's horrid."

"Don't you like it?"

"Of course I don't. It's ridiculous; it won't be allowed. My patience! what would Meg say?" (Alcott 1924:202-3)

Laurie's disclosure worries Jo, and she eventually confides in her mother:

That evening, while Meg was writing to her father, to report the traveler's safe arrival, Jo slipped upstairs into Beth's room, and, finding her mother in her usual place, stood a minute twisting her fingers in her hair, with a worried gesture and an undecided look.

"What is it, deary?" asked Mrs. March, holding out her hand, with a face which invited confidence.

"I want to tell you something, mother."

"About Meg?"

"How quickly you guessed! Yes, it's about her, and though it's a little thing, it fidgets me. . . . Last summer Meg left a pair of gloves over at the Laurences' and only one was returned. We forgot all about it, til Teddy told me that Mr. Brooke had it. He kept it in his waistcoat pocket, and once it fell out, and Teddy joked him about it, and Mr. Brooke owned that he liked Meg, but didn't dare say so, she was so young and he so poor. Now isn't it a *dreadful* state of things?"

"Do you think Meg cares for him?" asked Mrs. March with an anxious look.

"Mercy me! I don't know anything about love and such nonsense!" cried Jo, with a funny mixture of interest and contempt. "In novels, the girls show it by starting and blushing, fainting away, growing thin, and acting like fools. Now Meg does not do anything of the sort: she eats and drinks and sleeps like a sensible creature; she looks straight in my face when I talk about that man, and only blushes a little bit when Teddy jokes about lovers. I forbid him to do it, but he doesn't mind me as he ought. . . . I knew there was mischief brewing; I felt it; and now it's worse than I imagined. I just wish I could marry Meg myself, and keep her safe in the family."

This odd arrangement made Mrs. March smile; but she said gravely, "Jo, I confide in you, and don't wish you to say anything to Meg yet. When John comes back, and I see them together, I can judge better of her feelings toward him."

"She'll see his in those handsome eyes that she talks about, and then it will be all up with her. She's got such a soft heart, it will melt like butter in the sun if any one looks sentimentally at her. She read the short reports he sent more than she did your letters, and pinched me when I spoke of it, and likes brown eyes, and doesn't think John an ugly name, and she'll go off and fall in love, and there's an end of peace and fun, and cosey times together. I see it all! they'll go lovering around the house, and we shall have to dodge; Meg will be absorbed, and no good to me any more; Brooke will scratch up a fortune somehow, carry her off, and make a hole in the family; and I shall break my heart, and everything will be abominably uncomfortable. Oh, dear me! why weren't we all boys, then there wouldn't be any bother."

Jo leaned her chin on her knees, in a disconsolate attitude, and shook her fist at the reprehensible John. (Alcott 1924:262-6)

This excerpt illustrates the basic premises of symbolic interaction. As we will discuss, people attach symbolic meaning to objects, behaviors, and other people and develop and transmit these meanings through interaction. Symbolic interactionism is used in many types of theory and research, ranging from macrolevel topics, such as collective behavior, organizations, and social problems, to traditional microlevel social psychological topics, such as interpersonal interaction. Symbolic interactionists use a variety of methods, including introspection, fieldwork, interviews, participant observation, experiments, surveys, and the analysis of texts and other media. The breadth of symbolic interactionism makes a concise review difficult. In this chapter, we do not attempt to cover all of symbolic interactionism; rather, we focus on the aspects most relevant to our analysis of gender. These diverse aspects are unified by their reliance on a few key concepts and premises. We begin by discussing these foundational tools.

The Tools of Symbolic Interactionism

The most basic concept in symbolic interactionism is the *symbol.* Symbols are abstract meanings attached to objects, people, and behaviors. For example, some people wear religious symbols as necklaces: Christians often wear tiny crosses, Jews wear Stars of David, and so on. These pieces of jewelry are not simply geometric shapes cast in gold or silver; they carry complex meanings about religion, faith, and personal identity. Similarly, Meg's glove takes on symbolic meaning in the example above. Mr. Brooke keeps it in his waistcoat pocket because it symbolizes Meg and his affection for her. To him, the glove is not simply a few pieces of gray cotton sewn together; rather it takes on more extensive symbolic meaning because it belongs to a woman he admires. Thus the first premise of symbolic interaction is that people behave toward symbols not on the basis of the concrete properties of the objects but on the meanings that these objects have for them.

Note, however, that the glove carries a very different set of meanings for Jo. To her, the glove comes to symbolize the prospect of Meg's being taken away from the family—which would be, in her eyes, "a dreadful state of affairs." Thus a symbol can have different meanings for different people, and these meanings can also change over time. At first, Meg's glove symbolizes little beyond a protective covering for the hand; over time, however, it comes to have much more abstract meaning for Jo, her mother, and Mr. Brooke.

How do meanings become associated with objects? A second premise of symbolic interactionism is that meaning develops through *interaction*. The transformation in the meaning of the glove for Jo occurs through her conversation with Laurie. She then passes this new symbol on to her mother in their subsequent conversation. Meaning-making is thus a creative activity that occurs through language, which is itself a symbolic system. Without language, humans would not have the capacity to create symbols and communicate them to others.

Some symbolic meanings are unique to particular individuals or groups. For example, a song or story may take on a particular symbolic meaning for a couple, or a specific item of clothing may develop into a good luck charm for an individual. More often, however, the development of meaning relies on a symbolic system shared by many people in a culture. Meg's glove symbolizes romance to both Jo and Mr. Brooke not simply because they independently attach romantic meaning to an object. Rather, both Jo and Brooke (as well as ourselves as readers) share a symbolic universe in which ideas about "romance" include the sentimentalization of objects belonging to the beloved. Again, these meanings are conveyed through interaction, and especially through language. Jo learns about love by reading books: She knows that "in novels, the girls show it by starting and blushing, fainting away, growing thin, and acting like fools." All of these behaviors symbolize "love," and Jo compares Meg's behavior to these symbolic actions to determine whether she is in love with John Brooke. Thus these meanings are not constructed anew in every interaction; in many cases, individuals draw on a shared system of cultural meaning and adapt it to a new situation.

Note, however, that these symbolic meanings are gendered. In the quote above, Jo describes what she believes to be the signs of love in women: blushing, fainting, and so on. John Brooke has shown none of these signs, yet Jo is certain he is in love with Meg. For men, love is symbolized in different ways. Brooke romanticizes Meg's glove but is otherwise stoic about his feelings until Laurie teases him. Once he is able to "scratch up a fortune somehow," however, he will be able to "carry Meg off." Meg, in contrast, is unlikely to scratch up her own fortune and carry *him* off; her task is to wait. Thus gender (and other social positions, as we discuss in more detail below) is a crucial part of these cultural systems of meaning, transmitted and performed through the basic tools of symbolic interaction: symbols, meaning, and interaction.

Who Are We? Self and Identity

The most basic requisite for symbolic interaction is the existence of social selves who come together to share information, emotions, goods—the full range of human activities. The images people have of themselves and of others shape how they present themselves. In turn, how they present themselves allows others to infer what actors privately think of themselves and of others. Without an explicit definition of self, we cannot interact successfully with others. In this section, we discuss how symbolic interactionists conceive of self and identity and how selves and identities are both constructed in and played out through interaction with others.

William James ([1890]1991) was the first modern social psychologist to attempt to define self. He wrote, "In its widest possible sense . . . a man's Self is the sum total of all that he can call his" (p. 279). People recognize that their attributes, possessions, and friends are associated with them and that others (as well as they themselves) categorize and evaluate them on the basis of these things. James, and George Herbert Mead (1934) after him, divided components of self into the "I," the self-as-knower, and the "Me," the self-as-known. The *I* is the experiencing, active, being. The *me* is a person's perception of himself or herself as an object. *Self-awareness*, or reflexivity, is the uniquely human capacity to be both subject and object to one's self, literally to be able to think (as a subject) about one's self (as an object). *Self* is all the consequences of this self- and other-awareness—our convictions, values, motives, and experiential history, carried in the spatial and temporal boundaries of our physical bodies.

Identity typically refers to the more public aspects of self. Identities locate a person in social space by virtue of the relationships and memberships that these identities imply. Thus we hold identities based on our memberships in social groups (both voluntary and ascribed) and on the character traits we enact in interaction and that others attribute to us. For Jo, a primary identity is sister. Her worry about the glove is based on her recognition that Meg may be considering another identity—lover or, perhaps, wife. The salience of particular identities, unlike selves, is sensitive to situational context. When John Brooke is visiting with Meg, his primary identity is potential suitor. When he is working with Laurie, his identity is tutor.

Although many theorists present the idea of the self as though it were a universal concept, on closer analysis, their definition may not be so generic. The full sentence in the James quote reads, "A man's Self is the sum total of all that he can call his, not only his body and his psychic powers, but his clothes and his house, his wife and his children, his ancestors and his friends, his reputation and works, his lands and horses, and yacht and bank account" (p. 279). This statement suggests that to have a self is to be a man. It is also to be a man with substantial means. It is also probably to be white. Although no contemporary self-respecting social psychologist would be caught dead using James's precise words, *Oleanna's* John suggests a similar definition as he rants to Carol about his tenure decision:

> When the possibility of tenure opened, I was covetous of it. I desired it, I was not pure of longing for security. What was the price of this security? To obtain tenure. Which tenure the committee is in the process of granting me. And on the basis of which I contracted to purchase a house. Now . . . you may not know what this means. To me it is important. A home. A Good Home. To raise my family . . . the home I'd picked out for my wife and son. (Mamet 1992:43-45)

William James would recognize John's self.

The genesis of self lies in children's perceptions and feelings about how others treat them. An idea of the self develops, based on three elements: our imagination of how we appear to others, our imagination of how others judge us, and our emotional reactions to those presumed judgments—that is, our feelings about ourselves. The self-concept thus arises through taking the role of particular others, seeing one's self as others do. Over time, children develop a sense of the *generalized other*, a composite viewpoint from the perspective of society as perceived by the individual. In *Oleanna*, John's description of his intellectual self-development reveals the emotional intensity of this process—and the lifetime consequences:

> If the young child is told he cannot understand. Then he takes it as a *description* of himself. What am I? I am *that which can not understand*. . . . They said I was incompetent. . . . And when I'm tested, the feelings of my youth about the very subject of learning come up. And I become, I feel "unworthy," and "unprepared." (Mamet 1992:16-17)

Through interactions with others, John developed a lasting sense of himself as unable to learn.

Approaches to conceptualizing self and identity vary in their emphasis on the structure of identity, on the one hand, and the processes and interactions through which identity is constructed, on the other. The structural approach developed out of early quantitative surveys using the venerable Twenty Statements Test (Kuhn and McPartland 1954)—answers to the question "Who am I?"—as a method for assessing identities.[1] Role identities, the characters and the roles an individual develops as an occupant of particular social positions, explicitly link social structures to persons. Jo's identities as sister, daughter, and friend (especially to Laurie) are not only personal identities—although they are that as well—but also social positions accompanied by culturally specific duties and expectations. Jo's later relationship to Professor Bhaer, a man who lives in the boarding house where she is a governess, is a clear example of the identity-structure connection. At first, Jo has no readily available identity to help define her relationship to the professor. Is he a housemate? An editor? A lover? Until the two acknowledge and enact their attraction to each other through a role relationship, there is no firm identity that connects them. Thus the full profile of an individual's role identities is explicitly connected to and mirrors the multifaceted nature of society.

According to Stryker (1980), these role identities are organized hierarchically, varying on the basis of their salience to the self and the degree to which we are committed to them. Identities are based in part on connections to other people. Our commitment to particular identities, then, is based on the number of ties to other people and the emotional strength of the ties associated with those identities. The greater one's commitment to an identity, the greater the salience of that identity. The greater the salience of the identity, the greater its influence on behavioral choices. Particular identities are more salient in some situations than in others. The student identity of Carol, the student in *Oleanna*, is likely excruciatingly salient throughout much of the play. The professional identity of John, the professor, is probably less salient in Act 1 but grows increasingly more salient as the play progresses. In Act 1, John can take this identity for granted; in later acts, this identity is threatened. Summed over situations and time, those identities to which we are most committed shape behavioral continuities and personal resistance to change—that is, a sense of self.

Other approaches to conceptualizing self and identity emphasize the processes through which identity is constructed in naturally occurring social situations. Because individual actors enter particular situations with their own agendas, negotiation about who each actor will be is a fundamental aspect of defining those situations. McCall and Simmons (1978) present a detailed model of those cognitive and expressive processes through which actors attempt both to perform their desired identities (cognitively devising or improvising their own roles and then performing them) and to encourage the other to perform the identities they want the other to perform (cognitively assessing the role the other is projecting and then *altercasting*, behaviorally trying to encourage the other into the role the actor wants them to play). Through these cognitive and expressive negotiations, particular identities are agreed on (or not), and situations are defined consensually enough to allow interaction to proceed.

The following excerpt from *Little Women*, in which Laurie proposes marriage to Jo, is a poignant example of the interactional approach. Jo has anticipated his proposal and done all she could to prevent it:

Something in his resolute tone made Jo look up quickly to find him looking down at her with an expression that assured her the dreaded moment had come, and made her put out her hand with an imploring: "No, Teddy, please don't!"

"I will, and you must hear me. It's no use, Jo: we've got to have it out, and the sooner the better for both of us," he answered, getting flushed and excited all at once.

"Say what you like then; I'll listen," said Jo, with a desperate sort of patience.

"I've loved you ever since I've known you, Jo; couldn't help it, you've been so good to me. I've tried to show it, but you wouldn't let me; now I'm going to make you hear, and give me an answer, for I *can't* go on so any longer."

"I wanted to save you this! I thought you'd understand—" began Jo, finding it a great deal harder than she expected.

"I know you did; but girls are so queer you never know what they mean. They say 'No' when they mean 'Yes,' and drive a man out of his wits just for the fun of it," returned Laurie, entrenching himself behind an undeniable fact.

"*I* don't. I never wanted to make you care for me so, and I went away to keep you from it if I could."

"I thought so; it was like you, but it was no use. I only loved you all the more, and I worked hard to please you, and I gave up billiards and everything you didn't like, and waited and never complained, for I hoped you'd love me, though I'm not half good enough—"

"Yes, you are; you're a great deal too good for me, and I'm grateful to you, and so proud and fond of you, I don't see why I can't love you as you want me to. I've tried, but I can't change the feeling, and it would be a lie to say I do when I don't."

"Really, truly, Jo?" He stopped short, and caught both her hands as he put his question with a look that she did not soon forget.

"Really, truly, dear." (Alcott 1924:402-3)

Laurie's first words allow Jo to impute his role as suitor; her response clearly casts him as friend rather than lover. Laurie has rehearsed this conversation many times before acting; he has already devised the role he wants to play and manages his self-presentation so as to make Jo listen. Nonetheless, Laurie cannot successfully altercast Jo as his future wife; ultimately, her definition of the situation prevails.

Identity construction is thus an intentional, strategic process, often entailing considerable negotiation. From this perspective, identities are social constructions created through interaction, with significant social and material consequences. The self is not the focus of this approach; rather, multiple identities provide the basis and motivation for interaction.

Gendered Selves and Identities

Gender is consistently one of the most frequent responses provided on the Twenty Statements Test. As we noted in Chapter 1, gender identity refers to the socially defined self-meanings one has as a female or male. Despite their basis in a presumed physiological dichotomy, these meanings are variable; they are constructed differently by those in different structural positions, particularly of race and of class. Even within individual actors, they vary depending on the time and situation. For example, one's gender identity might be quite different in childhood than in adulthood or old age.

Like all identities, gender identities are defined in part by our positions in social structures and institutions. In a study of the meanings of divorce, for example, Arendell (1992, 1995) suggests that the family is the primary social group that conveys and reinforces the meanings of gender. She demonstrates that masculine identities shape for some men the creation of paradoxical goals in marriage: They seek relationships in which they can be the dominant spouse, "befitting men in relationship with women according to the conventions of masculinity" (Arendell 1992), while at the same time they want relationships in which they are equal co-partners, sharing a high degree of intimacy and reciprocity. The improbability of simultaneously having both types of marriage is largely obscured by their gendered assumptions. In fact, the contradictions between these two sets of goals ultimately led to the divorces of many of the men in Arendell's study.

These masculine identities also generate a "masculinist discourse of divorce, constructed and anchored in interaction and reinforced by the stratified social order, [making] available a set of practices and dispositions that prescribed and reaffirmed these men's gendered identities" (Arendell 1992:173). Among these practices are these men's reliance on a "rhetoric of rights" due to one as a man or as a father; their attempts to reassert a self as autonomous, independent, and controlling; their attributions of problems in the marriage to fundamental differences between women and men (rather than to relationship-specific problems); and their distancing themselves from the relationship by defining their postdivorce families as "me" and "them" (the ex-wife and children). These cognitive and interactional practices both express and reaffirm these men's masculine identities, while at the same time reaffirming a traditional conception of family.

Gender identity is also shaped by an individual's position in other social hierarchies. Membership in racial, ethnic, and class-based groups interacts with gender to produce a wide range of gendered selves. For example, Karp (1986) studied a group of upper-middle-class professionals who had been poor or working-class as children. He found that individuals' original class positions shaped their responses to their present status as professionals. Those who had been upwardly mobile had difficulty "creating and sustaining a 'coherent self' that integrates older and newer social identities" and continued to "harbor feelings of uncertainty, inauthenticity, marginality, and dis-ease" (p. 20) because of their working-class origins, despite their current success. These women and men continued to feel like "strangers in an alien culture"—a very different conception of self than that of other upper-middle-class people who had not experienced such a class shift. Even within this group, however, gender was salient: "Working-class women of this generation no doubt felt the double discrimination of their class and gender. While the boys could believe in the American dream of advancement through their own work efforts, the girls typically did not see career as an avenue for mobility" (p. 33). Thus a person's self is influenced simultaneously by many social positions—including ethnicity, class, race, and gender.

Presenting Selves in Interaction

Our selves and identities serve as resources, as tools for interaction. We present particular aspects of ourselves in interaction so as to achieve the outcomes we desire. A key idea in social cognition is that our cognitive preconceptions of ourselves and others shape how we behave; this insight is also vital for understanding symbolic interactions. Our preconceptions of ourselves shape who we present ourselves to be; our preconceptions of others shape how we behave toward them. In the section that follows, we discuss the presentation of self, or impression management, emphasizing the actor's own goals. In the next section, we discuss the interactional consequences of our preconceptions of others, emphasizing the process of behavioral confirmation. Both impression management and behavioral confirmation have considerable potential for contributing to an account of gender hierarchy and stratification, as we elaborate below.

Impression Management

Impression management, sometimes referred to as *dramaturgy*, is the interactional presentation of self. Although some people are uncomfortable with this metaphor, our interactions with others do often resemble a theatrical performance. We behave differently (i.e., play different roles) with different people (or audiences). We dress differently (using different costumes and props) for different situations. We say some things directly to the people they concern; other comments we may say only behind their backs. In short, we present particular selves to particular others for particular reasons. Laurie's cessation of billiards, for example, is directly intended to win Jo's affection. Jo's everyday behavior with Laurie, in contrast, is directly intended to dissuade him from wanting to marry her. Impression management has also been observed in a multitude of laboratory experiments. In a study of job applicants, for example, von Baeyer, Sherk, and Zanna (1981) found that expectations about the gender role attitudes of male interviewers held by women applying for these jobs strongly shaped how these women dressed for the interviews and what gender role attitudes they expressed during the course of the interviews. Their behavior was likely intentional and goal oriented, designed to win them the job.

One cannot discuss the concept of impression management without referring to the work of Erving Goffman (1959, 1961). Goffman maintained that like actors on a stage, individuals in social situations manipulate the impressions they give off to manage others' perceptions of them. Whether the social situation is a classroom, a date, or a workplace, individuals modify their appearance and behavior in an attempt to control others' perceptions of them.

Consider the trial of O. J. Simpson. Simpson contended that he was not guilty of murdering his ex-wife, and in the courtroom he and his attorneys created an impression of beleaguered innocence. Simpson came to court dressed in somber, conservative clothing, maintained a serious expression, and was seen to shake his head or look horrified when evidence was presented. When, during the course of the trial, Simpson was asked to try on for size the gloves believed to have been worn by his ex-wife's murderer, he engaged in a "dramatic display" that "transfixed jurors":

> The episode began when, after a brief sidebar conference with defense lawyers, prosecutors handed Simpson the worn brown gloves—one of them with a bloodstain circled in silver ink.
>
> Looking relaxed and confident, Simpson pulled two latex gloves out of a box in front of him and yanked them over his hands. Then he carefully picked up the cashmere-lined leather gloves and tried to tug them on—raising his eyebrows, pursing his lips, and using other body language to convey difficulty.
>
> The Aris Isotoner gloves are designed to be snug. In fact, a prosecution witness had testified earlier in the day that customers favored the gloves because they fit almost like a second skin.
>
> But Simpson, shaking his head and grinning with an expression of incredulity, showed the jurors that he could not fully extend his fingers into the tips of the gloves.
>
> Raising his hands in front of him and flexing his fingers, he revealed that the extra-large gloves did not stretch all the way to his wrists.
>
> Prosecutor Christopher Darden, meanwhile, provided a running commentary about Simpson's glove-donning technique, and even asked Judge

Lance Ito to instruct Simpson to put the gloves on in a normal manner. Later, in a question to a witness, he implied that Simpson had been bending his thumb so the glove would not slip on easily.

Simpson jumped in himself, commenting, "Too tight."

Fascinated, the jurors leaned forward and craned their necks. They were clearly spellbound by the show. (Simon and Boyarsky 1995:A2)

In contrast, the prosecution was charged with proving Simpson's guilt. The prosecuting attorneys attempted to convey their own integrity, and their belief in Simpson's guilt, through their actions. Similarly, all the other actors involved in this social drama—the judge, the members of the jury, and the various witnesses called to testify in the case, for example—managed the impressions they gave off in the courtroom in order to achieve their own goals.

Like a theater, however, social situations often have a "backstage," an area separate from the "frontstage" performance visible to the audience. The behavior of actors in this backstage region may be very different from their frontstage demeanor. In a theater's backstage, actors put on makeup and are coached on their lines, stagehands construct and move scenery, and directors plan how to create the dramatic effects they desire. In the Simpson trial, it is likely that a backstage observer would have found attorneys planning strategy, witnesses rehearsing their testimony and nervously arranging their clothing, and all parties complaining about the duration and circus atmosphere of the trial to their friends and families—behaviors they would never have performed in the courtroom. Once they entered the courtroom, however, all these actors worked together to maintain the reality of the frontstage (i.e., the trial itself) and its separation from the backstage.

Note, however, that *backstage* and *frontstage* are relative terms: They are defined in relation to the specific role being played and the particular audience present at a given moment. Relative to Marcia Clark's role as the lead prosecutor in the Simpson trial, for example, the courtroom was a frontstage area, and her home was likely a backstage area. In her role as a mother to her two children, however, her home is the front stage.

The metaphor of dramaturgy translates easily to a court trial. Goffman argued, however, that *every* social situation is a dramaturgical performance—more subtle, perhaps, but nonetheless an active juggling of identities. Job applicants, for example, generally choose their clothes carefully, arrange their appearance neatly, and behave in ways that they hope will make them good candidates for the job. They may talk about their past successes at work, wax optimistic about their career goals, and neglect to disclose their past drug use or work conflicts. These same applicants may present a very different self with their friends, their families, their intimate partners, or their teachers.

This is not to say that self-presentations are dishonest. Some people feel that the concept of impression management implies an inauthenticity to human interaction. We suggest instead that self-presentation is simply a fact of social life. Our intentions may at times be to deceive, but more frequently they are benign: to help new acquaintances to quickly develop a picture of our "real selves," to have our talents recognized by a new boss, or to convey our sympathy to a bereaved friend. Most self-presentations are sincere attempts to show others who we "really are" in order to facilitate social interaction. Selves, after all, are not quickly and easily knowable. As Kollock and O'Brien (1994) note, "Minds are private, which is to say that our thoughts, desires, beliefs, and character cannot be directly perceived and evaluated. We are not a race of mind readers, and so we must depend on signs and symbols as substitutes for an underlying reality" (p. 128). Indeed, much impression management occurs below the level of awareness and is simply an immediate, seamless adjustment to changing social situations. Because norms and goals vary across situations, we present different aspects of ourselves in different circumstances. Each of these identities, however, may be authentic.

The Consequences of Impression Management. Presentations of self provide information that is necessary for interaction: "Information about the individual helps to define the situation, enabling others to know in advance what he [sic] will expect of them and what they may expect of him" (Goffman 1959:1). Actors engaged in this dynamic process of mutual impression management, Goffman says, develop a *working consensus*: an agreement about what sort of situation they are in and what sort of roles or identities they are playing. This public agreement need not correspond to the actors' private beliefs. But it is the publicly agreed-on definition of the situation that guides subsequent interaction. Once this agreement has been reached, it acquires a certain moral force. Actors can then expect to be treated in accord with this working definition and, in turn, have an obligation to behave in accord with this agreement.

These interactional negotiations often end up reproducing familiar cultural patterns. To present certain identities and positions, we must draw on symbolic representations of those identities. Laurie, in *Little Women*, has to conduct himself like the cultural image of a suitor; O. J. Simpson must act like a bereaved husband. As is often the case with symbols, there may be a good deal of slippage between a symbolic representation and our underlying emotions, identities, and experiences. Laurie's feelings about Jo, his best friend, may not fit perfectly the role of lover. Nonetheless, he—and we—must use familiar symbols in order to communicate. Over time, the reliance of members of a culture on a limited set of symbols may narrow the underlying range of emotions, identities, and realities; in other words, this process may affirm stereotypic understandings of positions such as husbands, wives, professors, students, or athletes. Blumstein (1991) has argued that the process of identity negotiation with our romantic partners can actually lead to changes in our sense of self: The wife who used to do her car repairs before she married may discover she is mechanically inept after years of her husband's telling her she should stay away from the car. More generally, through the performance of particular identities in our habitual interactions with those with whom we share everyday interactions, our identities may eventually ossify into our "true selves." As *Oleanna*'s John states eloquently, "You have to look at what you are, and what you feel, and how you act. And, finally, you have to look at how you act. And say: If that's what I *did*, that must be how I think of myself" (Mamet 1992:22).

Behavioral Confirmation

Impression management concerns how we present ourselves and the extent to which these self-presentations achieve our interactional goals. Self-presentations are shaped not only by our conceptions of selves, however, but also by our conceptions of others. As we noted briefly in Chapter 4, one of the more fascinating phenomena in human interaction is that we often confirm these preconceptions about other people through our very own behavior, a process known as *behavioral confirmation*. The best known example of this "Pygmalion effect" is the musical *My Fair Lady*, based on the play *Pygmalion* by George Bernard Shaw (which was itself based on a Greek myth). In this story, the elite Henry Higgins transforms a poor Cockney woman into an elegant and poised society lady; his treatment of her elicits the woman he wants her to be. The social psychological analogue is a study done by Rosenthal and Jacobson (1968). Teachers in an elementary school were given "information" about their students at the beginning of the school year. They were told that some of these students were potential late bloomers who would excel with the proper support and motivation. In reality, the students were randomly assigned to these labels. By the year's end, however, the students identified as late bloomers were performing as teachers had been told to expect. Why? The teachers behaved differently toward these students, providing them with careful feedback, teaching them more difficult material, and giving them more opportunities for responding in class. The teachers' expectations became a self-fulfilling prophecy: Because of the teacher's behaviors, the students who received additional attention did in fact perform more strongly.

This study of behavioral confirmation and the hundreds that have followed attest to the ubiquity of this general pattern: Initially false definitions of a situation can evoke behaviors that subsequently make the false belief true. Consistent with our emphasis on the structural circumstances within which interaction occurs, it is also true that such expectations are more likely to lead to a self-fulfilling prophecy if the expectation is held by a higher-status person—and we might speculate, if the expectations are held about a lower-status person. Higher-status individuals have more power with which to enforce their own preconceptions; lower-status individuals have less power with which to combat false expectations held by others. Indeed, there is some evidence that men are more likely than women to induce others to provide behavioral confirmation for their own beliefs, whereas women are more likely than men to provide behavioral confirmation for the beliefs of others (see Snyder 1984:254).

The implications of this process are profound. Consider physical appearance. A commonplace expectation in (at least) Western societies is that physically attractive people possess more socially appealing personalities than do those who are viewed as unattractive. In the study by Snyder, Tanke, and Berscheid (1977) mentioned in Chapter 4, male college students interacted very differently over the phone with female college students they believed to be attractive; their behaviors, in turn, elicited interactional responses from the women that confirmed the men's assumptions about the personality characteristics of attractive and unattractive women. Thus, although there is no inherent link between conventional good looks and personality, the expectation that physically attractive people will also be more socially attractive became a self-fulfilling prophecy.

It is not a great leap to move from characteristics such as attractiveness to status markers such as gender, race, or sexuality; evidence of behavioral confirmation is strong for all of these social positions. Gender stereotypes and expectations frequently serve as the basis for behavioral confirmation. In a study by Skrypnek and Snyder (1982), pairs of students negotiated a division of labor for gender-stereotypic tasks. The students were not able to see each other. One member of each pair was led to believe that the other person was either male or female. Through the process of negotiation, the target of this belief ended up choosing tasks consistent with the expectations of the interaction partner. Both women and men ended up choosing male-typed tasks if their partner thought they were a man; both women and men ended up choosing female-typed tasks if their partner thought they were a woman. Gendered behaviors, in other words, are in part the product of other people's beliefs about gender; this is the social construction of gender.

This process of gender construction begins as early as the moment of birth. Rubin, Provenzano, and Luria (1974) found that new parents perceived their male and female infants very differently, even though independent observers saw no differences between the baby boys and girls. For example, parents described daughters as softer, prettier, more delicate, and smaller than sons. A more recent study (Karraker, Vogel, and Lake 1995) found that two decades later, parents continue to perceive their newborns in stereotyped ways, although to a lesser degree than in the 1970s. These gendered perceptions likely affect parents' behavior toward and expectations of their children; indeed, there is a great deal of evidence that parents treat girls quite differently than they do boys (Beal 1994). In general, "mothers seem to be more emotionally warm and responsive with girls, and more encouraging of independence with boys. Fathers often spend more time with their sons and engage in more physical play with sons than daughters" (Karraker et al. 1995:688). These expectations function as self-fulfilling prophecies, eliciting gender-stereotypical behaviors from children.

Racial stereotypes also create self-fulfilling prophecies. Word, Zanna, and Cooper (1974) considered the behavior of white interviewers toward both white and black job applicants. When interviewing black applicants, interviewers maintained a "nonimmediate" interview style, one with greater physical distance, less eye contact, and less perceptual availability; made more speech errors (stutters, repetitions, incomplete sentences); and conducted shorter interviews. When they interviewed white applicants, interviewers used an "immediate" interview style, made fewer speech errors, and conducted longer interviews. In a follow-up, interviewers were trained to work with either an immediate or nonimmediate interview style and then used this style with both white and black applicants. Applicants subjected to the nonimmediate style performed less adequately and were more nervous than those exposed to the immediate style, regardless of their race. Performance differences between white and black job applicants thus reflected the interviewers' behaviors, not the applicants' qualifications.

The studies described above address gender, on the one hand, and race, on the other. None considers the possibility that gender and race may work together in creating cognitive preconceptions and ultimately confirming those preconceptions. Given the considerable research that attests to stereotypic conceptions about interactional patterns of women and men, we can assume that had Word et al. varied the gender, as well as the race, of the job applicants, the effects might have been even more extreme. Note, too, that the gender of the interviewer is not even mentioned, nor is the race of the interviewer varied. All of these possibilities complicate the process of behavioral confirmation.

These examples illustrate how beliefs lead us to test and ultimately to create reality through altering the behavior of others. Interestingly, this process does not require actual behavioral confirmation by the target; it can also occur through reconstructive memory. In the study by Snyder and Uranowitz (1978) described in Chapter 4, respondents were presented with information about the current sexual orientation of a woman about whom they had already been given a good deal of background information. As a result, these respondents reconstructed her biography to be consistent with their preconceptions of lesbian or heterosexual partnerships. Behavioral confirmation can even occur simply through people's awareness of expectations others hold for them. Steele and Aronson (1995) describe the possible effects of "stereotype threat," which they define as "being at risk of confirming . . . a negative stereotype about one's group" (p. 797). They demonstrate that the knowledge that others hold a negative stereotype about the intellectual ability of African Americans may interfere with the test performance of African American students. As a result, they may perform less competently than they otherwise would, thereby confirming the original stereotype. Thus cognitive and interactional strategies combine to create a powerfully reproductive system whereby preconceptions and stereotypes about ourselves and others are enacted and maintained.

Status Expectations

The idea of behavioral confirmation has also been central to another social psychological approach, expectation states theory (Berger, Conner, and Fisek 1974; Ridgeway and Walker 1995). Expectation states theory is much narrower in scope than the three theories around which we have organized this book, limiting its focus to "behavioral indicators of power and prestige" (Ridgeway and Walker 1995:288), such as participation in group discussions or influence over others. Although not generally identified as a symbolic interactionist perspective—indeed, its laboratory-based experimental methods and rigorous use of equations and graphs to model interaction are antithetical to much symbolic interactionist work (and more closely resemble social exchange)—we include it in this chapter because it shares several important assumptions with symbolic interactionism. These include a focus on the perceptions of actors, an assumption that these perceptions are socially constructed, and an emphasis on the social context of interaction. In addition, expectation states theory has addressed gender considerably more explicitly than any of the other theories we have considered so far.

Expectation states theory limits its empirical focus to small, task-oriented groups. Examples of this kind of group include a jury trying to ascertain the guilt or innocence of a defendant, a work group trying to solve a problem, or a family discussing how to allocate household chores. In these kinds of groups, members evaluate their own and each other's potential contributions to the group task in order to figure out how to reach the group's goal most effectively. Because group members generally share similar cultural beliefs, they tend to reach similar conclusions about each other's likely competence. These shared *performance expectations* are often self-fulfilling, resulting in a "power and prestige order" that favors those for whom the group has high performance expectations. This process works in two interlocking ways. First, individuals who have high expectations for themselves tend to contribute more to the group discussion, defend their opinions if challenged, and speak and act assertively. At the same time, others in the group, because they share these expectations, tend to allow the high-status members more opportunities to participate and evaluate their contributions more highly. Thus these individuals appear to be more competent and more influential relative to the rest of the group, regardless of their actual competence at the task at hand. A similar process occurs for actors who are expected to perform poorly: They expect less of themselves, defer more to others, are provided with fewer opportunities to participate, and if they do participate, their contributions are evaluated less favorably.

What do group members base these performance expectations on? According to the theory, expectations are based on *status characteristics*, attributes that are culturally associated with greater esteem and value (Berger et al. 1977). These can be *specific* characteristics, such as skills relevant to the particular task at hand, or *diffuse* characteristics that transcend particular situations, such as gender, race, education, and age. Expectation states theory argues that status characteristics are associated not only with greater social esteem but also with "implicit expectations for competence." For example, people in this society tend to accord greater status to men than to women: "Observers consider men to be more skillful and competent than women, even when there is no objective gender difference in performance" (Carli 1991:94). When a group includes both men and women, actors of both sexes tend to expect men to contribute more to the group's goal than women, even if gender is not relevant to the task at hand (Pugh and Wahrman 1983; Wagner, Ford, and Ford 1986). These expectations become self-fulfilling prophecies. Because of others' higher expectations of them, men tend to contribute more to group discussion, behave more assertively, and emerge as task leaders in group interactions (Wood and Karten 1986; Eagly and Karau 1991; Carli 1991). Moreover, evaluation of members' participation is based on a double standard: Men's performances are evaluated more favorably than women's, even if they are objectively identical (Foschi 1989, 1991). Thus this theory provides an explanation for how societal beliefs and values (such as the differential valuation of women and men) are reproduced in small-group, face-to-face interaction.

What is the relative influence of specific versus diffuse status characteristics? When information is available, specific status characteristics (such as specialized skills) can overcome the effects of diffuse characteristics (such as race or gender).

For example, if a mixed-sex group is attempting to solve a mathematics problem and one of the women in the group reveals that she is a mathematician, the high performance expectations stemming from her skills will likely overwhelm the low expectations stemming from her gender. It is important to note, however, that specific information is not always readily available: "Gender, like a few other statuses in our society (e.g., age and race), can be quickly discerned. When you see or hear a person, usually one of the first things you recognize is the person's sex." If gender is salient,

> gender becomes the basis for your initial performance expectations for your-self and the other. Information on other factors such as specific abilities . . . is usually not as quickly available as it is on gender and therefore is less likely to shape initial expectations. As a result, interaction proceeds on performance expectations based on gender. (Ridgeway 1993:183-4)

This theory thus helps to explain the pervasive influence of beliefs about gender on social life.

Resisting Expectations. We do not mean to imply that behavioral confirmation is seamless; this process can be curtailed. Perceivers can compensate for expec-tations they hold about others. If, for example, one has reason to expect that a person with whom one will interact is hostile, one might treat that person particularly warmly. In so doing, one is attempting to produce behavior that contradicts expectations. Even though this strategy tends to be successful in eliciting the desired behavior, however, it does not always overturn the original expectation. And again, this strategy may be dramatically more successful when enacted by a higher-status person than by a lower-status person. Ridgeway (1993) reports that in expectation states experiments, women who challenge low per-formance expectations by contributing assertively to group discussions can experience a "backlash" reaction because their behavior is perceived as illegiti-mate (Ridgeway 1982; Carli 1990; Butler and Geis 1990). In addition, the targets of such expectations may actively try to dispel perceivers' false expectations in an attempt to assert and confirm their own self-definitions. (This implies, of course, that they are aware of others' expectations.) The success of this strategy depends on how certain each party is of their own expectations, the intensity of these expectations, and the social structural power of the actors. At the beginning of Act 2 of *Oleanna*, for example, John has discovered that Carol has filed a complaint of sexual harassment against him and makes a speech that is clearly intended to convince her that he is genuinely concerned with the welfare of his students; that he is not, as he puts it, a bogeyman. His failure to convince her is eloquent testimony to the dramatic shift in each actor's power.

Interactional Repairs

Despite our best attempts at skillful self-presentations, interaction does not always proceed smoothly. On occasion, the identity we present is undermined:

For example, we may present ourselves as knowledgeable about a particular subject, but then find ourselves unable to answer our teacher's (or our students'!) questions. At other times, the working consensus about the definition of the situation breaks down. For example, a patient or doctor may become physically aroused during a medical exam, destroying the consensus that the examination of the patient's body is a medical, rather than a sexual, procedure (Emerson 1970).

In many cases, the audience may help to repair these kinds of interactional breakdowns by pretending not to notice the problem or by facilitating the actor's recovery from the gaffe. This kind of teamwork is another example of the way that people work together to maintain the "reality" of the frontstage (Goffman 1959). In other cases, the actor herself will undertake to repair the interactional breach. Often, this repair is effected by offering an *account*, a statement explaining why the breach occurred. Accounts are closely related to impression management, because they are a means of controlling others' perceptions.

There are two types of accounts: *justifications*, which acknowledge that a behavior occurred but deny that it was problematic, and *excuses*, which acknowledge that a behavior was problematic but deny responsibility for it (Scott and Lyman 1968). For example, in *Oleanna*, the professor admits to having touched the student but justifies that touch by denying that it had a sexual intent—rather, he says, he was attempting to comfort an obviously distraught student. In contrast, the professor might have admitted that the touch was sexual but attempted to excuse his behavior by explaining that he believed his advances to be welcome.

Note that justifications and excuses are both verbal repairs. Interaction relies not simply on behavior but fundamentally on language. Through language, identities, self-concepts, and impressions are constructed, justified, maintained, and altered.

Repairs and Social Structure

Once offered, accounts are not always honored. Whether an account is judged acceptable depends on the behavior in question, the situation, and the actors involved. For example, one's family might excuse tardiness that an employer would find unacceptable. A man might be excused for forgetting to attend a business meeting but not the birth of his child. Moreover, not everyone can call an individual to account: A professor might hold a student accountable for classroom performance, but another student could not. Thus interactional repairs are not always available or effective.

The acceptability of accounts is closely correlated with structural differences, social position, and power. For example, gender affects the legitimacy of accounts. "Overwhelming desire" might be accepted as an excuse for a man's sexual improprieties, because cultural beliefs about masculinity include the idea that men are driven by their sexual impulses. The same excuse might not work as well for a woman, because women's task in performing traditional femininity is to control their own and others' sexuality (Fox 1977).

Other social positions also affect whether one's accounts of questionable behavior will be honored, or even heard. Gallant (1992) describes the accounts given by 17th- and 18th-century slaveowners for the escape of their slaves and notes that "history hears the planter but not the slave" (p. 390). Slaves, because of their race and social position, were not entitled to give accounts; their understanding of situations, indeed their very selves, were not believed by white slave owners to be important or valuable. Individuals in stigmatized positions often find that their accounts are dishonored or disbelieved (Goffman 1963). Rosenhan's classic study (1973) demonstrates this fact forcefully. Eight mentally healthy research confederates managed to gain entry to mental hospitals as patients by claiming to hear voices. After entering the hospital, each patient behaved normally—yet in no case was the deception detected. Because these patients had been labeled insane, their subsequent behavior was interpreted as consistent with that label and their attempts to present themselves as sane were dishonored. The pseudopatients remained locked in the hospitals for an average of 19 days; the longest stay was 52 days.

The O. J. Simpson case provides a fascinating example of how an individual's multiple social positions can interact. Simpson was charged with murder in a culture where black men are often associated with danger and threat and their accounts dishonored. If he had been an average African American man, his case would probably have received little attention and been resolved far more quickly. Because of his other social characteristics, however—as a sports star with a fortune and an appealing public persona—Simpson received respectful treatment from police, a yearlong trial, gavel-to-gavel TV coverage, and scores of faithful fans insisting that "he couldn't have done it." Contrast this with the 1978 Georgia case of an unknown African American man, Gary X. Nelson. Nelson, accused of the rape and murder of a 6-year-old girl, "was represented by a lawyer who had never tried a capital case, was paid $15 to $20 an hour and had no investigator or experts. His closing argument was 255 words long." Nelson was sentenced to death and spent 11 years on death row before "new lawyers, at their own expense, found that crucial prosecutorial evidence, a hair on the victim's body, could not be validly compared to Nelson's hair—a fact mentioned in an FBI report that had never been disclosed" (see Egelko 1994:A3).

The Simpson case also illustrates how the meaning of social positions can change over time. The slaveowners' accounts described in Gallant's study likely received different reactions before and after the Civil War. O. J. Simpson's case would probably have received vastly different treatment prior to the civil rights movement. And the professor's abuse of power described in *Oleanna* would have aroused much less fury just 25 years ago—because the concept of sexual harassment had not yet been publicly constructed. Similarly, accounts may vary in acceptability across different cultures. For example, accusations of infidelity might justify a man's killing his wife in some cultures, but not in the United States. Thus accounts, like symbols, are dynamic and situationally variable.

Self-Presentation and Social Structure

Social structures, then, play a crucial role in face-to-face interaction, a fact that much symbolic interactionist work (and much social psychological research more generally) does not adequately acknowledge. Erving Goffman's work stands in sharp contrast to this general trend. Goffman was deeply interested in social structure and its effects on interaction. Presentations of self, Goffman (1976) argued, are closely tied to individuals' positions in social structures:

> It is plain that if an individual is to give and receive what is considered his [sic] ritual due in social situations, then he must—whether by intent or in effect—style himself so that others present can immediately know the social (and sometimes the personal) identity of he who is to be dealt with; and in turn he must be able to acquire this information about those he thus informs. Some displays seem to be specialized for this identificatory, early-warning function: in the case of gender, hair style, clothing, and tone of voice. (p. 2)

Presentations of self are thus manifestations of social structure in face-to-face interaction: they alert others to one's social positions even before interaction begins.

Goffman (1976, 1977) was particularly interested in the ways in which actors manage their presentations of gendered selves in social situations. Many people believe that "masculine" and "feminine" behaviors are simply automatic expressions of males' and females' underlying natures—a belief Goffman termed the "doctrine of natural expression." (Note the similarity between the doctrine of natural expression and essentialism, discussed in Chapter 1.) However, Goffman (1976) claims that "expression in the main is not instinctive but socially learned and socially patterned . . . And this is so even though individuals come to employ expressions in what is sensed to be a spontaneous and unselfconscious way, that is, uncalculated, unfaked, natural" (p. 7). Gender displays, then, are not so much representations of underlying difference between males and females but indications of actors' cultural competence—in other words, their ability to perform the culturally prescribed roles believed appropriate for males and females. This contention, of course, is fundamental to the social constructionist perspective discussed in Chapter 2. In addition, these displays signal to others that the actor is claiming a particular kind of self with a set of associated traits, abilities, privileges, and feelings. Through this display, the actor positions herself or himself in the social hierarchy.

Like other aspects of self-presentation, gender is actively manipulated in the service of particular goals. Take, for example, the gendered self-presentation of Marcia Clark, the district attorney in the Simpson trial. Although known as an effective prosecutor, Clark's demeanor was perceived to be "not feminine enough," and she was urged to "soften" her presentation of self. And in fact she did exactly this: She began wearing pastel colors, changed her hairstyle, and emphasized her status as mother in order to create a more "feminine" image. Clark's obvious transformations in the service of femininity present a particularly interesting case, because they show that the demands of gender interact with—and sometimes overwhelm—the demands of more local roles. Clark's goal in changing her appearance was clearly to create a more feminine impression; her media handlers (whom we might call professionals in the presentation of self) apparently felt that to be taken seriously, both by the jury members and by the larger viewing public, she had to "do gender" more traditionally. However, these same changes risked damaging her identity as a tough and intelligent prosecutor, possibly weakening her effectiveness in the courtroom. Perhaps the most fascinating aspect of this example of impression management is that everyone (media, public, and trial participants) presumably *knew* that Clark's metamorphosis was deliberate, strategic, and probably not at all true to her own character and beliefs—yet she did it anyway, and her efforts appeared to satisfy her critics. (A similar process can be seen in the chameleon style of First Lady Hillary Rodham Clinton, another nontraditional woman playing a public role.) Thus, although on some level we know that impressions are strategically managed, our faith in the "doctrine of natural expression"—the belief that the impressions people give off offer insight into their character—remains strong. (This case can also be interpreted as an example of the fundamental attribution error, discussed in Chapter 4: We tend to attribute others' behavior to their character rather than to situational influences.)

Impression management may go beyond the superficial level of appearances. Hochschild (1983), for example, describes the ways in which flight attendants and other service workers are instructed to manage not only their behavior but also their feelings. She calls this process "emotional work," which she defines as "the management of feeling to create a publicly observable facial and bodily display" (p. 7). Part of the flight attendant's job is to provide the appearance of enthusiastic, willing service for the passengers' comfort; they must suppress other emotions such as anger and resentment at treatment from inconsiderate passengers. Hochschild notes that these expectations for emotional work are not gender neutral. Women, for example, are disproportionately located in service jobs requiring emotional labor. Even when women and men occupy the same position, however, as in the case of flight attendants, women are expected to care emotionally for the passengers more than are their male counterparts.

Goffman's (1976, 1977) description of impression management challenges the belief that gender displays reveal individuals' essential natures. Nonetheless, he argues that these displays are far from trivial. Rather, they are the interactional expression of social hierarchy. Goffman notes that people who are socially subordinate—including women and "subordinate males" (those men who, by virtue of their youth, social class, sexual orientation, or other social positions, have less power than other men)—rarely challenge their place in the social structure. In fact, these people often defer to others. The explanation, Goffman argues, is pragmatic: By demonstrating that they acknowledge their subordination, they signal to those with more power that a direct display of dominance is unnecessary. (Note the parallels to exchange theory: The person with less power is exchanging his or her deference for the more powerful person's forbearance.) In most cases, these self-subordinating presentations are subtle, but:

> however trivial some of these little gains and losses may appear to be, by summing them all up across all the social situations in which they occur, one can see that their total effect is enormous. The expression of subordination and domination through this swarm of situational means is more than a mere

tracing or symbol or ritualistic affirmation of the social hierarchy. These expressions considerably constitute the hierarchy; they are the shadow *and* the substance. (Goffman 1976:6)

Thus these displays both express and reinforce power and stratification.

Resistance and Negotiation

In some situations, individuals may present themselves in accord with gender expectations, as we have discussed. In other situations, however, individuals may resist these traditional expectations, manipulating their self-presentation to avoid association with some stereotype. A good example of this process is women's self-protective behavior in public spaces. According to the research of Carol Brooks Gardner (1990), women know that being female suggests to others that they are vulnerable to attack, and they strategically alter their self-presentation to reduce their risk of becoming targets of street crime:

As aspiring criminals will have to depend on judgments of appearance to select prospective victims, so those who seek to escape victimization must depend on assessment of strangers' appearance and manipulation of their own in order to avoid crime. One way to cope with crime in public therefore will be to develop an array of behavioral strategies that are also appearance dependent; alternatively, people will curtail others' visual access in order to prevent being judged a suitable target. (p. 314)

Women may avoid certain parts of town or stay home after dark. They may dress "tough," walk with a confidence they do not feel, or choose their company (another woman, a man, or a dog) with an eye to safety. They may even feign the company of a male protector by leaving male belongings visible in their car or home or adding a man's name to their mailbox or answering machine message. These findings "remind us that public places are arenas for the enactment and display of power and privilege"—and that one basis of power is gender (Gardner 1989:55).

Although men generally do not engage in the kinds of self-protective behaviors described above, men's self-presentation may nonetheless be affected by their knowledge of women's concerns. Staples (1994), for example, describes the way in which his appearance as a large African American man affects the women with whom he shares public space:

My first victim was a woman—white, well dressed, probably in her early twenties. I came upon her late one evening on a deserted street in Hyde Park, a relatively affluent neighborhood in an otherwise mean, impoverished section of Chicago. As I swung onto the avenue behind her, there seemed to be a discreet, uninflammatory distance between us. Not so. She cast back a worried glance. To her, the youngish black man—a broad six feet two inches with a beard and billowing hair, both hands shoved into the pockets of a bulky military jacket—seemed menacingly close. After a few more quick glimpses, she picked up her pace and was soon running in earnest. Within seconds she disappeared into a cross street. (p. 156)

Staples goes on to describe the strategies he has developed to present himself as unthreatening, including walking slowly, keeping a comfortable distance away from others, and speaking hyper-politely to police officers. Finally,

> On late-evening constitutionals, I employ what has proved to be an excellent tension-reducing measure: I whistle melodies from Beethoven and Vivaldi and the more popular classical composers. Even steely New Yorkers hunching forward toward nighttime destinations seem to relax, and occasionally they even join in the tune. Virtually everybody seems to sense that a mugger wouldn't be warbling bright, sunny selections from Vivaldi's *Four Seasons.* It is my equivalent of the cowbell that hikers wear when they know they are in bear country. (p. 158)

Staples' self-presentation resists the stereotypical association of black men with danger and threat. Thus individuals attempt to present themselves in a manner that will help them to achieve their interactional goals.

Snow and Anderson (1987, 1993) found that street people in Austin, Texas, similarly resisted negative class-based stereotypes. The homeless people they studied tended to construct positive personal identities through three distinct forms of "identity talk." First, some individuals distanced themselves from the roles, people, and institutions associated with homelessness: "I'm not like the other guys who hang out at the 'Sally' [Salvation Army] . . . you can't really learn about street people from studying me, because I'm different" (Snow and Anderson 1987:1349). Alternately, some people embraced these roles, people, and ideologies: "It would have to be a bigger purpose than just money to get me off the streets, like a religious mission." "I'm a bum and I know who my friends are" (Snow and Anderson 1987: 1356-7). Finally, some people engaged in fictive storytelling, embellishing past accomplishments and fantasizing about future possibilities. Snow and Anderson also note that these forms of identity talk can be gendered. Homeless men's fictive stories, for example, "were generally organized around four themes: self-employment, money, material possessions, and the opposite sex." The content of these fantasies demonstrates that gender expectations condition even those who have become separated from other normative social institutions:

> That these four factors function as springboards for fanciful identities constructed by homeless men in particular is hardly surprising, given that success as an adult male in America is defined in large part in terms of job, money, possessions, and women. This thematic connection also suggests that, while homeless males tend to stand very much outside the normative order in their way of life, some of them are, nonetheless, very much of that order in their dreams and fantasies. (p. 1361)

Thus identities are not simply assigned; they are negotiated and can be resisted by those in stigmatized positions.

On occasion, resistance may entail playing into others' stereotypes. Ramos (1979) describes an interaction between an elementary school principal and the father of a Mexican American student accused of breaking a window, whom Ramos calls Mr. Perez. Although he knew Mr. Perez to be interactionally competent and articulate in English, Ramos observed quite a different presentation of self in Perez's interaction with the principal: "As I watched Mr. Perez talk with the principal, it occurred to me that he appeared to be both nervous and stupid. He spoke with broken English, and acted as though he did not understand the situation very well. . . . He conformed to the typification of a Mexican American who speaks little English, and who can only deal with people in informal situations" (pp. 141-2). When Ramos later asked Mr. Perez "why he had presented himself in such a demeaning way," Mr. Perez answered,

> Oh, I was pulling a *movida* [strategy]. You know, I came on like the dumb Mexican, all lost and confused. You know how that guy thinks of us most of the time. Besides, had I come on straight, he might have held me responsible for the window Freddy broke. I am not about to pay for a window my boy broke by accident. They ought to provide a bigger play area so that kids don't break a window every time they throw a ball. (p. 142)

Thus in some situations, strategies for resistance may actually involve using others' preconceptions for one's own ends.

It is important to recognize, however, that resistance is not always successful. The term *negotiation* implies that the interacting parties have equal opportunity to control the social identities presented; they come to the bargaining table with equal resources and together develop a joint definition of the situation. This image of fair negotiation is not always accurate, especially in the case of stigmatized groups. Those people with more resources and more power can exert more control over interaction and the negotiation of identities. Despite homeless individuals' attempts to present themselves favorably, they are deeply stigmatized by the rest of the population. Despite Staples' (1994) attempt to present himself as nonthreatening, he may be harassed by police officers who perceive all black men as dangerous. And despite a woman's attempts to present herself as less vulnerable, she may nonetheless be attacked by a man. Some people, in short, have more control over negotiation than others. Once again, social structural factors condition social interaction.

Conclusions

The symbolic interactionist approach to self and identity has clear connections to both social cognition and social exchange. Cognition is central to symbolic interaction: It is through thought that meanings come to be attached to symbols, and it is through thought that we are able to interpret these symbols. In addition, the negotiation of identities requires a set of cognitive processes. An actor must review her identities and select those she deems appropriate for a situation; at the same time she must review the identities she wants to impute to the other person. Put in the terms of social cognition, the actor must scan her self-schemas; on the basis of a cognitive appraisal of the situation, certain identities will be more salient than others. At the same time, she must scan the possible selves others might perform and coordinate her behavior strategically with these selves. Like all cognitive processes, this need not be—and perhaps most often is not—conscious. On the other hand, particular structural circumstances may make this everyday negotiation acutely conscious. Dorothy Allison (1994) offers searing examples of this selective screening. Writing of her negotiation of the interactive challenges of being poor, she avows,

> My people were not remarkable. We were ordinary, but even so we were mythical. We were the *they* everyone talks about—the ungrateful poor. I grew up trying to run away from the fate that destroyed so many of the people I loved, and having learned the habit of hiding, I found I had also learned to hide from myself. I did not know who I was, only that I did not want to be *they*, the ones who are destroyed or dismissed to make the "real" people, the important people, feel safer. . . . The habit of hiding was deeply set in me. . . . if I told the truth about my life, my family, my sexual desire, my history, I would move over into that unknown territory, the land of they, would never have the chance to name my own life, to understand it or claim it. (pp. 13-14)

Symbolic interaction is also linked to social exchange. Both theories take the interaction, rather than the individual, as their unit of analysis. However, the two theories offer quite different pictures of social interaction. Whereas empirical work in social exchange has focused mainly on the exchange of resources between actors, symbolic interaction focuses on the *meaning* of these resources as well as on the exchange of cognitive and behavioral manifestations of identities, adding a far more complex and subtle level of analysis. Moreover, exchange theory considers the resources possessed by each actor, and actors' positions in the social structure, to be the keys to understanding behavior. Thus actors are essentially interchangeable: The implication is that in the same structural position, every individual will behave similarly. Symbolic interactionism, in contrast, focuses much more on the selves of actors. The individual's self-concept, identities, and subjective interpretations of meaning guide behavior.

As a result, symbolic interactionism is able to explain the subtleties of interaction neglected by exchange theory. On the other hand, exchange theory's conceptions of social structure, inequality, and power are better developed than those of symbolic interactionism. In fact, the most frequent critique of symbolic interactionism is its failure to adequately address social structure and power. For example, Stryker and Statham (1985) write that

> symbolic interactionism's strength is its ability to conceptualize social actors who can construct their lines of action individually and cooperatively and who can also alter the social structural conditions within which they act. Its weakness is its inadequate conceptualization and analyses of the social structural constraints—ranging from minimal to virtually total—within which social action is constructed and its inability to deal with stability in individual and social behavior. (p. 313)

For example, although symbolic interactionism helps to illuminate how beliefs and expectations about other people are maintained and perpetuated, it does not always address the question of where these expectations originate, and why. What do they accomplish, and for whom? When they are resisted, who resists and who enforces them? To answer these questions, we must look beyond the interactional level and address more macrolevel issues of power, social structure, and inequality. Although we have discussed a number of studies that do integrate social positions and structures into their analyses, these studies do not constitute the mainstream of symbolic interactionist research. Identity work, meaning construction, and self-presentation are important, but so are material resources and structural positions. Without an understanding of factors such as stratification and power, the picture is incomplete.

This is acutely evident in the interactions between John and Carol in *Oleanna*. In Act 1, John has virtually all the power to set up the interaction, to decide who can speak and what they can say, to decide when the interaction starts and when it is over, and most important, to decide literally who each person will be. The interactional model that McCall and Simmons (1978) outline may not even apply to Carol: She may not be able to devise identities for herself and for John, so great is his power over her. In other words, substantial imbalances of power may short-circuit the negotiation of identities. Actors import into these interactions the full force of those structural positions they occupy. Although both social exchange and symbolic interaction offer analytic insight, neither alone can explain such an interaction.

Finally, both symbolic interactionism and social exchange theory assume that self-interest motivates human action: People act in ways that they believe will result in desirable outcomes for themselves. These two theories conceptualize self-interest in radically different ways, however. Because exchange theory conceptualizes the self narrowly as a possessor of resources and social position, self-interest can entail only the maximization of those resources. Symbolic interactionism's richer idea of self, however, results in a much broader conceptualization of self-interest. Individuals are believed to be motivated by many desires, including the admiration and well-being of significant others and the maintenance of valued identities, as well as the maximization of one's own resources. Thus self-interest may involve sacrificing resources to meet other goals.

Recent developments in social cognitive understandings of selves and identities also suggest future questions for symbolic interactionism. There is increasing interest in how an individual's various structural positions and social roles are integrated to form a social self. For example, how do being female, black, a grandmother, and having a professional job combine into a coherent identity? Self-schemas have been assumed to be organized as a relatively harmonious set of many distinct identities, some more salient than others. What happens to the definition of self-schemas if we think of these identities as not so separable but as always interconnected in complex and often contradictory ways, and experienced simultaneously (West and Fenstermaker 1995)? For instance, *Oleanna's* John is an arrogant college professor who grew up thinking he was stupid; *Little Women's* Jo is a woman who wants a career and does not want to marry but is also eager to have children. O. J. Simpson is a man who certainly beat, and may have brutally murdered, the woman he professed to love, but is eager to be a father to his children; he lives in a culture that often vilifies black men as dangerous, yet he was revered as a sports hero by people of all races. Because we are always selecting and performing various identities in complex, situated combinations, playing off of other actors doing the same things in the same situations, our models both of selves and of interactions must be considerably more complex.

How does symbolic interactionism correspond to the four approaches to gender we described in Chapter 2? Because of its theoretical allegiance to the social construction of self and identity, symbolic interaction is incompatible with essentialist approaches to gender. Because of its commitment to the ongoing, active nature of this construction, it is also somewhat incompatible with the socialization perspective, which tends to view gender as instilled in childhood and relatively static thereafter. It should be clear that symbolic interactionism is closely related to the social constructionist approach to gender; indeed, it is from this tradition that the social constructionist approach developed. As we have suggested throughout this chapter, symbolic interaction is also compatible with a structural approach to gender, although many practitioners of symbolic interactionism tend to de-emphasize or even ignore the effects of social structure. Although it is true that symbolic interactionists at the margins of the discipline (as well as many non-social psychologists who use symbolic interactionist ideas in their work) do attend to these issues, their research often goes unread by mainstream social psychologists. Thus this work, although important and illuminating, often does not affect the bulk of social psychological research.

We have now completed our overview of the three main theories of social psychology: social exchange, social cognition, and symbolic interactionism. Many social psychology textbooks and courses, however, are organized not by theory but by topic. We believe that the theoretical grounding presented in the preceding chapters can also illuminate the traditional topical areas of social psychology. To illustrate, we now turn to two of the most intriguing topics in social psychology: aggression and altruism.

Note

1. Respondents are asked to provide 20 short-phrase answers to the question "Who am I?" The most common categories of responses to this question are personality characteristics, social structural positions, and personal evaluations.

CHAPTER 6

Altruism and Aggression

Gendered Dynamics of Helping and Harming Others

Up to this point, our journey through social psychology has been organized by the major theoretical perspectives in this field. We have explored the ways in which social exchange, social cognition, and symbolic interactionism explain the relationships between individuals and the societies in which they live and the ways in which each perspective incorporates, facilitates, or impedes a gendered analysis of these relationships. At this point, we shift orientation from theory to topic.

A glance at the table of contents of virtually any social psychology text reveals a list of only loosely connected topics. Our choice to order the bulk of this volume by theories reflects our conviction that ideas provide a preferable organizational framework. As the reader has discovered, however, we have also discussed the details of socialization, stereotyping, attribution, impression management, the development and negotiation of selves and identities, and other central social psychological topics. In this chapter, we focus in considerably greater detail on two popular areas of social psychological research: altruism and aggression. We shift focus here to illustrate how using gender as an analytic lens allows us to make connections across specific topics.

Altruism and aggression each earn a full chapter in almost all social psychology texts. Typically, these chapters are located sequentially, in recognition that there is an intuitive link between helping and harming others. Altruism and aggression are assumed to be opposite behaviors. As is often true with opposites, however, their dynamics are more similar than they might at first appear. In this chapter, we consider the substance of the connections between them, drawing on a series of examples to show that gender and other systems of hierarchy form a good deal of this substance. We analyze explanations for altruism and aggression offered by the major social psychological theories. We then review the key questions that have organized research in each field, illustrating with empirical research and critiquing assumptions made about gender, race, sexuality, and class positions. We also discuss some of the implications of researchers' methodological preferences, and, finally, turn to thematic issues that crosscut these two fields. We begin with definitions, because neither altruism nor aggression is so easily defined as it might at first appear.

Definitions

John: I'll make you a deal. You stay here. We'll start the whole course over. I'm going to say it was not you, it was I who was not paying attention. We'll start the whole course over. Your grade is an "A." Your final grade is an "A."

Carol: But the class is only half over . . .

John: Your grade for the whole term is an "A." If you will come back and meet with me. A few more times. Your grade's an "A." Forget about the paper. You didn't like it, you didn't like writing it. It's not important. What's important is that I awake your interest, if I can, and that I answer your questions. Let's start over.

Carol: Over. With what?

John: Say this is the beginning.

Carol: Of what?

John: Of the class.

Carol: But we can't start over.

John: I say we can. I say we can.

Carol: But I don't believe it.

John: Yes, I know that. But it's true. What is The Class but you and me?

Carol: There are rules.

John: Well. We'll break them.

Carol: How can we?

John: We won't tell anybody.

Carol: Is that all right?

John: I say that it's fine.

Carol: Why would you do this for me?

John: I like you.

Carol: Um . . .

John: There's no one here but you and me.

Carol: All right. I did not understand. When you referred . . .

John: All right, yes?

Carol: When you referred to hazing.

John: Hazing.

Carol: You write, in your book. About the comparative . . . the comparative . . .

John: Are you checking your notes?

Carol: Yes.

Mamet (1992:26-27)

Altruism

This passage is the central "action" of Mamet's play *Oleanna*. In this scene, John offers to help Carol do better in his class, a direct response to her plea that she does not understand. What do we mean by the term *help? Helping behavior* refers simply to any act that provides assistance to another person. The motives or intentions of the helper are irrelevant. The consequences of the behavior define helping. Note that consequences can be both material (e.g., money or medical aid) and psychological (e.g., feeling supported).

If John were so busy that taking this time with Carol would cost him dearly in some other realm, we might label his behavior altruistic. *Altruism* refers to action performed voluntarily to help someone when the actor has no expectation of receiving a reward; some people define acts as altruistic only if the actor also incurs costs. Here, the intentions and motives of the helper are crucial. Although most acts of altruism are also acts of helping, this is not always the case. An act intended to be helpful, even at great cost to the helper, does not always have helpful consequences. Intervening in a fight, for example, can sometimes accelerate the conflict. Also, actions intended to be helpful are not always perceived as such. Consider the dynamics of chivalry: How does it feel to have someone offer to walk you home at night or to carry your groceries? One might feel flattered, relieved, humiliated, or annoyed.

Prosocial behavior is another related concept. This term refers to acts that are in accord with or support the norms of a given community or culture. Fighting in war generally is considered prosocial behavior, in that such service is consistent with the predominant values and norms of a society. This is an even broader category than helping, because some prosocial behaviors are not helpful to their immediate targets, even though they advance the interests of the relevant society.

Thus, to understand the general domain of positive actions, one must take into account the intentions and motives of the actor(s), the consequences of the action, and the perceptions and reactions of the person(s) being helped. We emphasize in the remainder of this chapter that the social contexts within which such actions occur are also important. Social behaviors are not benign; they reflect prevailing relationships of power. Helping and harming behaviors are no exception, as the following discussion demonstrates.

Aggression

Let us return to the extended example from *Oleanna*. John's offer appears to be altruistic: He will spend extra time to help Carol understand the class material. As we find out in Act 2, however, Carol does not interpret this offer as altruism. Rather, she perceives it, and John's consoling hug, as an aggressive attempt at sexual harassment. As the play continues, the physical aggression becomes clearer, culminating in a scene in which John physically assaults Carol. The focus of the play shifts from altruism to aggression.

Defining aggression appears simple. Aggression, most people would agree, is any behavior that hurts someone else: hitting someone, shooting someone, stabbing someone, and so on. But what if the harm is unintentional? A driver might hit a pedestrian crossing the street, causing severe injury, but is this accidental injury really aggression? On the other hand, what if a person tries to shoot someone, but misses? Most people would define this act as aggressive, even though it does not result in harm. Although intent is more difficult to assess than harm (because, as we noted in Chapter 5, minds are private), it is clearly an important component of aggression.

Motivation is also important. If a homeowner shoots and kills an armed robber who breaks into his or her house, is that shooting aggressive? When soldiers kill others during a war, are those deaths the result of aggression? (And if so, whose aggression—the soldiers' or their government's?) War and self-defense are two circumstances in which most people consider violence to be legitimate; indeed, they are often considered prosocial behavior. Discipline is another such situation: Many people approve of using physical punishment to control children, and the death penalty is accepted by many people as punishment for the most heinous crimes. These normative uses of aggression are culturally defined as *prosocial*, in contrast with criminal violence, collectively defined as *antisocial*.

It is important to note that what is defined as prosocial and as antisocial reflects the systems of power that prevail in a given society. Thus political changes can also lead to changes in definitions of aggression. Until the last few decades, for example, many states had laws that allowed husbands to beat their wives; some states still permit husbands to force their wives to have sex against their will (a behavior that legally constitutes rape in any other situation). Most states have now redefined these behaviors as wife battering and marital rape. There are also cross-cultural differences in what is defined as antisocial aggression. In some countries, it is permissible for male family members to kill a woman whose sexual virtue has been questioned—an action that would be severely punished in the United States.

Whose viewpoint is considered when defining aggression? Most people would define rape as an aggressive act, but definitions of a sexual encounter can be contested. If a woman says she was raped, but the man says they engaged in consensual sex, how does one decide whether his behavior was in fact aggressive? If the woman did consent to intercourse but did so not out of desire but rather emotional coercion, fear, or threats of injury or death, was it aggression? And what about the status of words? Some people believe that words, as well as actions, can be violent: If a man regularly threatens to kill his wife but never actually does so, are his words aggressive? These examples make clear the importance of interpretation and meaning—and power—in defining aggression and violence. As we noted in our discussion of symbolic interaction in Chapter 5, the same behavior can carry different meanings in different contexts. In one situation, shooting someone might be considered aggressive; in another, it might be considered patriotic or heroic.

Social psychologists often distinguish three types of aggression. In *instrumental aggression*, actors know their actions will hurt others but use aggression strategically to achieve a specific outcome, such as discipline, obedience, or material gain. *Expressive aggression*, in contrast, results from emotions such as anger and is intended simply to harm another. In *indirect aggression*, actors use manipulative methods, such as gossiping, exchanging friends, trying to win others to one's side, excluding from groups, and so on (Björkqvist 1994:182) to harm others. These forms of aggression are not always separable: Consider, for example, parents who strike their children out of anger but with an ultimate goal of control or discipline. Breines and Gordon (1983) also note that violence can be expressive on an individual level but instrumental on a collective level: A given incident of wife battering, for example, can express individual anger, but large-scale patterns of battering can be "an important ingredient in the continued subordination of women; even to women not directly victimized, these attacks teach lessons" (p. 515).

Helping versus Harming

Helping is positive behavior, with consequences that presumably benefit another person, whereas aggression is negative behavior meant to hurt another person. In one sense, helping behavior is often reactive: we notice that someone else needs help, and we react by providing it. Aggression, in contrast, is more often proactive; actors generally initiate aggression. Furthermore, although both behaviors involve an interaction between two actors, the relationship between the actors is fundamentally different. The person providing help and the person receiving help are often treated as participants in a relationship. Indeed, the receipt of help creates indebtedness, which is itself the basis of a relationship. As we discussed in Chapter 3, the norm of reciprocity suggests that the provision and receipt of help are a basis for social relationships. For example, a Thanksgiving Day news story in the *Seattle Times* reported the formation of an enduring relationship based on the rescue of a man stranded in river floods by two men who happened to be driving by. The potential victim was so grateful that he had made one of his rescuers a regular part of his family holiday gatherings (Routman 1995:A1). Thus helping often generates reciprocal relationships.

In contrast, aggression is generally not the basis for formation of a relationship. Whereas helping brings people together, aggression separates them. The parallel to a norm of reciprocity is a norm of retaliation, but in practice, people do not always retaliate against aggression, whereas they usually do reciprocate helping. What keeps targets of aggression from retaliating? The structural power of the aggressor and of the person against whom aggression is directed determine whether retaliation is possible. If the aggressor has significantly more power, retaliation is unlikely. Helping behavior thus often generates a relationship, whereas aggression does not.

Social Psychological Explanations of Altruism and Aggression

The social psychological theories that we have reviewed in earlier chapters present very different approaches to social behavior. Each of these theories has been used to explain both altruistic and aggressive behavior. In the next section of this chapter, we discuss the explanations that each theory provides for altruism and aggression, paying close attention to the relationships between these behaviors and gender.

Essentialist/Biological Perspectives

Altruism. In Chapter 2, we noted that social psychological patterns of gendered behavior have been attributed to biological differences between the sexes. Although most social psychologists reject this essentialist perspective as an outdated theory of gender, biological factors continue to be the basis for one theory of altruism and helping behavior. The basic logic is that altruism toward one's own offspring helps those offspring survive, thus contributing to the maintenance of one's gene pool. This implies that people should be most altruistic toward those who are most closely linked genetically to themselves, they should be more altruistic toward healthy than unhealthy offspring, and mothers should be more altruistic toward offspring than are fathers, based on the numbers of offspring each sex can produce in a lifetime.

This perspective has specific implications for patterns of helping behavior by gender. Social scientists have hypothesized that, due to their different reproductive processes, women and men differ in their sensitivity to distress and emotional cues. Indeed, women are more likely than men to intervene at low levels of harm to others, women have more intense responses to others' expressions of emotion than do men, and girls report more distress than do boys (Piliavin and Charng 1990). Whether these patterns require a genetic explanation is debatable, however. Women may report more distress and intervene at different levels of harm than do men due to gender-based patterns of socialization, cognitive schemas and behavioral expectations, or interactional demands. Piliavin and Unger's (1985) review of empirical research suggests no gender-related differences in physiological arousal or in impulsive responses to emergency situations. Thus, although biological factors may well shape helping, many other social and cognitive factors are also influential.

Aggression. Commonsense understandings also attribute aggressive behavior to biological factors: It is widely believed that people are aggressive because of their genes, their hormones, their fight-or-flight instinct, their innate natures, their responses to pain or discomfort, or their unconscious urges. Biological explanations are particularly common in discussions of gender and aggression. Some theorists argue, for example, that men tend to be more aggressive than women because it is evolutionarily useful for them to be so: Aggressive males are likely to mate with more females than nonaggressive males and will therefore produce more offspring. Others argue that men tend to be more aggressive than women because of their higher concentrations of testosterone.

Clearly, biology plays some part in human aggression. Physiological arousal—excitement generated by physical activity, danger, emotional interaction, or the use of alcohol—can generate aggression. Most social psychologists agree, however, that biological factors alone cannot explain human aggression. Biological influences on aggression are filtered through social situations and structures. For example, alcohol increases aggression by reducing inhibitions against aggression and increasing both attention to potential threats and vulnerability to social pressures to aggress (Taylor and Sears 1988). These inhibitions, cues, and pressures are socially, rather than biologically, defined. Recent research on hormones has demonstrated that their effects are quite complex: Some studies have found no differences in testosterone (or other hormone) levels between aggressive and nonaggressive people (e.g., Constantino et al. 1993); other studies have found that aggressive behavior may increase testosterone levels rather than the other way around (Rose, Bernstein, and Gordon 1975). Injections of high concentrations of testosterone are currently being explored as a way of *reducing* male fertility (Monmaney 1995:A1). These results suggest that hormones are not the sole source of aggression but, rather, interact with other factors in shaping human behavior.

Another essentialist perspective, *frustration-aggression theory* (Dollard et al. 1939), argues that individuals are likely to behave aggressively when they have been prevented from achieving a goal. The emotional stimulation of frustration is presumed to trigger aggression. In one study, children who were forced to wait for a long time behind a wire screen before they were allowed to play with some enticing toys were very aggressive once they were admitted to the room—smashing the toys, throwing them across the room, and so on—whereas children who had not had to wait played with the toys nondestructively (Barker, Dembo, and Lewin 1941). We do not respond with aggression every time we are frustrated, however. Wife abuse, for example, has been attributed by some scholars to men's levels of frustration. Studies show, however, that men who batter their wives are often quite unaggressive in situations such as their workplaces (Kandel-Englander 1992). It is unlikely that they are frustrated only in their marital relationships; it is far more likely that they channel their frustration in different ways with different people, in accord with situational norms.

Equally telling are the overwhelming cross-cultural differences in aggression. Scott (1992) found enormous differences in his analysis of the murder rates in a variety of cultures: For example, the murder rate in the Gebusi society of New Guinea is nearly 800 times higher than the murder rate in Norway. It is implausible that biological factors account for this difference; clearly, there are cultural variations in what acts are even defined as murder. The large situational and cultural differences in aggression suggest that aggression is strongly influenced by social and cultural factors.

Social Learning Theory

Altruism. Generosity and other forms of helping behavior increase as children age. Most explanations for this trend derive from a social learning perspective. In most societies, children are explicitly taught to share and to help others. This behavior, like others, is learned through reinforcement principles and through modeling: Children consistently display greater generosity when they are exposed to generous as opposed to selfish models. Parents, other adults, and the media are all effective models of helping (see Piliavin and Charng 1990). Episodes of *Sesame Street*, for example, are rife with models of helping (Sprafkin, Liebert, and Poulos 1975). Adults also learn to help via reinforcement and modeling: A simple statement of gratitude for an act of generosity strongly increases adults' tendencies to repeat this behavior (Moss and Page 1972). Learning to help, in other words, continues throughout life.

Social norms reinforce helping behavior. The norm of social responsibility is pervasive: We should help those who depend on us. Parents help their children (and the law will take the children away if parents fail in this responsibility); in turn, children are supposed to care for their parents when they become elderly. A norm of reciprocity dictates that we should help those who help us. Norms of social justice proscribe violations of equity, as we noted in Chapter 3. Cultures clearly vary in the intensity and perhaps even the content of these norms. Miller, for example, has shown that a general sense of responsibility for others is appreciably higher in India than in the United States (Miller, Bersoff, and Harwood 1990). Miller attributes this difference to a greater stress on interpersonal interdependence and social obligations in Hindu Indian culture. Similarly, definitions of social justice vary within nations and communities.

Aggression. Social learning theorists suggest that children learn aggression, like altruism, through reinforcement and modeling. Bandura's Bobo doll experiments (discussed in Chapter 3) demonstrated that children imitate the aggressive behavior they see adults perform, especially if they identify with the adults or see them rewarded for their aggression. Research on intergenerational family violence supports the predictions of social learning theory: Children who observed abuse in their families of origin or who were abused themselves are far more likely to abuse their own intimate partners or children (Gelles 1994). Children who are physically disciplined by their parents also have a greater risk of delinquency as adolescents and of committing violence both inside and outside the home as adults (Straus et al. 1991). Observing violent behavior on television leads children to behave more aggressively toward other people, especially when they have also witnessed parental abuse (Heath, Kruttschnitt, and Ward 1986). Children in these situations learn that aggression is an effective way to solve problems and later use this behavior when they confront similar problems in their own lives.

Social learning also helps explain adult aggression. In one study, Black and Bevan (1992) measured aggression levels in people waiting to see both aggressive and nonaggressive movies, as well as in people who had just viewed these movies. People who had just viewed an aggressive film had higher levels of aggression than the other groups. Moreover, people who chose to see the aggressive film had higher levels of aggression even before entering the movie theater. These researchers conclude that "films featuring violence attract an audience with a propensity for aggression, [and] that viewing these films heightens this tendency" (pp. 42-43).

Do these increased levels of aggressive feelings translate into real-world behavior? Ethical concerns prevent researchers from investigating this question directly; indirect evidence, however, suggests that media coverage may indeed increase actual aggression. Phillips (1983, 1986), for example, found that the daily rate of homicide in the United States nearly always increased during the week after a heavyweight boxing match, when the match was well publicized. These patterns had racial and gender implications: After white boxers lost fights, there was a corresponding increase in murders of white (but not black) men; conversely, after black boxers lost fights, there was an increase in murders of black (but not white) men (Aronson, Wilson, and Akert 1994). Violence has also been found to increase after hijackings (Bandura 1973), riots at sporting events (Dunand 1986; Rime and Leyens 1988), and wars (Archer and Gartner 1976, 1984).

Research on pornography also suggests that viewing violent material may increase the likelihood of behaving aggressively. One study asked undergraduate men whether they would "force a woman to have sex against her will" if they knew they would not be caught. More than half (57%) said they would do so, after they had viewed violent pornography. Even when they had not viewed violent pornography, 25% to 30% reported they would do so (Donnerstein 1983; Briere and Malamuth 1983).[1] The most negative effects of pornography are associated with viewing materials that combine sexual content with violence. One study of widely available video pornography found that four-fifths of the films contained sexually explicit scenes depicting male domination or exploitation of women. Three-fourths of these videos depicted male physical aggression against women; half of them showed rape (Cowan et al. 1988). Thus the pornography that is most common is also potentially the most dangerous. Representations of violence do not affect all people equally, however; they have stronger effects on those predisposed to aggression.

Social Exchange

Altruism. Social exchange theorists view at least some acts of helping as exchanges: When one person provides help to another, resources are transferred. Several of the social norms mentioned above are based on principles of social exchange. The reciprocity norm, for example, prescribes equality of exchange. Norms of social justice are also guided by equity principles. Overbenefited people may give some of their resources to someone who has been shortchanged (a restoration of justice). Even those who are not involved in a direct exchange may transfer resources to others; people donate to charities, which in turn distribute those resources to people in need.

The social exchange perspective is particularly relevant to the reactions of those who receive help. When the provision of help is largely one way, the recipient becomes indebted to the helper. Unidirectional helping threatens equity, creates a power imbalance, and may lower the recipient's self-esteem (and, conversely, heighten the donor's self-esteem). Thus people are more likely to ask for help if they think they can repay it (Fisher, Nadler, and Whitcher-Alagna 1982). In real-world relationships between social equals, the possibilities for eventual repayment are considerably greater than in the brief interactions in laboratory studies. When participants in a helping encounter differ in their structural power, however, unidirectional helping is more problematic. *Oleanna's* John explicitly breaks the academic rules (starting the class over) to help Carol. His certainty that he can do this with impunity communicates his status and legitimacy and underscores Carol's lack of power. The same act that is intended to help Carol also reinforces John's power over her. This ostensibly unidirectional helping in fact has benefits for John and costs for Carol.

People do weigh the costs and benefits of action and inaction. Among the costs of helping are the possibility of looking foolish, physical danger, messiness of possible blood or vomit, lost time, legal complications, and so forth. Benefits of action include the psychological reward of feeling good about one's self and social approval. The intensifying need of the other party is a primary cost of inaction; guilt is also highly likely. The overall profile of costs and benefits eventually determines what one decides to do.

Perceived costs and benefits are particularly important in shaping gendered patterns of helping (Piliavin and Unger 1985). Many of the empirical differences between women and men in giving and receiving help relate to differences in their perceptions of the costs and benefits of helping. Providing physical help is often more costly for women, for example, because women tend to be physically smaller than men and because gender norms support the physical dominance of men over women. Reliance on the principles of social exchange in helping behavior may also differ by gender and class: Middle-class boys, for example, are more likely than less advantaged boys or girls of any class to consider whether or not gifts will be reciprocated when deciding whether to offer gifts (Dreman and Greenbaum 1973). The principles of social exchange thus explain helping better for some groups of actors than others.

Aggression. As we noted in Chapter 3, social exchange research has rarely addressed aggression. Indeed, the theory's focus on individual choice directs attention away from interactions that may be involuntary for one or more of the participants or that are based on emotion rather than on rational choice. Moreover, as Molm (1987) notes, research on social exchange has generally been restricted to the exchange of resources and rewards; her exploration of the use of punishment is a first step in the application of social exchange theory to studying aggression. She finds that the use of punishment varies according to the structural situations of the exchange partners: Those actors with less access to reward power are more likely to punish their exchange partners (Molm 1989a, 1989b). Note, however, that "punishment" in these experiments is operationalized as taking a few cents away from one's experimental partner—a far cry from aggression outside the laboratory.

Despite this neglect of aggression, we suggest that exchange theory could be fruitful for understanding coercive situations. If aggression is viewed as a resource that actors may use to achieve their goals, then coercive interactions can be conceptualized as situations in which the power imbalance between the actors is extreme. Interestingly, many researchers working outside social psychology have used an implicit exchange perspective to understand aggression and violence. Gelles (1985), for example, examines wife battering as a rational strategy used by men to maintain dominance over their wives. He hypothesizes that men weigh the costs and benefits of possible actions and choose to beat their wives, because this promises high rewards and relatively low costs. Similarly, much criminal justice theory is based on the idea that aggressive crimes can be deterred by making the perceived costs of crime higher than the perceived benefits. (However, research shows that punishment acts as a deterrent only when it is both certain and nearly immediate—circumstances rarely realized in our criminal justice system [Bower and Hilgard 1981]. In the real world, even the death penalty does not deter violent crime, perhaps because only rarely are homicides punished by death.)

Some researchers have also used exchange theory to explain reactions to violence, such as the reactions of women to battering. When discussing an abusive relationship, people may ask, "Why didn't she just leave?" Exchange theory predicts that a woman will decide whether to leave or stay in an abusive relationship based on the costs and benefits associated with each choice. Leaving might entail a risk of incurring greater injury, the possibility of becoming homeless, and the risk of losing custody of one's children, although it also has the benefit of escaping from repeated abuse. Staying might provide the benefit of love and affection when violence is not imminent, financial support for oneself and one's children, and social status, but at the risk of further assault. According to exchange theory, the balance of these perceived costs and benefits determines the woman's decision to stay or leave.

Social Cognition

Altruism. Helping behavior is the outcome of a cognitive decision-making process. First, we must notice that something is happening that might require help and then we must decide whether help is required. When we are in a hurry, tired, sick, or preoccupied, we are less likely to attend to the environment around us and thus to notice potential crises. Defining the situation as one that requires help is also not as straightforward as it might appear. People tend not to offer help in ambiguous situations, because of their concerns about appearing foolish. In one often-cited study, students sitting with others in a room rapidly filling up with smoke just continued to sit there, afraid of reacting inappropriately (Latane and Darley 1968). Normative conventions also affect the likelihood of intervention. In a study by Shotland and Straw (1976), strangers were much less likely to intervene in a fight between a man and a woman when they thought the two were married. Both general norms of privacy about intimate relationships and patriarchal conceptions about the rights of husbands over their wives discouraged these strangers from intervening.

If help is required, we must decide whether we are capable of helping. This also entails deciding what sort of help is needed and how to provide it. We also assess our own sense of responsibility to provide help. One factor in assessing personal responsibility is the number of other available bystanders. The greater the number of others available who might help, the less likely any given person is to act (Schwartz and Gottlieb 1980). In the murder of Kitty Genovese, the incident with which we began this book, this diffusion of responsibility is likely the major reason why her neighbors waited so long to call the police. Each of them thought someone else would take action. Once we have decided that intervention is called for and that we are capable of such action, we engage in the cost-benefit analyses suggested by social exchange theory. Social cognition and social exchange models thus intersect in the individual calculations of costs and benefits.

The social positions of those in need of help and those who offer help shape the cognitive assessment of costs and benefits of helping. Perceptions and judgments about who needs help, who is more capable of providing help, and whose need is legitimate derive from the structural positions of those involved. For example, the costs and benefits of both helping and inaction are gendered. Both socialization and social norms suggest that looking foolish might be more troublesome for men than women, that blood or dirt might be more troublesome for women than men, that men may feel they have more of the physical and technical skills necessary for some forms of intervention, or that women might feel more concern about the welfare of others and thus feel more guilt should they fail to intervene.

Structural constraints on helping are not always straightforward, however. As we have noted, gender stereotypes cast women as less competent and more dependent than men. Thus women are offered more assistance than men in some situations. This also means, however, that women are expected to take precautions to avoid being in need. Because of their perceived greater physical and sexual vulnerability, women are expected to avoid walking alone at night, to avoid spending time with strangers, and so forth. When they are assaulted in such situations, both women and men are more likely to blame them. In one study, respondents attributed considerably more blame to women who were assaulted when they had been hitchhiking than to women assaulted while jogging or to men assaulted while engaging in either activity (Howard 1984a). Thus stereotypes of women's greater vulnerability can generate both sympathy and blame, depending on attributions about their behavior.

Aggression. Cognition also plays an important role in aggression. One influential cognitive process involves the *priming* effects of aggressive cues. The presence of objects symbolizing aggression can provoke aggressive behavior. In one study, for example, college students who had seen a gun behaved more aggressively than those who had seen a badminton racket (Berkowitz and LePage 1967). Thus the presence of objects associated with aggression primes aggressive behavior by making aggressive thoughts and feelings more accessible, even if the objects themselves are not used.

Words may also prime aggression. Another study found that respondents exposed to words related to aggression (e.g., *insult, stab,* or *anger*) wrote stories containing more aggression, anger, and violence and expressed more interest in watching violent films than those exposed to nonaggressive words (Langley et al., 1992). This process may help explain the effects of viewing media violence on aggressive behavior. These materials may indeed provide models of aggression for viewers to imitate, as social learning theory argues. However, they may also prime aggressive thoughts and memories that make aggressive behavior more cognitively accessible to individuals.

Priming effects also occur through the activation of social schemas. For example, "one common television script is that the bad guy provokes the good guy, who retaliates. The child who has learned this script from television might in later life be too quick to retaliate to minor insults" (Taylor, Peplau, and Sears 1994:451). Similarly, the finding that children who experience or witness abuse are more likely to abuse as adults could also be explained by the transmission not of specific behaviors but of scripts about the proper roles of women and men and the appropriate responses to frustration in intimate relationships.

Attribution is another cognitive process that helps explain aggression. Individuals are far more likely to respond aggressively to attacks they perceive to be intentional, for instance, than to attacks they perceive to be accidental or beyond the control of the instigator (Berkowitz 1986). Apologizing for provocative behavior, however, reduces aggressive responses (Schwartz et al., 1978). The apology presumably alters the attribution. Other evaluations are also significant. As discussed in Chapter 3, many social behaviors stimulate cognitive calculations of equity and justice. Not getting what one expects or feels one deserves can result in perceptions of unfairness. In particular, provocation that is perceived to be unfair produces stronger aggressive reactions than provocation perceived as legitimate.

Stereotypes also influence aggression. Whom would you expect to be more aggressive: a football player or a librarian? A young person or a very old person? A man or a woman? A black man or a white man? A white woman or an Asian American woman? A straight man or a gay man? A middle-class woman or a working-class woman? Most people have expectations about whom they expect to be aggressive. These expectations likely depend on one's own and others' social positions; a white man might expect that a black man would be more likely to aggress, whereas a black man might expect more aggression from a white man. In one study, for example, white participants characterized women as passive and men as aggressive far more than black participants did (Smith and Midlarsky 1985). Thus expectations about aggression are conditioned by membership in and stereotypes about different social groups.

Stereotypes also influence social psychological research on aggression. Despite the fact that men as well as women can be sexually assaulted, for example, there were no studies of male sexual assault victims until fairly recently (Howard 1984a). This gap in research is likely due to prevailing stereotypes of men as victimizers and protectors rather than as victims. Similarly, stereotypes of women as nonaggressive victims inhibits analysis of the ways in which women do aggress, as we discuss in greater depth below.

Symbolic Interaction

Altruism. The concepts of symbolic interaction seem well suited to explaining helping encounters. How we define situations through interaction is clearly related to the resolution of those ambiguous situations in which helping might be required. Negotiating the identities we want to perform and the identities we want others to adopt is a major task in potential helping situations; the identity implications of needing help, of being helped, and of offering help are not trivial. In one scene in *Little Women,* for example, the March girls have spent Christmas morning gathering together their presents for each other and eagerly awaiting their holiday breakfast. Just as they gather at the table, their mother returns from a last-minute errand with an announcement:

"Merry Christmas, little daughters! . . . But I want to say one word before we sit down. Not far away from here lies a poor woman with a little newborn baby. Six children are huddled into one bed to keep from freezing, for they have no fire. There is nothing to eat over there; and the oldest boy came to tell me they were suffering hunger and cold. My girls, will you give them your breakfast as a Christmas present?"

They were all unusually hungry, having waited nearly an hour, and for a minute no one spoke; only a minute, for Jo exclaimed impetuously:

"I'm so glad you came before we began!"

"May I go and help carry the things to the poor little children?" asked Beth eagerly.

"I shall take the cream and the muffins," added Amy, heroically giving up the articles she most liked. (Alcott 1924:27)

In that long minute between Mrs. March's question and the girls' responses, we can well imagine the sorts of identity debates going on in their private thoughts: They must choose between the self-satisfaction of a fine meal and the costs of seeming—and judging themselves as—selfish.

The consequences of social encounters depend on these situational definitions. In *Oleanna,* John and Carol fail to achieve a common working definition of their situation. From John's perspective, he provided help to a student. From Carol's perspective, he took advantage of her vulnerability. Their failure to achieve a mutual definition has disastrous consequences: John loses tenure and physically assaults Carol. The consequences for John are explicit in the play; the negative consequences for Carol, although not articulated, are not hard to imagine. Students who file complaints of sexual harassment, even when those complaints are judged valid, often are ostracized by faculty and other students alike; their academic and working environments may become so aversive that they drop out of school.

Symbolic interactionists maintain that the ability to take the role of the generalized other is partly a function of one's position in social structures (Schwalbe 1991). Actors located in relatively complex social structures, such as bureaucratic organizations, are exposed to a greater variety of roles and therefore have more opportunities to take the role of a generalized other. Greater opportunity does not necessarily translate into use of those opportunities, however. John has clearly had the experience of being a student—and one who struggled academically—as well as the experience of being a professor. Nonetheless, he fails to reflect on Carol's perspective. One's social power shapes how much one has to take the perspective of others and, therefore, how likely one is to recognize others' needs and to offer help.

In addition, the symbolic interactions through which helping encounters are performed are themselves deeply social. Social norms of "appropriate" gendered and racialized behavior guide self-presentation and impression management. In one field experiment, white female students high in racial prejudice helped black victims in an emergency more slowly than white victims but only when there were passive bystanders present. When there were no bystanders, all respondents helped the victims equally quickly (Gaertner, Dovidio, and Johnson 1982). These respondents' self-presentations appeared to be based on concerns about the appraisals of others.

Eagly and Crowley (1986) argue that gender differences in patterns of helping are derived from the symbolic meanings of what they refer to as the social roles of women and men. Agency and a sense of self as a "good provider" are fundamental to the male gender role; chivalry, therefore, is part of the successful portrayal of masculinity. Chivalry depends on having someone to help, however: women. Being helpless and passive are part of the female gender role. The performance of both chivalry and the "damsel in distress" entail identity management. Management of the female role is particularly complex; another part of the female gender role is to care for the personal and emotional needs of others.

Aggression. Symbolic meaning and interpretation are central to aggression. The priming effect of guns is a case in point: Although the participants in the Berkowitz and LePage (1967) study did not use the gun in their aggressive behavior, its symbolic connotation of aggression prompted them to behave aggressively. Interestingly, symbolic interaction has rarely addressed aggression, perhaps because its model of humans as meaning-makers downplays the role of power and hierarchy in interaction. The theory describes individuals actively interpreting the world around them, an image at odds with the realities of coercion and force. Nonetheless, the few symbolic interactionist studies of aggression do demonstrate the rich potential of this theory.

Felson's (1978) provocative analysis of the impression management of aggression, for example, suggests that aggression is often an "attempt to seek or restore face, self-esteem, status, or power" (p. 205). Actions that are perceived to attack the identity of another person—for example, calling someone dishonest or unkind—threaten that person's identity. One strategy for preventing or repairing that damage is to respond aggressively: "A successful counterattack is one effective way of nullifying the imputed negative identity by showing one's strength, competence, and courage" (p. 207).

This kind of identity work is deeply gendered. Consider the effects of being called a "girl": A woman may bristle at or be complimented by such a term, but a man may feel compelled to fight, to resist what he perceives as a stigmatizing identity. Indeed, many male high school coaches frequently call their players "girls" or "ladies" to pump them up before a game. Aggression is a central theme of many cultural stereotypes of masculinity: "a 'real man' is a strong, heterosexual protector, capable of taking care of himself and, if necessary, guarding his and others' safety aggressively" (Stanko 1990:110). Many men report that, as boys, they were compelled to fight other boys to prove their masculinity. Recent analyses of sports and war link men's participation in these activities to the need to prove their masculine identity (Messner and Sabo 1994; Connell 1995; Enloe 1993).

Masculine identity rests on two contradictory forms of aggressive behavior. Many men establish a masculine identity by protecting and defending—sometimes aggressively—"their" women and children, and, often, others as well. In this case, aggression is perceived to be prosocial behavior. However, some men also confirm their masculine identity through antisocial aggressive behavior, such as crime and violence. A number of authors have suggested that gang rape, for example, is as much an interaction between men (on the symbolic level) as an act of violence against a woman. In their study of gang rape in college fraternities, Martin and Hummer (1993) conclude that "fraternity norms and practices influence members to view the sexual coercion of women, which is a felony crime, as a sport, a contest, or a game. . . . This sport is played not between men and women but between men and men. Women are the pawns or prey in the interfraternity rivalry game; they prove that a fraternity is successful or prestigious" (p. 128). Harry's (1990) discussion of heterosexual men's violent aggression against lesbians and gay men similarly suggests that this violence is often an attempt to reaffirm their heterosexuality. Thus aggression can be a strategy for constructing a valued masculine identity.

Unlike men, women rarely manage their identities by enacting aggression. Cultural stereotypes locate women as the targets, not the perpetrators, of aggression or protection. These stereotypes may themselves increase women's vulnerability: Because some women do not believe that they can defend themselves, they may not try to do so, instead relying on men for protection. Their inaction then confirms both the stereotype of women as needing protection and women's own identities as feminine actors.

Women and men may also differ in their interpretation of the events precipitating aggression. Shotland and Craig (1988) found that women interpreted behaviors such as smiling or speaking in a low voice as friendly, whereas men perceived these behaviors as indicating sexual interest. Similarly, Muehlenhard (1988) found that women perceived initiating a date, wearing sexy clothes, drinking alcoholic beverages, allowing the man to pay dating expenses, and going to his apartment as normative behaviors, whereas men interpreted them as signs of sexual interest. Men also rated force (having sex with a woman against her wishes) as more justifiable than did women. It is easy to see how these conflicting interpretations could facilitate date rape.

Summary

As we have emphasized in this discussion, each of the major social psychological theories can be used to explain some aspects of both helping and aggressive behaviors. No one of these theories is sufficient by itself, but taken together, they can account for much of the variability in these forms of behavior. There are, however, systematic omissions in the sorts of questions these theories address. In particular, each of them tends to minimize the role of structural factors and power in helping and aggression. We turn to these topics in the next section.

Structural Patterns of Helping and Aggression

In the preceding review of theories of helping and aggression, we have deliberately foregrounded what is at best a minor theme in the prevailing emphases of these fields: the effects of social structural positions. In the following section, we offer a systematic analysis of the demographics of altruism and aggression. We focus on a few key questions: Who is more or less likely to offer help? Who is more or less likely to receive help? Who is more or less likely to be aggressive? Who is more or less likely to be the target of aggression? What kinds of situational factors and what kinds of individual differences make altruism or aggression more or less likely?

Who Provides Help?

According to gender stereotypes, helping encounters should be gendered. As competent, active, and strong, men should be more likely to provide help; as helpless, passive, and weak, women should be more in need of and likely to receive help. Early studies of altruism consistently reported that, under similar conditions, men offer help more than women and women receive more help than men (Krebs 1970).

Research conducted since 1970, however, paints a different picture. Piliavin and Unger's (1985) extensive review of gender and helping suggests that gendered patterns of helping behavior are not so clear-cut. There is consistent evidence that women respond more empathically than men to the distress of others. Because women are also more willing to report affective responses than men, due to differential socialization, it is difficult to interpret this finding. Women report providing their friends with more personal favors, emotional support, and counseling about personal problems. In laboratory studies, women donate more money than do men (Lerner and Frank 1974). Women also seem to value helping more than do men (e.g., Hales and Fenner 1973). The subtleties of these patterns are intriguing: Calabrese and Cochran (1990) report, for example, that although women (and Asian men) are less likely to cheat than white men, they are more likely to cheat when their cheating helps others succeed, whereas white men are more likely to cheat for their own personal gain.

Women do not always provide more help than men do, however. Men are more likely to provide help than women when women perceive helping as more dangerous, an audience witnesses the act, and other potential helpers are available (see Piliavin and Charng 1990). Men are more likely to provide help that requires physical strength, such as lifting someone who has collapsed. Differential expertise is also relevant, and assumptions about expertise vary along explicitly gendered lines. Men are more likely to offer help for car problems (West,

Whitney, and Schnedler 1975) or when shopping tasks involve buying a cigar (Dovidio et al. 1978). Women are more likely to offer help to children (Wunderlich and Willis 1977) or to assist with laundry (Dovidio et al. 1978).

Other social positions also influence the provision of help. We noted above that involvement in more complex social structures enhances opportunities to role-take and thus those in more advantaged financial circumstances might be more helpful. When we consider low-cost helping, there is some support for this prediction: Upper-middle-class residents of two cities were more likely than lower-middle-class residents to return unstamped lost letters (Lowe and Ritchey 1973); "middle-class" people (as assessed by their clothes) were more likely to return a dropped wallet than "lower-class" people (Diener et al. 1973). Opposite patterns have been found in higher-cost helping, however, both in semicontrolled studies (Yarrow, Scott, and Waxler 1973) and real-world patterns. Poorer people give higher proportions of their incomes to charities, for example, than those who are wealthy. Indeed, contributions of the wealthy steadily declined during the Reagan era of the 1980s, whereas contributions of those with lower incomes steadily increased (*Giving USA* 1986).

Who Receives Help?

There are also gendered patterns in the receipt of help. Following logically from patterns of who provides help, women are helped more (by men) in automobile mishaps, thefts, or dropped goods. Men are helped more (by women) in situations involving children or housecare. In less gender-typed situations, such as lending money or stapling questionnaires, gender differences in the receipt of help disappear (see Piliavin and Unger 1985).

Other social positions also affect the receipt of help. Predictions about these effects are based on intergroup dynamics. In-group favoritism, majority bias against a minority group, or majority support of a minority group have all been found— more evidence that the effects of social positions depend on situation and context. In some public situations, racial dynamics seem to play little role. Both black and white shoppers, for example, provided assistance to both black and white shoppers who spilled a bag of groceries (Wispe and Freshley 1971). Helpers (race unidentified) did not distinguish between Mexican and English surnames in returning unstamped lost letters (Lowe and Ritchey 1973). Biases against racial minority groups are found in other public situations, however. In one study, both male and female white adults performed a small favor more often for white than for Asian requestors, and in another, whites predominantly helped other whites whose cars were disabled, whereas blacks did not show a racial preference (West et al. 1975).

Some of these contradictions are due to situated costs and benefits. One field experiment found, for example, that a minor helping gesture was offered more to blacks than to whites (by helpers whose race was not identified) when it was cost-free but more to whites than blacks when there was a small financial cost (Brown and Reed 1982). Not surprisingly, racial prejudice is more evident in anonymous helping. Whites were more likely to mail a "lost" application for graduate school, for example, when the enclosed photograph showed a white rather than a black applicant (Benson, Karabenick, and Lerner 1976). Political nuances are also significant: In one study, blacks were assisted more if they identified themselves with the older, conservative label "Negro" rather than the (then) radical label "Black" (Katz, Cohen, and Glass 1975). Although the terms in this study are dated, the patterns are likely not.

Because of this resilience of racial prejudice, there is a good deal of evidence that blacks help each other. Blacks were particularly likely to provide low-cost assistance to other blacks on a predominantly white college campus, for example, where they may have felt a special solidarity with and responsibility to other minority students (Wegner and Crano 1975). Studies of racial patterns in effectiveness of volunteer counselors also suggest that among both blacks and whites, intraracial effectiveness in helping is the norm (Morrow-Howell, Lott, and Ozawa 1990).

Underscoring the influence of social prejudices, a few recent studies show that sexual orientation also determines the receipt of help. Both women and men (whose sexual orientation was not assessed) were more likely to do a favor for a male heterosexual caller than for a male homosexual caller (Shaw, Borough, and Fink 1994). Both women and men (again, whose sexual orientation was not assessed) were more likely to provide change for heterosexual than for homosexual requestors of either gender; this pattern did not change when an explanation for the request was provided (Gray, Russell, and Blockley 1991; Tsang 1994).

Cultural context also shapes the provision and receipt of helping. The tendency to favor one's in-group is considerably stronger in collectivist than in individualist cultures. Because the interests of the individual in collectivist cultures are often subordinated to the needs of the group, members of collectivist cultures are more likely to share resources with in-group members. Chinese and Japanese respondents offered more help than did U.S. respondents to others whom they perceived to be members of their own national group, for example; these same respondents were less likely than U.S. respondents to help those perceived to be from a different national group (Leung and Bond 1984).

The receipt of help based on gender differs in (at least) one significant respect from the receipt of help based on race, class, sexuality, or nationality. Social psychologists generally interpret the latter in terms of intergroup conflicts and intragroup favoritism. Research on gendered patterns in helping does not suggest even the possibility of intergroup conflict—that is, that women or men might discriminate against each other in the provision and receipt of help. Rather, researchers treat women and men as members of a common group, differing only in their abilities and styles of helping and vulnerabilities to needing help. In contrast, researchers assume potential in-group preferences based on other social positions. Thus a systematic structural analysis is at least partially evident in analyses of the effects of race, class, sexuality, or nationality on helping behavior, in contrast to the consistent focus on individual traits in analyses of the effects of gender.

Who Is Aggressive?

Sociobiologists argue that sex differences in aggression result from innate differences between women and men. To support their arguments, these theorists point to a large body of evidence that suggests that men tend to engage in more real-world physical aggression than do women. In 1987, for example, only 11.1% of all those arrested for violent crimes were women (Simon and Landis 1991:46).[2] Laboratory experiments also have found that men, on average, behave more physically aggressively than women, as Maccoby and Jacklin (1974) concluded in their influential review of such research. Others, however, have challenged the conclusion that there are large, stable gender differences in aggression. Recent meta-analyses of aggression research demonstrate that if differences do exist, they are not nearly as large as prior analyses suggest: Hyde (1986) found that gender accounted for only 5% of the variation in aggression in the 143 studies she analyzed. Moreover, most of the studies in Maccoby and Jacklin's review involved children; gender differences among adults are far smaller than among children (Eagly and Steffen 1986). More recent laboratory studies and meta-analyses have concluded that women and men have similar capacities for aggression (Macaulay 1985; White and Kowalski 1994). Thus, if there are gender differences in aggression, they are far smaller than stereotypes suggest. Moreover, it is clear that the sexes are more similar than they are different: Most men, like most women, commit little aggressive violence.

Gender has not been a central theoretical construct in most other social psychological theories of aggression, although all have discussed gender differences in aggressive behavior. Most theories are gender neutral: Frustration-aggression theory, for example, posits that women and men will respond similarly to frustration. Examining this theory with a gendered lens, however, suggests some problems. If aggression results from frustration, then what are we to make of the fact that women tend to engage in far less real-world physical aggression than do men? It is unlikely that women's lives are less frustrating than men's. How then can social psychology explain gender differences in aggressive behavior?

Social learning theory provides one answer: Women may be equally capable of violence, but these capacities are encouraged in men and inhibited in women. Girls rarely observe women modeling aggressive behavior and are punished more harshly than boys for behaving aggressively. These gendered consequences of aggression continue into adulthood. A businessman who behaves aggressively may be labeled a "star" or a "go-getter," for example, whereas a woman who behaves similarly may be labeled "pushy," "bitchy," or "abrasive." Women may learn that indirect aggression will serve them better than direct physical aggression. Eagly and Steffen's (1986) meta-analysis of 63 studies of adult aggression found that more than one-third of the gender differences observed in aggression could be accounted for by differences in guilt, anxiety, and concern about retaliation. Thus, whereas the principles of social learning theory are gender neutral, social norms and expectations are not, resulting in different patterns of aggressive behavior for women and men.

This analysis implies that if social norms and reactions to women's aggression were different, women would behave differently. Bandura's (1965) Bobo doll experiments support this hypothesis. Boys in these experiments behaved more aggressively than girls. However, when the children were rewarded for aggressive behavior, the girls' aggression increased to match the boys' level. Other studies show that women may act as aggressively as men when aggression is perceived as prosocial. Thus "sex" differences might be due not to differences in aggressive tendencies but to societal norms that lead women and men to define situational cues differently and lead people in general to respond more negatively to women's aggression. Because women are less frequently rewarded for aggression, they may choose other means to achieve their goals—not because of an innate aversion to aggression but because aggression is not a rewarding strategy for them.

The size of gender differences in aggression also varies by social situations. In one study, female and male undergraduates read vignettes in which one student prevented another from preparing for an examination in dance (a feminine context) or in body building (a masculine context) (Towson and Zanna 1982). The male participants advocated responding more aggressively than the female participants did, but only in the masculine situation. In the feminine situation, the gender difference disappeared. Again, the important factor is not sex but gender. Kogut, Langley, and O'Neal (1992) found that respondents' masculinity or femininity predicted aggression in some circumstances: "Women possessing more stereotypically masculine traits aggressed more following insult than did women less masculine in their gender role orientation" (p. 365). Similarly, Nirenberg and Gaebelein (1979) found that men with gender-traditional attitudes were more likely to aggress against both women and men. The important distinction, then, is not one's sex per se but how well one has learned to perform the traits and characteristics considered appropriate for one's gender.

Moreover, when women are aggressive, gender stereotypes suggest that they will act suddenly and emotionally, out of an instinct to preserve themselves or their children. Chronic domestic violence is expected from men but not from women; women may respond to domestic violence and kill an abuser in self-defense during an episode of battering, but they are not expected to premeditate retaliation or to behave aggressively when the abuser is helpless. In the well-publicized case of John and Lorena Bobbitt, for example, his chronic physical abuse of her did not seem to shock the nation, but her response—severing his penis with a knife while he slept—did.

Thus cognitive stereotypes, expectations, and social norms condition reactions to women's and men's aggression. Although violence by all actors is nominally disapproved, in practice, men's aggression is more readily accepted than women's. Boys are rewarded for fighting because it fits with gender expectations; girls are not (Thorne 1993). As adults, gender (and race and class) expectations continue to shape reactions to women's aggression. The criminal justice system treats women who violate gender expectations more harshly than those who do not. For example, "older, white, female suspects are less likely to be arrested than their younger, black, or hostile sisters" (Visher 1983:5). Women who murder their husbands typically receive far harsher punishments than men who murder their wives (White and Kowalski 1994). The reactions of women and men to the violence of other women and men do vary by gender: Women have more favorable attitudes toward rape victims and attribute more blame to rapists than do men, for example. Nonetheless, both women and men tend to hold female victims more responsible in rape cases than in other types of crime (White and Sorensen 1992).

These patterns are especially evident in reactions to women who kill their children. Consider the case of Susan Smith, the South Carolina mother who in 1994 strapped her two young sons into their car seats and allowed the car to roll into a lake, resulting in the boys' deaths. Later, she said she had intended to drown herself as well. Although Smith committed a dreadful crime, her actions were less physically violent than those of many murderers, and according to her account she sought relief from pain and misery, not harm to her sons. Yet she was publicly vilified in the press and called a "monster" by reporters and the public alike (Bragg 1995:A1), who clamored for her to receive the death penalty. Why? Because her behaviors did not match widespread stereotypes of what a "mother" should be like. The vehement public reaction to the drowning of her sons resulted not only from the fact that she caused the death of two young boys but from the fact that she did so *as a woman and a mother*—violating gender norms as well as more general moral norms. It may be useful to speculate what reaction would have ensued had the boys' father committed this act. Ironically, gender may also explain why Smith was sentenced to life imprisonment rather than the death penalty; the United States has historically been reluctant to execute women (Sullivan 1995:A2).

Other social positions also influence aggression and social reactions to it. The connection between race and real-world aggression is dramatically illustrated by crime statistics. Black men (13% of the U.S. male population) have higher arrest rates than do other racial or ethnic groups (LaFree 1995) and constitute nearly 50% of those in prison (Chambliss 1995:250). In contrast, some experimental studies have found no racial differences in aggression or have found blacks to be less aggressive than whites (e.g., Luchterhead and Weller 1976). There are several explanations for the disparity between experimental findings and arrest patterns. First, there are racial inequities in criminal justice responses to violence: Blacks are more likely to be arrested than whites for the same crime and are more likely to be imprisoned if convicted (Bridges and Crutchfield 1988; Crutchfield et al. 1995). These patterns also reflect social class biases. "Violent street crime tends to be committed by powerless men, but powerful men also commit crimes, although they are less likely to be charged or convicted of them" (Basow 1992:312). Moreover, wealthier men tend to commit white-collar, rather than violent, crimes.

Race is also crucial in the interpretation of violence. Duncan (1976) showed white undergraduates a videotape of an ambiguous situation (one person shoving another) and asked respondents to assess the violence of the shove. The students judged the behavior to be more violent when the perpetrator was black rather than white and also attributed the violence to the person when the perpetrator was black but to the situation when the perpetrator was white. Similar results were obtained with black respondents in a later study. Duncan suggests that the concept of violence was more accessible when a black person was seen committing the same act.

Research by Howard and Pike (1986) suggests that the effects of race on attributions about aggression are not as straightforward as stereotypes (and some laboratory studies) might suggest. Research participants (white and Asian American) were asked to describe their reactions to an interview with a man who had been arrested on a disorderly conduct charge. Some participants were told the man was black; others, that he was white. The race of the actor affected attributions of blame but in an unexpected way: "Subjects were more likely to blame the actor when he was white than when he was black, and to blame society when the actor was black as opposed to white" (p. 163). The authors' speculative explanation is that these college students' knowledge of racism and discrimination in the criminal justice situation influenced their attributions.

Class stereotypes also influence aggression and social reactions to it. Many people believe that poor and working-class people are more likely to be aggressive than members of upper classes. The reasoning behind this assumption is economic: Because financial problems often cause frustration and because the poor presumably have more financial problems than the rich, the poor must be more aggressive. There is some evidence that violence is more frequent in poorer families and neighborhoods. A recent study by Roff (1992) found that social class during childhood was the second most significant predictor of adolescent delinquency, after childhood measures of aggression; respondents in low or middle social classes were most at risk for delinquency.

On the other hand, some forms of aggression occur fairly consistently across social classes, especially those that occur within families, such as domestic violence and child sexual abuse. What is not consistent is aggressors' treatment by the criminal justice system: In general, middle- and upper-class offenders are treated more leniently than poor or working-class offenders (see Reiman 1995). The prevalence of *private* violence across all classes suggests that social class affects the forms in which aggression is expressed but not the tendency to aggress. Messerschmidt's (1993) study of crime among different race and class groups supports this point: Crime existed across all social categories but took different shapes for men from different racial and socioeconomic groups, because these groups had different resources, different opportunities for aggression, and different stakes in the mainstream culture.

Cultural norms may underlie the relationship between ethnicity and aggression. Kaufman, Gregory, and Stephan (1990) studied differences in the reactions of Anglo and Hispanic students to being an ethnic minority in their schools. Hispanic students were more moody, but not more aggressive, in classrooms where they were a minority. Anglo students, however, were more aggressive in parallel situations. Kaufman et al. attribute this difference to cultural norms: They maintain that Hispanic culture emphasizes individual effort to be likable and easygoing, whereas Anglo culture permits more overt aggression. Similarly, Moghaddam, Taylor, and Wright (1993) note that Japanese children are taught to avoid or withdraw from potentially aggressive situations, whereas Western children are taught to confront and retaliate against aggression:

> In Japanese culture, parents actively discourage quarreling and encourage their children to yield rather than fight on. When Japanese children are faced with an argument or a fight, their mother will likely tell them "*Makeru ga*

kachi," which means "To lose is to win." In the Japanese household, the child
who yields is honored. (Moghaddam et al. 1993:124)

Similarly, Lambert (1971, cited in Moghaddam et al., 1993) suggests that
Mexican and U.S. parents respond differently to children's aggression because
of different degrees of interdependence in their respective extended families. One
Mexican mother explained her punishment of her child's aggression in this way:
"I cannot permit my son to fight with the child next door in the Mexican town,
because he is my brother's child and if our children don't get along, then my
brother and I may come to a parting of the ways and that may lead to great
problems" (Lambert, quoted in Moghaddam et al. 1993: 125-6). In contrast, an
American mother said, "If he can't get along with one child, he can always play
with someone else. There are many children around to *choose* from" (p. 126). In
the Mexican community, families are so interdependent that conflict would be
devastating; this interdependence was not found in the U.S. community. The
place of the family in the larger community, which varies cross-culturally, thus
affects parental responses to aggression.

Who Are the Targets of Aggression?

Social positions such as gender, race, sexuality, and class also affect patterns
of victimization (both actual and stereotypic). Stereotypes suggest that women
are not only nonaggressive bystanders but are also disproportionately the victims of violence. Women are believed to need protection (from men) against
violence (paradoxically, also from men). Indeed, women's fear of being victimized by violence is greater than men's in every racial, ethnic, age, and social class
group (Gordon and Riger 1989), despite the fact that men are more likely to be
the targets of every kind of violence except rape (Koss 1993). Experimental
research reports the same results; research participants are likely to aggress more
against men than women in experimental settings (Eagly and Steffen 1986).
Gender stereotypes mask men's victimization, however, facilitating a sense of
vulnerability in women and a sense of self-sufficiency in men. Part of the reason
for men's greater victimization, of course, lies in lifestyle differences. Men are far
less likely than women to restrict their activities because of fear or to take safety
precautions in their homes or on the street (Gordon and Riger 1989). Social norms
also make men more legitimate targets for many forms of aggression. Again,
however, social context is crucial: Women may be chivalrously protected from
aggression in public places, but domestic violence statistics suggest that these
normative restrictions do not apply in private.

Most aggression is also intraracial (LaFree 1995), in part because of the
extensive everyday segregation of racial groups in the United States (Massey and
Denton 1993). Interracial violence, however, has received far more social psychological attention. Interracial (and interethnic) aggression are also topics of great
social concern, because these have been the basis for wars and riots, as well as
much everyday violence. Cognitive social psychologists suggest that the targets
of violence are often dehumanized by aggressors—a process in which different
beliefs and values are attributed to individuals or groups, making them seem less

than human and rationalizing aggression against them. Dehumanization is particularly easy when the target is a member of an easily definable out-group, such as a different racial or ethnic group. Although many people would like to believe that racism and discrimination have largely disappeared, unobtrusive studies of white and black helping behavior, aggression, and nonverbal communication indicate that whites' behavior often appears antiblack, despite survey data reporting a decrease in expressed antiblack attitudes (Crosby, Bromley, and Saxe 1980).

Because of the greater likelihood that people of color are poor, they also have a far greater risk of being victimized by violence than do whites. The relationship between social class and the risk of victimization has not been studied extensively by social psychologists, but it is well-known that poorer people are more likely to be the targets of crime because they tend to live in more vulnerable neighborhoods and have fewer resources with which to defend themselves (by installing security systems, driving rather than walking or taking public transportation, or working in safe environments).

Sexual orientation also affects individuals' risk of violence. Violence against lesbians and gay men appears to be escalating (Herek and Berrill 1992), and those who are more visibly homosexual are at greater risk (Harry 1990). This kind of violence and the homophobic attitudes that support it are closely linked to gender norms: "Although gender identity is distinct from socioerotic identity, the two are closely related. Heterosexuality is equated ideologically with 'normal' masculinity and 'normal' femininity, whereas homosexuality is equated with violating norms of gender." As a result, "gay people are stigmatized not only for their erotic behavior, but also for their perceived violation of gender norms" (Herek 1992:97).

Coda: Helping and Harming—Lessons from Opposition

As we noted at the beginning of this chapter, altruism and aggression are assumed to be opposite behaviors. As is often true with opposites, however, their dynamics are more similar than they might at first appear. In the concluding section of this chapter, we consider what the research traditions on altruism and aggression share and where they differ. This analysis reveals important insights about the assumptions underlying social psychological research, as well as the structural contexts of these behaviors. We focus in particular on the implications of prevailing methodological strategies and thematic issues that crosscut these two fields of research.

Research versus Reality

The methodological approaches of these two literatures are very similar. Both have relied heavily on the experimental paradigm dominant in most social psychological research. This paradigm requires random assignment of research participants to experimental conditions, strict control of extraneous factors, and tight manipulation of independent variables—requirements that are not easily adapted to studying real-life situations or long-term relationships between family members, romantic partners, or coworkers. Instead, most research has been conducted in short-term laboratory settings, often with unacquainted college student participants.

A common scenario in a laboratory study of aggression, for example, entails exposing participants to aggressive cues (or not exposing them to such cues, in control conditions). Participants might enter a waiting room in which guns are present or watch a film about boxing. Participants then experience some sort of provocation from a confederate of the experimenter, followed by an opportunity to administer electric shocks, supposedly to the person who has provoked them. (Often, the person is ostensibly in another room, so participants do not see the target receive their aggression.) This sort of laboratory scenario is far removed from "real-world" aggression such as murder, assault, or verbal confrontations between friends, coworkers, or family members. Most of us are never asked to administer electric shocks to others, especially to strangers whom we have never met. Thus, "The social psychologist curious about the violent phenomena of murder, riots, and war may well end up studying and understanding the shock-setting behavior of deceived college students, the Bobo doll hammerings of TV-watching children, and the horn-honking of frustrated motorists" (Lubek 1979:266). (Situations in studies of helping, such as picking up a stranger's dropped parcels or giving someone the change for a phone call, are, not surprisingly, more common in everyday life, although even these are hardly the most common forms of everyday helping.) Laboratory situations also constrain the possibility of retaliation for aggression or reciprocation of altruism. Because results of these laboratory studies are often generalized to real-world situations, it is important to ask what patterns are missed by these approaches, a topic we take up below.

Everyday Helping

Findings that men provide more help and women receive more help are due in part to the experimental research tradition, which focuses on the forms of help performed more often by men, such as physical labor and help with male-typed tasks. There has been much less attention to patterns of emotional support and indirect helping (especially with female-typed tasks, forms of behavior that women may be more likely than men to perform). Only when we consider real-world helping relationships do these patterns emerge.

What sorts of help are provided in everyday life? In a socioeconomic context in which most people experience substantial demands both at work and at home, the occasional necessity of both receiving and offering help is ubiquitous. What about the everyday patterns of caring, nurturing, and offering minor (sometimes major) but never-ending assistance to family, friends, or neighbors (see Cancian and Oliker, forthcoming)? As the U.S. population is steadily aging and the economic circumstances of adult children are relatively worse than in recent generations, patterns of intergenerational assistance have received increasing attention from demographers and public policy analysts (Lye, forthcoming).

Do structural circumstances shape the provision or receipt of such assistance? Like behavior studied in experimental contexts, everyday helping is systematically patterned by gender, race, class, and other structural positions (Hogan, Eggebeen, and Clogg 1993). Helping in daily family life is pervasively gendered, as, for example, DeVault's (1991) ethnography *Feeding the Family* reveals. DeVault demonstrates that virtually all tasks of home maintenance and support are differentially allocated by gender. Intergenerational support is also deeply gendered: Older adults with one or more daughters are far more likely to receive assistance in old age than those with only sons (Spitze and Logan 1990). Adult women are three times as likely as adult men to live with an aging parent and are more likely to exchange, rather than just receive, support. Controlling for resources, needs, family structure, and closeness of ties across generations, gender persistently affects the provision, but not the receipt, of aid (Hogan et al. 1993).

Lye et al. (1995) suggest that the origins of these patterns lie at least partially in childhood. American men invest less time and emotional resources in their children than do women, and after a divorce they contribute considerably fewer financial resources to their children. These patterns persist throughout the life span; even as grandparents, men provide less support to their adult children and their grandchildren than do women. Both girls and boys thus learn that the provision of support is more appropriate for women than for men. The type of assistance is also gendered: Sons are more likely to give financial or household assistance (e.g., with repairs, transportation, or work around the house) to their parents, and daughters are more likely to provide advice and homecare (e.g., physical care, cooking, or cleaning). To fail to to consider everyday helping is to miss the major and asymmetric contribution of women.

Research on racial patterns of intergenerational helping shows contradictory results. It is a common assumption that families of minority racial groups exchange more support (based most often on ethnographic studies, e.g., Stack 1974). Hogan et al. (1993) assert, however, that large-scale representative surveys do not find stronger support networks among minority families than among white families. On the basis of data from the 1987-88 National Survey of Families and Households, for example, Hogan et al. report that blacks are consistently less likely than whites to engage in any form of intergenerational assistance. The number of children in a family, however, is crucial to interpreting these patterns. Black families tend to have more children than white families. Thus one reason that black adult children receive comparatively less assistance than do whites from their parents is because more siblings compete for this support. Moreover, black parents are likely to have less disposable income than white parents to share with their children. Exchanges of practical and financial assistance are not necessarily indicators of emotional ties. Lye and Klepinger (1995) note that black and Hispanic adult children report higher quality relationships with their parents than do whites.

Intragroup solidarity is a powerful factor in shaping patterns of real-world support. Thus support comes not only from family but also from friends and coworkers. Black professionals, for example, are likely both to have had and to have served as mentors to other black professionals (Kalbfleisch and Davies 1991). Similarly, most providers of daily help for those living with AIDS are gay men and lesbians. (Interestingly, the few experimental studies that address effects of sexual orientation have focused on receiving rather than providing help, despite the fact that lesbians and gay men are active agents in real-world helping.)

Considering everyday altruism is also crucial for understanding cross-cultural patterns of helping others. One set of studies comparing patterns of helping across six countries (Kenya, Mexico, the Philippines, the United States, Japan, and India) found considerable differences in levels of children's helping behavior (Whiting and Whiting 1975; Whiting and Edwards 1988). Kenyan, Mexican, and Filipino children showed the highest levels of helping, with Indian and Japanese children in the middle range; U.S. children showed the lowest levels of helping. These cross-cultural differences in helping behavior are correlated with children's daily responsibilities. Helping was least likely in communities where children competed in school and were rarely responsible for farm or household chores. Helping was most common where children had to cooperate with other family members in performing many chores, especially where older siblings were required to share in the care and raising of other children.

Everyday Aggression

Unlike helping behavior, physical aggression is not an everyday event in the lives of most individuals. Although the newspapers are filled with incidents of physical violence, and social psychologists have emphasized physical aggression in their research, the forms of aggression most individuals are likely to encounter in their daily lives are verbal arguments. As with altruism, focusing on extraordinary forms of aggressive behavior has diverted attention from other types of aggression, which may show different patterns by gender, race, class, and sexuality.

Researchers have implied, for example, that women do not engage in active, physical aggression—indeed, perhaps in any aggression at all. Many early studies did not even include women as respondents, assuming that aggression in women was not common enough to study. Moreover, most studies have focused on physical violence, which has skewed findings about the relationship between aggression and gender. As discussed above, studies have found significant, albeit small, gender differences in physical aggression (Eagly and Steffen 1986; Björkqvist et al. 1992). Gender differences in indirect and verbal aggression (such as spreading rumors or ignoring a person) are even smaller (Eagly and Steffen 1986; Lagerspetz, Björkqvist, and Peltonen 1988). Scholarly emphasis on physical aggression has thus minimized those situations in which men's and women's aggression may be more similar.

The dominance of the experimental paradigm that has so shaped research on altruism has also contributed to these patterns of findings about aggression. Eagly and Steffen (1986) maintain that experimental situations "manifest the four conditions associated with larger sex-of-subject and sex-of-target effect sizes: a laboratory setting, physical aggression, a semiprivate context, and required aggressive behavior." The result is that "the best known and most popular methods for studying human aggression . . . happen to be those that are most likely to elicit greater aggression in men than women and greater aggression toward men than women" (pp. 325-6).

Women are more likely to be aggressive in private contexts, such as the home, than in less private situations, such as laboratory experiments. Research on child abuse, for example, shows that women commit a considerable amount of such abuse (although men's rate of abuse is higher when time spent with children is controlled [Gelles 1994; Margolin 1992]). Ignoring everyday aggression also makes invisible the many situations in which women are more frequent targets of aggression: domestic violence, sexual harassment in the workplace and on the street, bullying in schools, and child sexual abuse. These patterns have been explored more by sociologists and social workers than by social psychologists.

Some empirical studies on domestic abuse have reported that women engage in a considerable amount of aggression against their partners (e.g., Straus and Gelles 1986, 1990). Some researchers go so far as to contend that wives and husbands have equal levels of aggression (e.g., Steinmetz 1977/78). Recent research also reports a considerable amount of battering in lesbian relationships (Renzetti 1988, 1992; Lockhart et al. 1994). The issue of female aggression is contentious: Some scholars (and activists) fear that examining women's aggression may detract attention from the fact that women are overwhelmingly the targets, rather than the perpetrators, of aggression. They point out, for example, that studies that find reciprocal battering often ignore the frequency, motivations, or consequences of violence. A single episode of self-defense may be counted as equivalent to an ongoing pattern of instigation. These writers contend that when these factors are taken into account, women suffer far greater victimization than do men (Dobash et al. 1992).

Research clearly does show that women are capable of aggression and do engage in aggressive behavior in certain situations. Women and men do not appear to differ on personality measures of aggressivity or hostility (Frodi, Macaulay, and Thorne 1977; Hyde 1986) or everyday anger (Averill 1982; Tavris 1989). Laboratory studies show that when there is no risk of being recognized (and therefore no risk of retaliation), women may behave as aggressively as men (Björkqvist and Niemelä 1992:14). In most real-world situations, however, women are not as physically aggressive as men. Why? First, men's aggression tends to have more damaging consequences, because men tend to be larger and stronger than women and are generally taught how to use their bodies more effectively than women. Second, women tend to believe that behaving aggressively is more dangerous to themselves than men do; this belief is an important mediator of sex differences in aggression (Eagly and Steffen 1986). Third, men's physical violence tends to be ongoing, whereas women's tends to be episodic and more frequently in self-defense. (Ironically, this may mean that women are more likely to engage in severe violence, because that may be the only way they believe they can overcome men's perceived physical advantages.) Fourth, men's violence is facilitated by expectations for masculinity. One important reason for the relative persistence of men's aggression, toward both women and other men, is that when conflict arises, backing down risks the loss of masculinity. Being aggressive, in other words, is performing masculinity. Finally, men's aggression is reinforced by greater social power, both within a relationship and in the broader social environment. Compare the situation of a traditional wife, who is dependent on her husband for financial survival and who risks losing her children if she leaves the marriage, with that of her husband, who has the financial and professional resources to support himself. In this context, wife battering has a very different meaning than husband battering.

Thus women and men may have the same capacity for aggression, but this capacity is tempered by socialization, structural circumstances, and the symbolic meanings associated with aggression. Ultimately, these differences result in women's subordination. The stereotype that men are more aggressive than women permits men to maintain power and dominance over women by fostering fear and dependence in women and by restricting access to the competitive realms of the economy, polity, and military (White and Kowalski 1994). Indeed, some have argued that domestic violence represents not a "breakdown in social order," but "the reflection of a power struggle for the *maintenance* of a certain kind of social order" (McGrath, discussed in Breines and Gordon 1983: 511).

Instrumentality and Expressiveness

The distinction between goal-directed behavior, on the one hand, and behavior motivated by emotions, on the other, also cuts across altruism and aggression. As we have noted, helping behavior can be instrumental: People can provide help to others in order to meet their own goals. Helping behavior can also be provoked by the rush of adrenaline in observing an emergency or by the depth of compassion from seeing someone in pain. Similarly, aggressive behavior can be either instrumental or expressive. People may hurt others to bring about desired ends, or they may lash out in anger or fear. Indeed, the line between aggression and altruism disappears in some forms of instrumental aggression: Prosocial aggression, such as fighting a war, entails aggression toward some people while helping others.

The distinction between instrumental and expressive behavior is gendered. At the level of stereotypes, instrumentality is more closely related to the male stereotype of rationality, whereas emotional expression is a central component of the female stereotype. Thus stereotypes suggest that men should behave more instrumentally and women more emotionally, both when they help and when they harm others. Research suggests a more complex picture, however. The altruism literature portrays women more often as emotional, compassionate, expressive helpers, and men as thoughtful, organized, goal-oriented helpers. The literature on aggression also presents women as emotional aggressors (e.g., they might aggress in defense of their children), consistent with these stereotypes. Men's aggression is also portrayed as expressive, driven by hormonal, biological urges, however, rather than as instrumental. Indeed, in one of the many fascinating contradictions of gender, women are often held responsible for controlling the aggressive behavior of "their" men.

Just as we have questioned the assumption of gender differences in aggression, we also question the validity of a distinction between instrumental and expressive behavior. Is helping expressive or instrumental when a head of household spends a good deal of his or her time at home planning, preparing, and cleaning up after meals for the family? Is aggression expressive or instrumental when that same head of household speaks sharply to a child who has transgressed family rules? Goal-oriented behavior can be laden with feeling, as a participant in DeVault's (1991) study of family caring indicates: " 'If you have a real discussion at the dinner table, you can give a person a chance to let you in on their life. . . . It's a time when you can show that you really care about that person in more than just a caretaking role' " (pp. 33-4).

Similarity, Difference, and Power

We have argued that the capacities of women and men to help others, the occasional vulnerabilities of women and men to needing help, the capacities of women and men to engage in aggressive behavior, and the capacities of women and men to be victimized by others are not inherently different. Both women and men share these strengths and these vulnerabilities. Yet much research in these areas (and in social psychology more generally) appears to assume that there are innate or at least deeply rooted differences between women and men in both helping behavior and aggression. By conducting research in situations and with methods most likely to elicit gender differences, social psychological researchers themselves have contributed to the widespread cultural belief in gender difference (held even by those who struggle to escape these stereotypes). Because beliefs shape behavior, social psychological research (and cultural practices more generally) contributes to a self-perpetuating system that creates, affirms, and entrenches gender difference. We have emphasized that social structural factors shape these potentials and possibilities into the gendered patterns that researchers have not only discovered but, in part, created. Difference enters in through the location of women and men in their particular social structural circumstances and is deepened by the cultural traditions that ossify these circumstances into the regularities of individual lives and the histories of social groups. Difference is exaggerated; similarity is made invisible.

Power

The gaps in these (and other social psychological) areas indicate a larger pattern: widespread inattention to issues of power and dominance in research on both helping behavior and aggression. Power relationships structure who can offer help to whom, who can request help from whom, who can receive help from whom, and who cannot refuse to be helped when help is offered. Power defines what constitutes helping and who legitimizes the definition. Who determines whether help is necessary? Who determines the means of help? Is an act helping when it reproduces social dependencies? Are recipients of help more visible if they are women, poor, people of color, or some combination of these? Are agents of helping more acclaimed if they are men, wealthy, white, or some combination of these? Similarly, power shapes who aggresses against whom, who are the targets of aggression, what forms aggressive behavior takes, and what is defined as aggression.

Sprague's (1995:19) distinction between forms of helping that encourage independence and forms of helping that sustain dependence illustrates how the act of helping someone can reaffirm one's own power. People who provide help often do so (likely unintentionally) in a way that perpetuates their own role as helper rather than teaching others how to provide for themselves. The perspective of both parties is crucial. We can assume that *Oleanna's* John views his gesture of helping as benign. Carol will not pass the class without his help, and he thinks that making her come to his office regularly for private tutoring sessions is the best way to help her. From Carol's perspective, however, this form of helping is intrusive. John's mode of tutoring enforces Carol's reliance on him; he does not show her better study techniques, suggest she join study groups of other students, or show her other techniques that would allow her to develop her study skills. In short, John ensures that Carol will continue to depend on him.

This example also suggests that the boundary between helping and aggression is fragile. Why are some forms of public assistance defined as helping? Why is the fact that one of six children in this country lacks decent nutrition not an indication of societal aggression? Why is helping rarely analyzed in terms of the structural advantages of the helper and the structural disadvantages of those who are given assistance? Indeed, the transfer of resources from those who are wealthy to those who are poor is an excellent case in point. When those with resources contribute money to those with less, it is celebrated as charity. That such contributions provide tax write-offs is often unremarked. When we consider the profile of research in altruism and aggression, the centrality of power is inescapable—yet it is too often unacknowledged.

Summary

We have analyzed research on helping behavior and aggression through a gendered lens. Research in each of these areas has been deeply influenced by prevailing cultural assumptions about gender, as well as about race, class, and sexuality, yet in large part these assumptions have been neither acknowledged nor incorporated in these analyses. Thus these assumptions have framed the nature of the questions asked—and the questions not asked—about both helping behavior and aggression. We have shown, in contrast, that gender is a central organizing principle of these types of social behaviors. Moreover, the embeddedness of both research traditions in cultural stereotypes about gender, race, ethnicity, social class, and sexuality underlies structural similarities in the emphases and omissions of each line of research. Thus, although helping and harming others may seem to be polar opposites, a gendered analysis reveals their interdependence.

Notes

1. See Segal (1993) for discussion of problems with this research, however.

2. We must be cautious, however, in using arrest data as a measure of aggression, because arrests are influenced by factors such as the opportunity to participate in criminal activity (Eagly and Steffen 1986:309) and the biases of the criminal justice system (Visher 1983).

CHAPTER 7

Conclusions

Reprising a Gender Lens on Social Psychology

A Case in Point

In the preceding chapters, we discussed in detail why social psychological theories need to integrate gender into their analyses and how they might do so. In this final chapter, we summarize the key themes of a gendered lens on social psychology and show how the various social psychological theories might work together to explain patterns of social interaction. The implications of a gender lens might be better understood through example. We have cited a good deal of experimental work throughout the book, but we deliberately choose our example from everyday life rather than from the lab. Why? The many constraints of experimental work—the barrenness of the social context, the deliberate removal of effects often found in everyday life, the strict control over the circumstances— have limited the generalizability of findings of social psychological research, as we have stressed throughout the book. The experimental method provides a degree of rigor available in no other method, and therefore we can feel confident about the internal validity of such research. But because we are interested in asking the sorts of questions less amenable to the laboratory context, we turn now to broader arenas. And so, we trace the circumstances of a contemporary couple as they negotiate the demands of everyday life.[1]

Eve and Adam have known each other for 10 years. They have lived together for seven years; when they moved in together, they allocated household work relatively evenly, although Eve did a bit more cooking and cleaning, whereas Adam did more of the outside maintenance work. They married when they decided to move to a new city and pursue graduate degrees. They both brought strongly egalitarian beliefs and expectations to the relationship; they identify as feminist and generally progressive (in contrast to many members of both their families). When they married, she retained her own name, a decision that both sets of parents greeted with consternation.

Time passed. Both graduated from their programs, she with a master's degree in social work, he with a law degree. He secured a prestigious clerkship; she found a position with a local well-respected counseling center. With all the years it took for them to attain this point in their professional careers, they became cognizant of a decision they had put off—having children. They decided to get pregnant, and during the first year of their postdegree jobs, Eve had a baby. She took a 6-month maternity leave and then returned to work.

In another year and a half, Eve became pregnant again. Both Eve and Adam had long felt that it is not fair to raise a child without siblings, and they preferred their children to be fairly close in age. Both agreed that two children were enough, recognizing both the financial and emotional costs of having more children to raise. At this point, Eve was well ensconced in her job. She was the assistant director of one branch of the center and poised to take over the directorship when that person retired in a few more years. Adam was also doing well at the firm he joined when he completed his clerkship. In a few more years, he had a good chance of earning a partnership.

But now they would have two children. Eve planned to take a maternity leave again, but this time they had some serious talks about just how much attention kids need. In addition, they weighed their relative incomes, noting that Adam earned far more as an attorney (and had the potential for far greater future earnings) than Eve did at the counseling center. Reluctantly, Eve decided to take an open-ended leave from her position to become a full-time parent. She reasoned that she could still take on clients on an ad hoc basis and bring in some income to the household and that she would have a good deal more control over her time and much more time to spend with her children. This, too, would free up more time for Adam, for whom the pressures of a potential partnership were growing intense. Both felt pleased with this decision and thought it best for the entire family.

Let's check in five years later. Eve and Adam have two children, ages seven and five (plus a few pets now). Eve has elected not to return to her position. The director did retire, and another younger member of the group took her position. Eve is seeing a few clients in the room they remodeled in the basement. Adam has become a partner in his law firm and now finds himself busier than ever at work. Eve is responsible for primary child care. She also contributes a small but fairly steady income to the family through her counseling activities. Adam contributes the bulk of the income, considerably more than Eve could have done in her profession. Adam spends time with the kids on Sundays, his dedicated day off. He also arranges to work at home on evenings when Eve is seeing clients. Eve and Adam are content with this arrangement. It seems fair to all, it clearly provides an excellent income for the family, and the kids always have a parent available to them.

Eve and Adam's story does two things. First, it illustrates many of the points of the theories we have presented throughout this volume. Second, a close analysis of this vignette reveals a host of ways in which gender dynamics shape social behavior. An even closer look also reveals how systems of class and sexuality shape social behavior.

Traces of Social Psychological Theories

Let's look at Eve and Adam again, but this time through the lenses of the several social psychological theories. The basic tenet of behaviorism and social exchange theories is that social behavior is motivated by self-interest and the desire to gain rewards (and avoid punishments). Eve and Adam move to a new city to pursue graduate work; we can assume that the costs of moving were not as considerable as the advantages to them of studying in this particular community. When they have a second baby, Eve leaves her job; Adam does not. Cost-efficiency is one component of their decision calculus: The family will have a good deal more money if Adam continues to work. This same cost-benefit logic may also explain why Eve, rather than Adam, took a parental leave. Without further information, we cannot know whether they made any explicit exchanges. But we can assume that Eve's adoption of more parenting responsibility was part of an exchange for cutting back so heavily on her paid work. Similarly, Adam's restriction of his structured parenting responsibilities to one day probably reflects an exchange for his many hours of paid work. These exchanges were likely based in part on the relative resources of the two partners: time, skills, money, and so on. This analysis of cost-benefit assessment is one of the strengths of exchange theory.

Exchange theory argues that individuals choose to behave in particular ways as a function of their resources and alternatives. What exchange theory does not address, however, are the dynamics of these choice processes. Understanding these processes requires another social psychological theory, social cognition. One important backdrop for understanding Eve and Adam's negotiations about work and family is that both partners endorse strongly feminist and progressive social and political beliefs. Presumably, these convictions shape many of their behavioral decisions: to pursue careers, to work in fields where they can help others. On the other hand, both live (and have grown up) in a culture that has particular gender expectations and stereotypes; these presumably also influence Eve and Adam's ideas about the appropriate roles of men and women—for example, about who might be a better primary caretaker of their children.

In addition, Eve and Adam have to make a number of difficult decisions. They have to weigh information to decide where to go to graduate school, whether to have a first child, whether to have a second child, whether either of them should stop working for pay, and so forth. (Note that each of these decisions will underlie future exchanges that they make in their relationship.) We might speculate that a bit of selective memory also comes into play. Would the Eve and Adam who began graduate school with their strong beliefs have believed they would be where they ended up seven years later, and happily so? We as readers also make attributions about Eve and Adam and the reasons for their choices. We construct our own explanations for why they made the choices they did and our own evaluations that follow from these attributions.

Social comparisons are also crucial to how each person deals with these conflicts—indeed to how they define them. Because truly egalitarian relationships are still a rarity (see Schwartz 1994), Adam can feel good about himself for being willing to share tasks in their early years together. Even if the sharing is not quite equal, the fact that he does some of the cooking, even some of the laundry, makes him stand out by comparison from some of the men in couples they know. Both Eve and Adam may feel that their objectively unequal work allocations are egalitarian, due to gendered expectations of even greater asymmetry and social comparisons with other couples whose work allocations are less equal.

Eve and Adam's attitudes and stereotypes are important in their choices about work and family. But how do these beliefs and attitudes develop? How, in everyday interaction, do situations become defined, identities negotiated, meanings shared? This is the realm of symbolic interaction. Much symbolic interaction also underlies this vignette, although we have not presented the details of these interactions. Both Eve and Adam have strongly developed senses of themselves and the kind of lives they want to lead. In making all the decisions they go on to make, they rely on a host of culturally significant symbol systems. Spouse, professional, and parent are all symbols, and the meaning that each of these symbols has for Eve and Adam is a strong influence on the life choices they make. *Professional* may now be a symbol available to both women and men, but the symbol *parent* has historically had different meanings for women and men. (Consider, for example, the different connotations of the words *mother* and *father*: Fathering a child implies little more than participating in the child's conception; mothering a child implies a far greater investment of time, energy, and care.) As a result, women may experience a certain tension between these positions of professional and parent. And of course, there are undoubtedly many negotiations and situations that have needed defining to get Eve and Adam to this point. Although we cannot eavesdrop on their conversations, their situation is familiar enough to many readers that we can likely imagine some of the identity management and altercasting that has gone on. And lest we forget their own parents, it is clear that a great deal of negotiation and impression management must have been involved in providing accounts to their parents and in-laws for Eve's decision to keep her own surname, possibly about how they chose their children's surnames, probably about her decision to return to work after their first child was born.

Thus these three social psychological theories offer three different lenses, or ways of viewing the world. Social exchange sees a world full of rational decision-makers: individuals weighing the costs and benefits of different lines of action, assessing the resources and alternatives available to the relevant players in an interaction, and behaving in the ways that they perceive will be most beneficial. Social cognition sees a world of information-processors: individuals struggling to deal with the mass of stimuli available in the world, using tools such as categories, schemas, and stereotypes to guide behavior. Finally, symbolic interactionism sees a world of meaning-makers: individuals making sense of the world by developing symbols and identities, managing impressions, and defining situations through negotiation with others.

Which of these lenses is correct? In fact, each lens offers a valid picture of the world. People are decision-makers, information-processors, and meaning makers all at the same time. None of these perspectives offers the *only* valid picture of the world, however. Looking at the world through only one of these lenses is like using only one sense to perceive the world. What we hear when we listen is true, but what we smell, taste, feel, and see is also true. Using all our senses together provides a more complete representation of reality than any one sense can provide alone.

We also believe that each social psychological lens has some significant gaps. In the preceding chapters, we noted the specific blind spots associated with each theory. One critique applies equally to all three theories, however: None of the perspectives offers a satisfactory analysis of social structure and how it affects individual thoughts and behaviors. Social structure rarely enters explicitly into social cognitive and symbolic interactionist work. Structure plays a more prominent part in social exchange theory, but as we pointed out in Chapter 3, this theoretical emphasis rarely extends into empirical research. The distribution of resources—and therefore power—in society is highly structured: Some people (men, whites, upper classes) tend to have many more resources, and therefore much more power, than others (women, people of color, working classes). For example, none of the theories addresses why it is that Adam is likely to make more money than Eve. One explanation involves gender socialization and ongoing expectations that push women and men to choose different types of work. But another equally important explanation involves the biases of the labor market, which segregates women and men into different jobs despite their preferences and which pays women less than men even if they are performing the same tasks. Thus the structure of the labor market makes it more financially feasible for Adam to continue working and Eve to stop, rather than vice versa. Although Eve and Adam treat this as a choice, it is clearly a constrained choice. Moreover, the class structure of the society is what allows them to make this choice at all. Couples who do not belong to the middle and upper classes do not have the luxury of such a choice; both partners in such couples must work for pay. Both Eve and Adam benefit from class privilege in ways they do not even seem to realize. Social psychologists, however, have paid little attention to these kinds of structural factors and how they affect the patterning of power in relationships.

Because of this inattention to structure and power, social psychology has also generally failed to problematize social positions such as gender, race, and class. As we have discussed extensively in the preceding chapters, social psychologists have tended either to ignore gender, to view it as synonymous with biological sex, or to accept sex difference as an explanation in itself rather than as something to be explained. Although work on gender and social psychology is becoming both more widespread and more nuanced, the mainstream of social psychology continues without understanding how central gender is to the processes it describes. In contrast, our contention throughout this book is that no social psychological topic can be fully understood without seeing how deeply and pervasively it is gendered. Moreover, gender cannot be fully understood without analyzing its intersections with other social statuses.

Approaches to Gender

We have identified four basic perspectives that dominate scholarship on gender: essentialist, socialization, social constructionist, and structural. Each would analyze Eve and Adam's situation differently. In this section, we briefly reprise these four perspectives, using the vignette above to elaborate some central gendered themes. We also note how these perspectives on gender might map onto the three social psychological theories discussed earlier.

Essentialism, of course, argues that Eve and Adam make the choices they do because child care, maintenance work, breadwinning, and so on are built into their genes, their hormones, or some other part of their "natures." We will not repeat our critiques of this theory here; we simply note again that these theories take as explanation the very phenomena we consider it crucial to explain. Moreover, they cannot adequately explain the considerable historical, cross-cultural, and interpersonal differences in these sorts of behaviors. Essentialist assumptions can be found in both the social exchange literature and the social cognition literature, but this perspective is entirely incompatible with symbolic interaction, which sees gendered identity and behavior as negotiated, not fixed.

The other major social psychological theories argue that gender is learned, constructed, or structured, rather than innate. The socialization perspective suggests that Eve and Adam learned their various skills, behavioral tendencies, and personality patterns as they were growing up, by watching family members, friends and neighbors, or other models on television or in the movies. Adam learned that breadwinning is an important role for men, and Eve learned that caretaking is a valued occupation for women. These lessons may also have shaped their career choices, as well as their later decisions about the division of labor in their own home. Note that the socialization perspective draws from both social cognition (people learn particular schemas or scripts for behavior) and social learning theory (they learn through being rewarded for particular behaviors or watching others receive rewards). This perspective does not, however, provide an easy explanation for the fact that both Eve and Adam have developed ideological positions at odds with those of their parents.

The social constructionist approach, in contrast, looks at the ways in which both individuals construct gender (and other identities) through their actions. For Adam, becoming a lawyer and supporting his family may be a way of enacting his masculinity; on the other hand, his help with domestic work and his willingness to negotiate about family arrangements no doubt help to maintain his view of himself as progressive. For Eve, bearing and caring for children may be a way of constructing femininity; her continued (although greatly reduced) part-time work may help her maintain her view of herself as an independent woman. Both Eve and Adam—and others around them—must negotiate and redefine the situation at every stage in their relationship. For example, when they marry, Eve keeps her own surname. Her choice is worthy of comment only in a world still structured by naming conventions—fundamental components of identity—that are asymmetric by gender. Her in-laws actually question the depth of the relationship because she would not take their name. In other words, these respective actors' definitions of the situation are dramatically different. To Eve's in-laws, the choice of surname indicates a tenuous commitment to their family; to Eve, it may symbolize personal identity and independence. The social constructionist perspective draws on both cognition and symbolic interaction to understand these kinds of choices.

Finally, the structural perspective on gender looks beyond individual characteristics and cognitions and focuses instead on the structural positions and associated resources of the two partners. Adam is an attorney (a relatively well-paid and prestigious profession) and a man in a society that privileges masculinity. Eve, in contrast, is a social worker (a relatively poorly paid and low-prestige profession) and a woman. Structuralism notes the ways in which Eve and Adam's relative positions in the social structure result in gendered outcomes: Eve stays home with their two children and does the majority of the domestic work, and Adam brings home the money to support the family. We would expect that as a result, Adam would have more power than Eve in their relationship. Perhaps the most important point about this structural analysis is that it shows how gendered outcomes can occur even without conscious intentions on the part of the actors involved. Both Eve and Adam consider themselves progressive and feminist; they would argue that they have made practical rather than ideological choices and would no doubt be shocked to realize the degree to which their lives have become traditionally gendered. But a number of relatively minor decisions (set in motion long ago) have culminated in a highly traditional work-family arrangement because of the gender (and class) inequities of the social structure. Both social cognition and social exchange are central to this structural perspective.

As with the three social psychological theories, no one of these four approaches to gender is complete by itself; again, we must use more than one lens to fully understand social situations. To see these multiple lenses at work, consider Eve and Adam's decisions about parenting. Although most new parents these days believe that children benefit from having the attention of two parents, and expect that both fathers and mothers will be actively involved in parenting, it is the rare father who takes paternity leave when his child is born. Lest we attribute this to individual intransigence, the structure of the workplace rarely allows this. Many organizations now have maternity policies in place; far fewer have paternity policies. And even when they do, social influence often dictates that men shouldn't use them or their careers will suffer (Olson, forthcoming). Moreover, the occupational structure of society generates sex segregation and discrimination such that men generally earn more than women; thus a man's taking paternity leave generally has economic as well as symbolic costs.

Even if Even and Adam held identical jobs, however, others would likely see them, and their occupational and personal choices, differently. Consider this scenario: A male employer has just been told that one of his key male employees is planning to get married. How would this employer respond? There is a good chance that he would respond with happiness and, perhaps, relief that this long-term bachelor is finally "settling down." Now consider a slightly different scenario: The same employer has just heard the same news but from a key *female* employee. Is his reaction the same? Probably not. The employer's mind may turn to the future; he may fear that she will have children and leave the company or at least demand maternity leave. Marriage for a female employee suggests instability; for a male employee it suggests maturity and increased stability. Thus gender is invoked not only by the distribution of jobs and wages but also by the images and assumptions of those in the occupational sphere.

When Eve and Adam have their second child, the gendered norms come even more acutely into play. Adam compares himself to his law firm colleagues. They are working 70-hour weeks; he, in contrast, has promised he will be home at least three nights a week for dinner and all day Sunday. Eve compares herself to other women who have chosen to leave potential careers or work part-time in order to care for their kids. Both Eve and Adam have referential frameworks that are highly gendered because the structures of work and family life are highly gendered. It is worth noting that these gendered expectations are so fundamental that both Eve and Adam feel satisfied with their situation. This need not be a sort of self-serving blind spot on Adam's part or self-delusion on Eve's. Social structures shape each everyday decision about the allocation of work and family responsibilities. These decisions involve the jockeying of exchanges of time, money, and energy; they are based on frameworks of cultural schemas so familiar that most of us don't even remark on them; and they are negotiated between partners in an ongoing stream of symbolic interactions.

In our view, each of these perspectives has something to offer. Although we have found fault with essentialist perspectives throughout this book, the essentialist position does remind us that our lives are influenced (although not determined) by biological potentials. At a minimum, the physiological differences among people—the ability to bear children, or not; the ability to see and hear and move easily; the ability to overpower another person—affect the lives of individuals and do so in patterned ways. We believe, however, that even these biological potentials are filtered through cultural beliefs and understandings. How these potentials are understood and developed by individuals and groups has a far greater impact on our lives than does raw biology. Indeed, the pervasive cultural belief in the significance of biology may be as important a determinant of behavior as biology itself. The belief that women and men are predisposed by biology to prefer and excel at different tasks is as responsible for the gendered division of labor as any biological difference and has long served to justify gender inequality.

Although we believe the nonessentialist positions contribute more to our understanding of social life, each has its strengths and limitations as well. We agree with the socialization approach that gender is learned and maintained through modeling, rewards, and punishments; however, we believe that gender is more dynamic and fluid than most socialization perspectives suggest. We draw from the structural approach the insight that gender is structured by social position: Much of what we understand to be gendered behavior is driven not by individual characteristics (whether innate or learned) but by one's positions in various social hierarchies. However, we also believe that it is necessary to combine this approach with the social constructionist perspective, which pays much greater attention to the ways in which gender is negotiated in interaction against a backdrop of cultural expectations. We suggest that to truly understand social interaction, we need a multilevel model of gender that incorporates the strengths of each approach.

We have also argued throughout this book that any approach to gender must incorporate the ways that other social positions, such as race, class, age, and sexual orientation, intersect and interact with gender. The O. J. Simpson trial that transfixed the nation in 1994 and 1995 was not simply a case of one person accused of murdering two others, but of a man accused of murdering a woman (and her friend) within a social system that affords men far greater power than women. However, the case was also not reducible to gender alone. O. J. Simpson is not simply a man; he is a black man, a wealthy man, a famous man, a heterosexual man, a middle-aged man, an able-bodied man, and a father. Nicole Brown Simpson was not simply a woman; she was a white woman, a wealthy (but economically dependent) woman, a relatively unknown woman, a hetero-sexual woman, a conventionally beautiful woman, an able-bodied woman, and a mother. These statuses are always present; one is always all of one's statuses, and it is impossible to experience—or analyze—one status without the others. Thus our models of social life need to envision, elaborate, and incorporate the ways in which these statuses coexist and interact. Social scientists are only beginning to develop the tools to do this; we suggest that this is an urgent need in social psychology as well as in the study of gender and other social positions.

Before we close, there is a bit more to say about Eve and Adam. Some readers may find it difficult to identify with Eve and Adam. The referential groups tapped by this example will not accord with everyone's situations and experiences. For example, individuals without enough money or educational opportunities to obtain graduate degrees, to have careers available, or to have the choice to stop working even if they wanted may find few similarities between Eve and Adam's professional dilemmas and their own. The following variation might be more resonant with these readers' experiences. Suppose that Eve and Adam are poor rather than relatively well-off as they are in the original example. What if neither had attended college, let alone graduate school, and both were working in relatively low-prestige, low-paying jobs—he as a school bus driver, she as a waitress—when their first child was born. It is unlikely, first of all, that either employer would have offered them a paid or even an unpaid parental leave. It is true that the recent Family and Medical Leave Act mandates that companies with more than 50 employees offer unpaid leave to new parents. However, the majority of U.S. companies have fewer than 50 employees and therefore are not required to offer such leave. Those companies that offer the most generous leave policies—including paid or partially paid parental leave—are generally large, wealthy companies with many employees. Thus those people who have access to the most generous leave policies are also those people who are better-off to begin with.

Even if Eve and Adam had had the option of taking an unpaid parental leave, it is unlikely that they would have been able to afford to do so. For a family that is barely scraping by on two incomes, adding a new baby and at the same time losing one income might mean financial disaster. The important decisions to be made might involve how to juggle shift work rather than which income to keep.

Alternatively, suppose that the couple had the same economic and educa-tional statuses as in the first example, but were both female or both male. In this case, the couple (call them Eve and Anna) cannot legally marry. Their decision to have a child will be considerably more complicated: They must either find a sperm donor or try to adopt a child, a goal that is prohibited in some states because of their sexual orientation. If they do succeed in having a child, on the other hand, they will have to deal not only with the usual pressures of parenthood but also with added pressures resulting from the stereotypes and prejudices of others. In each case, the active referential frameworks, choices, options, expectations, and stereotypes differ. These alternative versions of the saga of Eve and Adam remind us of the importance of the full array of social positions for understanding human behavior. All of these positions—economic resources, racial and ethnic histories, sexual orientation, gender—together shape actors' social behavior.

Final Messages for the Reader

We have summarized what we see as the most important themes of this volume. We have illustrated precisely what we mean by a gender lens in working with this example of Eve and Adam and their deliberations as they make important life decisions. We close by suggesting questions we think it would be useful to emphasize in your own future endeavors. Some of you are researchers, some of you are teachers, some of you are students, and we know all of you are readers. We keep each of these roles in mind as we offer the following questions and principles to consider when conducting, teaching, or evaluating social psychological research.

About Theories

Assumptions: What assumptions are made? What possibilities are left out?

Implications: What are the implications of this perspective for those in varying social positions? Has this question ever been asked?

Historical Context: How have political and social trends shaped the questions that are asked and the answers that are posed?

About Social Resources and Human Action

Inequality: What is the distribution of resources, access, opportunity, options, and consequences? Which groups are advantaged; which are disadvantaged?

Choice: Do individuals have choices? Which ones? Do some have more choices than others? Who structures whether choice is available?

Agency: In what realms do/can (some) people act as agents? Which people?

About Social Groups

Position: Be aware, always, of structural positions such as gender, race, class, sexuality, and age. Explore how these positions work together as well as separately. For example, how do gender and social class jointly determine Eve and Adam's choices about family and work? How would their experiences differ if they were people of color? If they were both the same sex?

Difference and Similarity: Always consider differences within groups, not just between groups. Be as aware of similarity as of difference. Where difference is emphasized, ask why. (Where similarity is emphasized, also ask why.)

Sex versus Gender: Keep in mind that sex and gender are distinct terms, based in distinctly different theories, with distinctly different implications. Be aware that gender is not fixed/homogeneous/dichotomous/individual.

About Everything

Power: How is the behavior or pattern in question shaped by power? Who has power over whom? What is this power based on? How is this power exercised and for what ends? Are power differences revealed or masked? Why?

These questions often go unasked in traditional social psychology. As a result, research and theorizing have left out important groups, perspectives, and questions. Asking these questions, and taking these issues seriously, will lead us closer to a full understanding of social interaction. This understanding, in turn, will help us better address some of the most important questions facing us as individuals, communities, and societies.

Note

1. We are indebted to Barbara Risman for the basic outlines of this example (Risman, forthcoming).

REFERENCES

Abzug, Bella. 1995. "A Message from NGO Women to U.N. Member States, the Secretariat, and the Commission on the Status of Women." Speech delivered at the Final Preparatory Meeting for the Fourth World Conference on Women, April 3. (Press release from the Women's Environment and Development Organization [WEDO], 212-759-7982).

Alcott, Louisa May. 1924. *Little Women*. Akron, OH: Saalfield.

Allison, Dorothy. 1994. *Skin: Talking About Sex, Class, and Literature*. Ithaca, NY: Firebrand.

Anderson, Susan M. and Sandra Lipsitz Bem. 1981. "Sex Typing and Androgyny in Dyadic Interaction." *Journal of Personality and Social Psychology* 41:74-86.

Archer, Dane and Rosemary Gartner. 1976. "Violent Acts and Violent Times: A Comparative Approach to Postwar Homicide Rates." *American Sociological Review* 41:937-63.

———. 1984. *Violence and Crime in Cross-National Perspective*. New Haven, CT: Yale University Press.

Archibald, W. Peter. 1978. *Social Psychology as Political Economy*. Toronto: McGraw-Hill.

Arendell, Terry. 1992. "The Social Self as Gendered: A Masculinist Discourse of Divorce." *Symbolic Interaction* 15:151-81.

———. 1995. *Fathers and Divorce*. Thousand Oaks, CA: Sage.

Argyle, Michael. 1994. *The Psychology of Social Class*. New York: Routledge.

Aronson, Elliot, Timothy D. Wilson, and Robin M. Akert. 1994. *Social Psychology: The Heart and the Mind*. New York: HarperCollins.

Ashmore, Richard D. and Frances K. Del Boca, eds. 1986. *The Social Psychology of Female-Male Relations: A Critical Analysis of Central Concepts*. New York: Academic Press.

Averill, James R. 1982. *Anger and Aggression: An Essay on Emotion*. New York: Springer-Verlag.

Bandura, Albert. 1965. "Influences of Models' Reinforcement Contingencies on the Acquisition of Imitative Responses." *Journal of Personality and Social Psychology* 1:589-93.

―――. 1969. *Principles of Behavior Modification.* New York: Holt, Rinehart & Winston.

―――. 1973. *Aggression: A Social Learning Analysis.* Englewood Cliffs, NJ: Prentice Hall.

―――. 1977. *Social Learning Theory.* Englewood Cliffs, NJ: Prentice Hall.

―――. 1986. *Social Foundations of Thought and Action.* Englewood Cliffs, NJ: Prentice Hall.

Bandura, Albert, Dorothea Ross, and Sheila A. Ross. 1963. "Imitation of Film-Mediated Aggressive Models." *Journal of Abnormal and Social Psychology* 66:3-11.

Bandura, Albert and Richard H. Walters. 1963. *Social Learning and Personality Development.* New York: Holt, Rinehart & Winston.

Barker, R., T. Dembo, and K. Lewin. 1941. "Frustration and Aggression: An Experiment with Young Children." *University of Iowa Studies in Child Welfare* 18:1-314.

Baron, Reuben M., Linda Albright, and Thomas E. Malloy. 1995. "Effects of Behavioral and Social Class Information on Social Judgment." *Personality and Social Psychology Bulletin* 12:308-15.

Bayton, James A., Lois B. McAlister, and Jeston Hamer. 1956. "Race-Class Stereotypes." *Journal of Negro Education* 25:75-78.

Basow, Susan A. 1992. *Gender: Stereotypes and Roles.* Pacific Grove, CA: Brooks/Cole.

Beal, Carole R. 1994. *Boys and Girls: The Development of Gender Roles.* New York: McGraw-Hill.

Begley, Sharon. 1995. "Three Is Not Enough." *Newsweek,* February 13, pp. 67-69.

Bem, Daryl J. 1970. *Beliefs, Attitudes, and Human Affairs.* Belmont, CA: Brooks/Cole.

Bem, Sandra L. 1974. "The Measurement of Psychological Androgyny." *Journal of Consulting and Clinical Psychology* 42:155-62.

―――. 1975. "Sex Role Adaptability: One Consequence of Psychological Androgyny." *Journal of Personality and Social Psychology* 31:634-43.

―――. 1993. *The Lenses of Gender: Transforming the Debate on Sexual Inequality.* New Haven, CT: Yale University Press.

Bem, Sandra Lipsitz and Ellen Lenney. 1976. "Sex Typing and the Avoidance of Cross-Sex Behavior." *Journal of Personality and Social Psychology* 33:48-54.

Benson, P. L., S. A. Karabenick, and R. M. Lerner. 1976. "Pretty Pleases: The Effects of Physical Attractiveness, Race, and Sex on Receiving Help." *Journal of Experimental Social Psychology* 12:409-15.

Bergen, Elizabeth. 1991. "The Economic Context of Labor Allocation: Implications for Gender Stratification." *Journal of Family Issues* 12:140-57.

Berger, Joseph, Thomas L. Conner, and M. Hamit Fisek. 1974. *Expectation States Theory: A Theoretical Research Program.* Cambridge, MA: Winthrop.

Berger, Joseph, M. Hamit Fisek, Robert Z. Norman, and Morris Zelditch Jr. 1977. *Status Characteristics in Social Interaction: An Expectation States Approach.* New York: Elsevier.

Berk, Sarah Fenstermaker. 1985. *The Gender Factory: The Apportionment of Work in American Households.* New York: Plenum.

Berkowitz, Leonard. 1986. "Situational Influences on Reactions to Observed Violence." *Journal of Social Issues* 42(3):93-106.

Berkowitz, Leonard, and Anthony LePage. 1967. "Weapons as Aggression-Eliciting Stimuli." *Journal of Personality and Social Psychology* 7:202-7.

Björkqvist, Kaj. 1994. "Sex Differences in Physical, Verbal, and Indirect Aggression: A Review of Recent Research." *Sex Roles* 30:177-88.

Björkqvist, Kaj, Karin Österman, and Ari Kaukiainen. 1992. "The Development of Direct and Indirect Aggression Strategies in Males and Females." Pp. 51-64 in *Of Mice and Women: Aspects of Female Aggression,* edited by K. Björkqvist and P. Niemelä. San Diego, CA: Academic Press.

Björkqvist, Kaj and Pirkko Niemelä. 1992. "New Trends in the Study of Female Aggression." Pp. 3-16 in *Of Mice and Women: Aspects of Female Aggression,* edited by K. Björkqvist and P. Niemelä. San Diego, CA: Academic Press.

Black, Stephen L. and Susan Bevan. 1992. "At the Movies with Buss and Durkee: A Natural Experiment on Film Violence." *Aggressive Behavior* 18:37-45.

Blau, Peter M. 1964. *Exchange and Power in Social Life.* New York: Wiley.

Blood, Robert O., Jr. and Donald M. Wolfe. 1960. *Husbands and Wives.* New York: Free Press.

Blumstein, Philip. 1991. "The Production of Selves in Personal Relationships." Pp. 305-22 in *The Self-Society Dynamic: Cognition, Emotion, and Action,* edited by J. A. Howard and P. L. Callero. New York: Cambridge University Press.

Blumstein, Philip and Pepper Schwartz. 1983. *American Couples: Money, Work, and Sex.* New York: Morrow.

Bornstein, Kate. 1994. *Gender Outlaw: On Men, Women, and the Rest of Us.* New York: Vintage.

Bower, Gordon H. and Ernest R. Hilgard. 1981. *Theories of Learning.* Englewood Cliffs, NJ: Prentice Hall.

Bragg, Rick. 1995. "Susan Smith: Victim or Monster? Image Is a Life-or-Death Matter to Mother Who Drowned Two Sons." *Seattle Times* (Seattle, WA), July 9, p. A1.

Bramel, Dana and Ronald Friend. 1981. "Hawthorne, the Myth of the Docile Worker, and Class Bias in Psychology." *American Psychologist* 36:867-78.

Breines, Winnie and Linda Gordon. 1983. "The New Scholarship on Family Violence." *Signs: Journal of Women in Culture and Society* 8:490-531.

Brewer, Marilynn B. 1988. "A Dual Process Model of Impression Formation." In *Advances in Social Cognition*, Vol. 1, edited by T. K. Srull and R. S. Wyer. Hillsdale, NJ: Erlbaum.

Brewer, Marilynn B., Valerie Dull, and Layton Lui. 1981. "Perceptions of the Elderly: Stereotypes as Prototypes." *Journal of Personality and Social Psychology* 41:656-70.

Brewer, Marilynn B., Hing-Kay Ho, Ju-Young Lee, and Norman Miller. 1987. "Social Identity and Social Distance among Hong Kong Schoolchildren." *Personality and Social Psychology Bulletin* 13:156-65.

Bridges, George S. and Robert D. Crutchfield. 1988. "Law, Social Standing, and Racial Disparities in Imprisonment." *Social Forces* 66:699-724.

Briere, John and Neil M. Malamuth. 1983. "Self-Reported Likelihood of Sexually Aggressive Behavior: Attitudinal Versus Sexual Explanations." *Journal of Research in Personality* 17:315-23.

Brines, Julie. 1993. "The Exchange Value of Housework." *Rationality and Society* 5:302-40.

———. 1994. "Economic Dependency, Gender, and the Division of Labor at Home." *American Journal of Sociology* 100:652-88.

Broverman, Inge K., Susan R. Vogel, Donald M. Broverman, Frank E. Clarkson, and Paul S. Rosenkrantz. 1972. "Sex-Role Stereotypes: A Current Appraisal." *Journal of Social Issues* 28(2):59-78.

Brown, Clifford E. and Mark D. Reed. 1982. "Race, Cost, and Car-Status: Interacting Variables Using the Lost-Letter Technique." *Psychological Reports* 51:303-8.

Bussey, Kay and Albert Bandura. 1984. "Influence of Gender Constancy and Social Power on Sex-Linked Modeling." *Journal of Personality and Social Psychology* 47:1292-1302.

Butler, Dore and Florence L. Geis. 1990. "Nonverbal Affect Responses to Male and Female Leaders: Implications for Leadership Evaluations." *Journal of Personality and Social Psychology* 58:48-59.

Calabrese, Raymond L. and John T. Cochran. 1990. "The Relationship of Alienation to Cheating among a Sample of American Adolescents." *Journal of Research & Development in Education* 23(2):65-72.

Campbell, Donald T. 1967. "Stereotypes and the Perception of Group Differences." *American Psychologist* 22:817-29.

Cancian, Francesca and Stacey Oliker. Forthcoming. *For Love and Money: A Gendered View of Caring*. Thousand Oaks, CA: Pine Forge Press.

Cantor, Muriel G. 1987. "Popular Culture and the Portrayal of Women: Content and Control." Pp. 190-214 in *Analyzing Gender*, edited by B. B. Hess and M. M. Ferree. Newbury Park, CA: Sage.

Carli, Linda L. 1990. "Gender, Language, and Influence." *Journal of Personality and Social Psychology* 50:941-51.

———. 1991. "Gender, Status, and Influence." Pp. 89-113 in *Advances in Group Processes*, Vol. 8, edited by E. J. Lawler, B. Markovsky, C. Ridgeway, and H. A. Walker. Greenwich, CT: JAI.

Carlson, Rae. 1971. "Sex Differences in Ego Functioning: Exploratory Studies of Agency and Communion." *Journal of Consulting and Clinical Psychology* 37:267-77.

Carrigan, Tim, R. W. Connell, and John Lee. 1985. "Toward a New Sociology of Masculinity." *Theory and Society* 14:551-604.

———. 1987. *Toward a New Sociology of Masculinity*. Boston: Allen & Unwin.

Chambliss, William J. 1995. "Crime Control and Ethnic Minorities: Legitimizing Racial Oppression by Creating Moral Panics." Pp. 235-58 in *Ethnicity, Race, and Crime: Perspectives across Time and Place*, edited by D. F. Hawkins. Albany: State University of New York Press.

Cherry, Frances. 1995. *The "Stubborn Particulars" of Social Psychology: Essays on the Research Process*. New York: Routledge.

Chodorow, Nancy. 1978. *The Reproduction of Mothering: Psychoanalysis and the Sociology of Gender*. Berkeley: University of California Press.

Chow, Esther Ngan-Ling. 1985. "The Acculturation Experiences of Asian American Women." Pp. 238-51 in *Beyond Sex Roles*, 2d ed., edited by A. Sargent. St. Paul, MN: West.

Cline, Rebecca J. and Karen E. Musolf. 1985. "Disclosure as Social Exchange: Anticipated Length of Relationship, Sex Roles, and Disclosure Intimacy." *Western Journal of Speech Communication* 49:43-56.

Cohen, Claudia E. 1981. "Person Categories and Social Perception: Testing Some Boundaries of the Processing Effects of Prior Knowledge." *Journal of Personality and Social Psychology* 40:441-52.

Coleman, Richard Patrick, Lee Rainwater, and Kent A. McClelland. 1978. *Social Standing in America: New Dimensions of Class*. New York: Basic Books.

Collins, Patricia Hill. 1990. *Black Feminist Thought: Knowledge, Consciousness, and the Politics of Empowerment*. London: HarperCollins.

Connell, R. W. 1987. *Gender and Power: Society, the Person, and Sexual Politics*. Stanford, CA: Stanford University Press.

———. 1995. *Masculinities*. Berkeley: University of California Press.

Constantino, John N., Daniel Grosz, Paul Saenger, and Donald W. Chandler. 1993. "Testosterone and Aggression in Children." *Journal of the American Academy of Child and Adolescent Psychiatry* 32:1217-22.

Cook, Karen S., Gary Alan Fine, and James S. House, eds. 1995. *Sociological Perspectives on Social Psychology*. Boston: Allyn & Bacon.

Cook, Karen S. and Karen A. Hegtvedt. 1986. "Justice and Power: An Exchange Analysis." Pp. 19-41 in *Justice in Social Relations*, edited by H. W. Bierhoff, R. L. Cohen, and J. Greenberg. New York: Plenum.

Cook, Karen S., Jodi O'Brien, and Peter Kollock. 1990. "Exchange Theory: A Blueprint for Structure and Process." Pp. 158-81 in *Frontiers of Social Theory: The New Syntheses*, edited by G. Ritzer. New York: Columbia University Press.

Cota, Albert A. and Kenneth L. Dion. 1986. "Salience of Gender and Sex Composition of Ad Hoc Groups: An Experimental Test of Distinctiveness Theory." *Journal of Personality and Social Psychology* 50:770-76.

Cowan, Gloria, Carole Lee, Daniella Levy, and Debra Snyder. 1988. "Dominance and Inequality in X-Rated Videocassettes." *Psychology of Women Quarterly* 12:299-311.

Crocker, Jennifer and Brenda Major. 1989. "Social Stigma and Self-Esteem: The Self-Protective Properties of Stigma." *Psychological Review* 96:608-30.

Crosby, Faye J. 1982. *Relative Deprivation and Working Women.* New York: Oxford University Press.

Crosby, Faye, Stephanie Bromley, and Leonard Saxe. 1980. "Recent Unobtrusive Studies of Black and White Discrimination and Prejudice: A Literature Review." *Psychological Bulletin* 87:546-63.

Crutchfield, Robert D., Joseph L. Weis, Rodney L. Engen, and Randy R. Gainey. 1995. *Racial and Ethnic Disparities in the Prosecution of Felony Cases in King County.* Final Report to the Washington State Minority and Justice Commission, November.

Deaux, Kay. 1976. *The Behavior of Women and Men.* Monterey, CA: Brooks/Cole.

———. 1984. "From Individual Differences to Social Categories: Analysis of a Decade's Research on Gender." *American Psychologist* 39:105-16.

———. 1995. "How Basic Can You Be? The Evolution of Research on Gender Stereotypes." *Journal of Social Issues* 51(1):11-20.

Deaux, Kay and Brenda Major. 1990. *A Social-Psychological Model of Gender.* New Haven, CT: Yale University Press.

Deaux, Kay and Laurie L. Lewis. 1984. "The Structure of Gender Stereotypes: Interrelationships among Components and Gender Labels." *Journal of Personality and Social Psychology* 46:991-1004.

Della Fave, L. Richard. 1980. "The Meek Shall Not Inherit the Earth: Self-Evaluations and the Legitimacy of Stratification." *American Sociological Review* 45:955-71.

Deutsch, Morton. 1975. "Equity, Equality, and Need: What Determines What Value Will Be Used as the Basis for Distributive Justice?" *Journal of Social Issues* 31(3):137-50.

DeVault, Marjorie L. 1991. *Feeding the Family: The Social Organizational of Caring as Gendered Work.* Chicago: University of Chicago Press.

Devine, Patricia G. 1989. "Stereotypes and Prejudice: Their Automatic and Controlled Components." *Journal of Personality and Social Psychology* 56:5-18.

Devine, Patricia G. and Andrew J. Elliot. 1995. "Are Racial Stereotypes Really Fading? The Princeton Trilogy Revisited." *Personality and Social Psychology Bulletin* 21:1139-50.

Devine, Patricia G. and Sara M. Baker. 1991. "Measurement of Racial Stereotype Subtyping." *Personality and Social Psychology Bulletin* 17:44-50.

Diener, Edward, Karen L. Westford, Scott C. Fraser, and Arthur L. Beaman. 1973. "Selected Demographic Variables in Altruism." *Psychological Reports* 33:226.

Dobash, Russell P., R. Emerson Dobash, Margo Wilson, and Martin Daly. 1992. "The Myth of Sexual Symmetry in Marital Violence." *Social Problems* 39:71-91.

Dollard, John, Leonard William Doob, Neal E. Miller, Orval Herbert Mowrer, and Robert R. Sears. 1939. *Frustration and Aggression*. New Haven, CT: Yale University Press.

Donnerstein, Edward. 1983. "Erotica and Human Aggression." In *Aggression: Theoretical and Empirical Views*, Vol. 1, edited by R. G. Geen and E. Donnerstein. New York: Academic Press.

Dovidio, J. F., J. C. Campbell, S. Rigaud, J. Yankura, L. Rominger, and R. Pine. 1978. "Androgyny, Sex-Roles, and Helping." Unpublished manuscript, Colgate University, Hamilton, NY.

Dreman, S. B. and Charles W. Greenbaum. 1973. "Altruism or Reciprocity: Sharing Behavior in Israeli Kindergarten Children." *Child Development* 44:61-88.

Dunand, Muriel A. 1986. "Violence et Panique dans le Stade de Football de Bruxelles en 1985: Approche Psychosociale des Evénements [Violence and Panic in the Brussels Football Stadium in 1985: A Psychosocial Approach to These Remarkable Events]." *Cahiers de Psychologie Cognitive* 6:235-66.

Duncan, Birt L. 1976. "Differential Social Perception and Attribution of Inter-Group Violence: Testing the Lower Limits of Stereotyping Blacks." *Journal of Personality and Social Psychology* 34:590-98.

Eagly, Alice H. and Linda L. Carli. 1981. "Sex of Researchers and Sex-Typed Communications as Determinants of Sex Differences in Influenceability: A Meta-Analysis of Social Influence Studies." *Psychological Bulletin* 90:1-20.

Eagly, Alice and M. Crowley. 1986. "Gender and Helping Behavior: A Meta-Analytic Review of the Social Psychological Literature." *Psychological Bulletin* 100:283-308.

Eagly, Alice H. and Steven J. Karau. 1991. "Gender and the Emergence of Leaders: A Meta-Analysis." *Journal of Personality and Social Psychology* 60:685-710.

Eagly, Alice H. and Valerie J. Steffen. 1986. "Gender and Aggressive Behavior: A Meta-Analytic Review of the Social Psychological Literature." *Psychological Bulletin* 100:309-30.

Eccles, Jacquelynne S. and Janis E. Jacobs. 1986. "Social Forces Shape Math Attitudes and Performance." *Signs: Journal of Women in Culture and Society* 11:367-89.

Eckhoff, Torstein. 1974. *Justice: Its Determinants in Social Interaction*. Rotterdam, Netherlands: Rotterdam University Press.

Egelko, Bob. 1994. "The Rich Don't Live on Death Row." *Seattle Times* (Seattle, WA), September 6, p. A3.

Emerson, Joan P. 1970. "Behavior in Private Places: Sustaining Definitions of Reality in Gynecological Examinations." Pp. 74-97 in *Recent Sociology*, No. 2, edited by P. Dreitsel. New York: Macmillan.

Emerson, Richard M. 1972a. "Exchange Theory, Part I: A Psychological Basis for Social Exchange." Pp. 38-57 in *Sociological Theories in Progress*, Vol. 2, edited by J. Berger, Jr., M. Zelditch, and B. Anderson. Boston: Houghton Mifflin.

———. 1972b. "Exchange Theory, Part II: Exchange Relations and Networks." Pp. 58-87 in *Sociological Theories in Progress*, Vol. 2, edited by J. Berger, Jr., M. Zelditch, and B. Anderson. Boston: Houghton Mifflin.

England, Paula and Barbara Stanek Kilbourne. 1990. "Feminist Critiques of the Separatist Model of Self." *Rationality and Society* 2:156-71.

England, Paula and George Farkas. 1986. *Households, Employment, and Gender: A Sociological, Economic, and Demographic View.* New York: Aldine de Gruyter.

Enloe, Cynthia. 1993. *The Morning After: Sexual Politics at the End of the Cold War.* Berkeley: University of California Press.

Espiritu, Yen Le. 1996. *Asian American Women and Men: Labor, Laws, and Love.* Thousand Oaks, CA: Sage.

Evans, M. D. R., Jonathan Kelley, and Tamas Kolosi. 1992. "Images of Class: Public Perceptions in Hungary and Australia." *American Sociological Review* 57:461-82.

Fausto-Sterling, Anne. 1985. *Myths of Gender: Biological Theories About Women and Men.* New York: Basic Books.

———. 1993. "The Five Sexes: Why Male and Female Are Not Enough." *Sciences* 32(2):20-5.

Felson, Richard B. 1978. "Aggression as Impression Management." *Social Problems* 41:205-13.

Ferree, Myra Marx. 1991. "The Gender Division of Labor in Two-Earner Marriages: Dimensions of Variability and Change." *Journal of Family Issues* 12:158-80.

Ferree, Myra Marx and Elaine J. Hall. Forthcoming. "Rethinking Stratification from a Feminist Perspective: Gender, Race and Class in Mainstream Textbooks." *American Sociological Review.*

Festinger, Leon. 1957. *A Theory of Cognitive Dissonance.* Stanford, CA: Stanford University Press.

Fine, Michelle and Susan M. Gordon. 1989. "Feminist Transformations Of/Despite Psychology." Pp. 147-74 in *Gender and Thought: Psychological Perspectives*, edited by M. Crawford and M. Gentry. New York: Springer-Verlag.

Fisher, Jeffrey D., Arie Nadler, and S. Whitcher-Alagna. 1982. "Receipient Reactions to Aid." *Psychological Bulletin* 91:33-54.

Fiske, Susan T. and Steven L. Neuberg. 1990. "A Continuum of Impression Formation, from Category-Based to Individuating Processes: Influences of Information and Motivation on Attention and Interpretation." Pp. 1-74 in *Advances in Experimental Social Psychology*, Vol. 23, edited by M. P. Zanna. San Diego, CA: Academic Press.

Fiske, Susan T. and Shelley E. Taylor. 1991. *Social Cognition.* (2nd Ed.) New York: McGraw-Hill.

Fitzgerald, Louise F. 1993. "Sexual Harassment: Violence Against Women in the Workplace." *American Psychologist* 48:1070-76.

Fong, Stanley L. and Harvey Peskin. 1969. "Sex-Role Strain and Personality Adjustment of China-Born Students in America: A Pilot Study." *Journal of Abnormal Psychology* 74:563-67.

Forbes, Jack D. 1992. "The Hispanic Spin: Party Politics and Governmental Manipulation of Ethnic Identity." *Latin American Perspectives* 19(4):59-78.

Ford, Clellan S. and Frank A. Beach. 1951. *Patterns of Sexual Behavior.* New York: Harper.

Form, William and Christine Hanson. 1985. "The Consistency of Stratal Ideologies of Economic Justice." *Research in Social Stratification and Mobility* 4:239-69.

Foschi, Martha. 1989. "Status Characteristics, Standards, and Attributions." Pp. 58-72 in *Sociological Theories in Progress: New Formulations,* edited by J. Berger, M. Zelditch and B. Anderson. Newbury Park, CA: Sage.

———. 1991. "Gender and Double Standards for Competence." Pp. 181-207 in *Gender, Interaction, and Inequality,* edited by C. Ridgeway. New York: Springer-Verlag.

Fox, Greer Litton. 1977. " 'Nice Girl': Social Control of Women through a Value Construct." *Signs: Journal of Women in Culture and Society* 2:805-17.

Frankenberg, Ruth. 1993. *White Women, Race Matters: The Social Construction of Whiteness.* Minneapolis: University of Minnesota Press.

Friedman, Debra and Carol Diem. 1993. "Feminism and the Pro- (Rational-) Choice Movement: Rational-Choice Theory, Feminist Critiques, and Gender Inequality." Pp. 91-114 in *Theory on Gender/Feminism on Theory,* edited by P. England. Hawthorne, NY: Aldine de Gruyter.

Frodi, Ann, Jacqueline Macaulay, and Pauline R. Thorne. 1977. "Are Women Always Less Aggressive Than Men? A Review of the Experimental Literature." *Psychological Bulletin* 84:634-60.

Gaertner, Samuel L., John F. Dovidio, and Gary Johnson. 1982. "Race of Victim, Nonresponsive Bystanders, and Helping Behavior." *Journal of Social Psychology* 117:69-77.

Gallant, Mary J. 1992. "Slave Runaways in Colonial Virginia: Accounts and Status Passage as Collective Process." *Symbolic Interaction* 15:389-412.

Gardner, Carol Brooks. 1989. "Analyzing Gender in Public Places: Rethinking Goffman's Vision of Everyday Life." *American Sociologist* 20(1):42-56.

———. 1990. "Safe Conduct: Women, Crime, and Self in Public Places." *Social Problems* 37:311-28.

Garfinkel, Harold. 1967. *Studies in Ethnomethodology.* Englewood Cliffs, NJ: Prentice Hall.

Gelles, Richard J. 1985. "Family Violence: What We Know and What We Can Do." In *Unhappy Families*, edited by E. N. Newberger and R. Bourne. Littleton, MA: PSG Publishing.

Gelles, Richard J. 1994. "Family Violence, Abuse, and Neglect." Pp. 262-80 in *Families and Change: Coping with Stressful Events*, edited by P. C. McKenzy and S. J. Price. Thousand Oaks, CA: Sage.

Giddens, Anthony. 1991. *Introduction to Sociology*. New York: Norton.

Gilligan, Carol. 1982. *In a Different Voice: Psychological Theory and Women's Development*. Cambridge, MA: Harvard University Press.

Giménez, Martha E. 1992. "U.S. Ethnic Politics: Implications for Latin Americans." *Latin American Perspectives* 19(4):7-17.

Giving USA. 1986. New York: American Association of Fund-Raising Council, Inc.

Goffman, Erving. 1959. *The Presentation of Self in Everyday Life*. New York: Doubleday.

———. 1961. *Asylums: Essays on the Social Situation of Mental Patients and Other Inmates*. Garden City, NY: Anchor.

———. 1963. *Stigma*. Englewood Cliffs, NJ: Prentice Hall.

———. 1976. *Gender Advertisements*. New York: Harper & Row.

———. 1977. "The Arrangement between the Sexes." *Theory and Society* 4:301-31.

Gordon, Margaret T. and Stephanie Riger. 1989. *The Female Fear: The Social Cost of Rape*. Urbana: University of Illinois Press.

Graham, Sandra. 1992. "Most of the Subjects Were White and Middle Class: Trends in Published Research on African Americans in Selected APA Journals, 1970-1989." *American Psychologist* 47:629-39.

Gray, Colin, Phil Russell, and Stephanie Blockley. 1991. "The Effects upon Helping Behaviour of Wearing Pro-Gay Identification." *British Journal of Social Psychology* 30:171-78.

Greenberg, Jerold. 1978. "Effects of Reward Value and Retaliative Power on Allocation Decisions: Justice, Generosity, or Greed?" *Journal of Personality and Social Psychology* 36:367-79.

Gurin, Patricia, Arthur H. Miller, and Gerald Gurin. 1980. "Stratum Identification and Consciousness." *Social Psychology Quarterly* 43:30-47.

Hales, Loyde W. and Bradford J. Fenner. 1973. "Sex and Social Class Differences in Work Values." *Elementary School Guidance & Counseling* 8:26-32.

Hansen, Ronald D. and Virginia E. O'Leary. 1983. "Actors and Actresses: The Effects of Sex on Causal Attributions." *Basic and Applied Social Psychology* 4:209-30.

Harry, Joseph. 1990. "Conceptualizing Anti-Gay Violence." *Journal of Interpersonal Violence* 5:350-58.

Hartmann, Heidi. 1993. "Comment on Brines and Fiorentine." *Rationality and Society* 5:375-85.

Hartsock, Nancy C. M. 1985. "Exchange Theory: Critique from a Feminist Standpoint." *Current Perspectives in Social Theory* 6:57-70.

Healy, Joseph F. 1995. *Race, Ethnicity, Gender, and Class: The Sociology of Group Conflict and Change.* Thousand Oaks, CA: Pine Forge Press.

Heath, Linda, Candace Kruttschnitt, and David Ward. 1986. "Television and Violent Criminal Behavior: Beyond the Bobo Doll." *Violence and Victims* 1:177-90.

Hegtvedt, Karen A. and Barry Markovsky. 1995. "Justice and Injustice." Pp. 257-280 in *Sociological Perspectives on Social Psychology,* edited by K. S. Cook, G. A. Fine, and J. S. House. Boston: Allyn & Bacon.

Heilbrun, Carolyn. 1973. *Toward a Recognition of Androgyny.* New York: Knopf.

Hendrick, Susan, Clyde Hendrick, Michelle J. Slapion-Foote, and Franklin H. Foote. 1985. "Gender Differences in Sexual Attitudes." *Journal of Personality and Social Psychology* 48:1630-42.

Herbert, Melissa. 1995. "Frederick the Great or Frederick's of Hollywood? The Accomplishment of Gender among Women in the Military." Paper presented to the Annual Meeting of The Pacific Sociological Association. San Francisco, CA, April.

Herek, Gregory M. 1992. "The Social Context of Hate Crimes: Notes on Cultural Heterosexism." Pp. 89-104 in *Hate Crimes: Confronting Violence against Lesbians and Gay Men,* edited by G. M. Herek and K. T. Berrill. Newbury Park, CA: Sage.

Herek, Gregory M. and Kevin T. Berrill, eds. 1992. *Hate Crimes: Confronting Violence against Lesbians and Gay Men.* Newbury Park, CA: Sage.

Herrnstein, Richard J. and Charles Murray. 1994. *The Bell Curve.* New York: Free Press.

Hess, B. B. and Myra Marx Ferree. 1987. *Analyzing Gender.* Newbury Park, CA: Sage.

Hochschild, Arlie Russell. 1983. *The Managed Heart: Commercialization of Human Feeling.* Berkeley: University of California Press.

Hoffman, Curt and Nancy Hurst. 1990. "Gender Stereotypes: Perception or Rationalization?" *Journal of Personality and Social Psychology* 58:197-208.

Hogan, Dennis P., David J. Eggebeen, and Clifford C. Clogg. 1993. "The Structure of Intergenerational Exchanges in American Families." *American Journal of Sociology* 98:1428-58.

Hollander, Jocelyn A. 1995. "Doing 'Studs': The Performance of Gender and Sexuality on Late-Night Television." Paper presented to the Annual Meeting of The Pacific Sociological Association. San Francisco, CA, April.

Homans, George C. 1974. *Social Behavior: Its Elementary Forms.* New York: Harcourt Brace and World.

Hossain, Ziarat and Jaipaul L. Roopnarine. 1993. "Division of Household Labor and Child Care in Dual-Earner African-American Families with Infants." *Sex Roles* 29:571-83.

Howard, Judith A. 1984a. "Societal Influences on Attribution: Blaming Some Victims More Than Others." *Journal of Personality and Social Psychology* 47:494-505.

———. 1984b. "The "Normal" Victim: The Effects of Gender Stereotypes on Reactions to Victims." *Social Psychology Quarterly* 47:270-81.

———. 1988. "Gender Differences in Sexual Attitudes: Conservatism or Powerlessness?" *Gender & Society* 1:103-114.

———. 1994. "A Social Cognitive Conception of Social Structure." *Social Psychology Quarterly* 57:210-27.

Howard, Judith A. and Kenneth C. Pike. 1986. "Ideological Investment in Cognitive Processing: The Influence of Social Statuses on Attribution." *Social Psychology Quarterly* 49:154-67.

Howard, Judith A., Philip Blumstein, and Pepper Schwartz. 1986. "Sex, Power, and Influence Tactics in Intimate Relationships." *Journal of Personality and Social Psychology* 51:102-9.

Hughes, Michael and David H. Demo. 1989. "Self-Perceptions of Black Americans: Self-Esteem and Personal Efficacy." *American Journal of Sociology* 95:132-59.

Hurtado, Aida, Patricia Gurin, and Timothy Peng. 1994. "Social Identities: A Framework for Studying the Adaptations of Immigrants and Ethnics: The Adaptations of Mexicans in the United States."*Social Problems* 41:129-51.

Hyde, Janet S. 1986. "Gender Differences in Aggression." Pp. 51-66 in *The Psychology of Gender: Advances through Meta-Analysis*, edited by J. S. Hyde and M. C. Linn. Baltimore, MD: Johns Hopkins University Press.

James, William. [1890] 1991. *The Principles of Psychology*, Vol. 1. Cambridge, MA: Harvard University Press.

Jones, Tricia S. and Martin S. Remland. 1992. "Sources of Variability in Perceptions of and Responses to Sexual Harassment." *Sex Roles* 27:121-42.

Jost, John T. and Mahzarin R. Banaji. 1994. "The Role of Stereotyping in System-Justification and the Production of False Consciousness." *British Journal of Social Psychology* 33:1-27.

Kahn, Arnold, R. E. Nelson, and William P. Gaeddert. 1980. "Sex of Subject and Sex Composition of the Group as Determinants of Reward Allocation." *Journal of Personality and Social Psychology* 38:737-50.

Kahn, Arnold S. and William P. Gaeddert. 1985. "From Theories of Equity to Theories of Justice: The Liberating Consequences of Studying Women." Pp. 129-148 in *Women, Gender, and Social Psychology*, edited by V. E. O'Leary, R. K. Unger, and B. Strudler Wallston. Hillsdale, NJ: Lawrence Erlbaum.

Kalbfleisch, Pamela J. and Andrea B. Davies. 1991. "Minorities and Mentoring: Managing the Multicultural Institution." *Communication Education* 40:266-71.

Kandel-Englander, Elizabeth. 1992. "Wife Battering and Violence Outside the Family." *Journal of Interpersonal Violence* 7:462-70.

Kanter, Rosabeth Moss. 1977. *Men and Women of the Corporation.* New York: Basic Books.

Karlins, Marvin, Thomas L. Coffman, and Gary Walters. 1969. "On the Fading of Social Stereotypes: Studies in Three Generations of College Students." *Journal of Personality and Social Psychology* 13:1-16.

Karp, David A. 1986. " 'You Can Take the Boy Out of Dorchester, But You Can't Take Dorchester Out of the Boy': Toward a Social Psychology of Mobility." *Symbolic Interaction* 9:19-36.

Karraker, Katherine Hildebrandt, Dena Ann Vogel, and Margaret Ann Lake. 1995. "Parents' Gender-Stereotyped Perceptions of Newborns: The Eye of the Beholder Revisited." *Sex Roles* 33:687-701.

Kashima, Yoshihisa, Michael Siegal, Kenichiro Tanaka, and Hiroko Isaka. 1988. "Universalism in Lay Conceptions of Distributive Justice: A Cross-Cultural Examination." *International Journal of Psychology* 23:51-64.

Katz, Daniel and Kenneth W. Braly. 1933. "Racial Stereotypes of One Hundred College Students." *Journal of Abnormal and Social Psychology* 28:280-90.

Katz, Irwin, Sheldon Cohen, and David Glass. 1975. "Some Determinants of Cross-Race Helping Behavior." *Journal of Personality and Social Psychology* 32:964-70.

Kaufman, Karen, W. Larry Gregory, and Walter G. Stephan. 1990. "Maladjustment in Statistical Minorities within Ethnically Unbalanced Classrooms." *American Journal of Community Psychology* 18:757-65.

Kelley, Johnathan and M. D. R. Evans. 1995. "Class and Class Conflict in Six Western Nations." *American Sociological Review* 60:157-78.

Kerbo, Harold R. 1976. "The Stigma of Welfare and a Passive Poor." *Sociology and Social Research* 60:173-87.

Kessler, Susan J. and Wendy McKenna. 1978. *Gender: An Ethnomethodological Approach.* New York: John Wiley.

Kluegel, James R. and Eliot R. Smith. 1986. *Beliefs about Inequality.* New York: Aldine.

Kogut, Diane, Travis Langley, and Edgar C. O'Neal. 1992. "Gender Role Masculinity and Angry Aggression in Women." *Sex Roles* 26:355-68.

Kollock, Peter, Philip Blumstein, and Pepper Schwartz. 1985. "Sex and Power in Interaction: Conversational Privileges and Duties." *American Sociological Review* 50:34-46.

Kollock, Peter and Jodi O'Brien. 1992. "The Social Construction of Social Exchange." Pp. 89-112 in *Advances in Group Processes,* edited by E. J. Lawler, B. Markovsky, C. Ridgeway, and H. A. Walker. Greenwich, CT: JAI.

———. 1994. *The Production of Reality: Essays and Readings in Social Psychology.* Thousand Oaks, CA: Pine Forge Press.

Koss, Mary P. 1993. "Rape: Scope, Impact, Interventions, and Public Policy Responses." *American Psychologist* 48:1062-69.

Krebs, D. L. 1970. "Altruism: An Examination of the Concept and a Review of the Literature." *Psychological Bulletin* 73:258-302.

Kuhn, Manfre H. and Thomas S. McPartland. 1954. "An Empirical Investigation of Self-Attitudes." *American Sociological Review* 19:68-76.

Kurdek, Lawrence A. 1993. "The Allocation of Household Labor in Gay, Lesbian, and Heterosexual Married Couples." *Journal of Social Issues* 49:127-39.

LaFree, Gary. 1995. "Race and Crime Trends in the United States, 1946-1990." Pp. 169-193 in *Ethnicity, Race, and Crime: Perspectives Across Time and Place,* edited by D. F. Hawkins. Albany: State University of New York Press.

Lagerspetz, Kirsti M. J., Kaj Björkqvist, and Tarja Peltonen. 1988. "Is Indirect Aggression Typical of Females? Gender Differences in Aggressiveness in 11-12-year-old Children." *Aggressive Behavior* 14:303-15.

Lambert, W. W. 1971. "Cross-Cultural Background to Personality Development and the Socialization of Aggression: Findings from the Six Culture Study." Pp. 49-61 in *Comparative Perspectives on Social Psychology,* edited by W. W. Lambert and R. Weisbrod. Boston: Little, Brown.

Landrine, Hope. 1985. "Race × Class Stereotypes of Women." *Sex Roles* 13:65-75.

Langer, Ellen J. 1989. *Mindfulness.* Reading, MA: Addison-Wesley.

Langer, Ellen J., A. Blank, and Benzion Chanowitz. 1978. "The Mindlessness of Ostensibly Thoughtful Action: The Role of 'Placebic' Information in Interpersonal Interaction." *Journal of Personality and Social Psychology* 36:635-42.

Langer, Ellen J., Susan Fiske, Shelley E. Taylor, and Benzion Chanowitz. 1976. "Stigma, Staring and Discomfort: A Novel-Stimulus Hypothesis." *Journal of Experimental Social Psychology* 12:451-63.

Langley, Travis, Edgar C. O'Neal, K. M. Craig, and Elizabeth A. Yost. 1992. "Aggression Consistent, Inconsistent, and Irrelevant Priming Effects on Selective Exposure to Media Violence." *Aggressive Behavior* 18:349-56.

Latane, Bibb and John M. Darley. 1968. "Group Inhibition of Bystander Intervention in Emergencies." *Journal of Personality and Social Psychology* 10:215-21.

———. 1970. *The Unresponsive Bystander: Why Doesn't He Help?* Englewood Cliffs, NJ: Prentice Hall.

Lerner, R. M. and P. Frank. 1974. "Relation of Race and Sex to Supermarket Helping Behavior." *Journal of Social Psychology* 94:201-3.

Leung, Kwok and Michael H. Bond. 1984. "The Impact of Cultural Collectivism on Reward Allocation." *Journal of Personality and Social Psychology* 47:793-804.

Leventhal, Gerald S., Jurgis Karuza, Jr., and William Rick Fry. 1980. "Beyond Fairness: A Theory of Allocation Preferences." Pp. 167-218 in *Justice and Social Interaction,* edited by G. Mikula. New York: Springer-Verlag.

Lockhart, Lettie L., Barbara W. White, Vicki Causby, and Alicia Isaac. 1994. "Letting Out the Secret: Violence in Lesbian Relationships." *Journal of Interpersonal Violence* 9:469-92.

Lopata, Helen Z. and Barrie Thorne. 1978. "On the Term 'Sex Roles.'" *Signs: Journal of Women in Culture and Society* 3:718-21.

Lowe, Roland and Gary Ritchey. 1973. "Relation of Altruism to Age, Social Class, and Ethnic Identity." *Psychological Reports* 33:567-72.

Lubek, I. 1979. "A Brief Social Psychological Analysis of Research on Aggression in Social Psychology." In *Psychology in Social Context,* edited by A. R. Buss. New York: Irvington.

Luchterhead, Elmer and Leonard Weller. 1976. "Effects of Class, Race, Sex, and Educational Status on Patterns of Aggression of Lower-Class Youth." *Journal of Youth and Adolescence* 5:59-71.

Lye, Diane N. Forthcoming. "Adult Child-Parent Relationships." *Annual Review of Sociology* 22.

Lye, Diane N. and Daniel H. Klepinger. 1995. "Race and Hispanic Ethnicity, Childhood Living Arrangements and Adult-Child Parent Relations." Unpublished paper, University of Washington, Seattle.

Lye, Diane N., Daniel H. Klepinger, Patricia Davis Hyle, and Anjanette Nelson. 1995. "Childhood Living Arrangements and Adult Children's Relations with Their Parents." *Demography* 32:261-80.

Macaulay, J. 1985. "Adding Gender to Aggression Research: Incremental or Revolutionary Change?" Pp. 191-224 in *Women, Gender, and Social Psychology,* edited by V. E. O'Leary, R. K. Unger, and B. Strudler Wallston. Hillsdale, NJ: Lawrence Erlbaum.

Maccoby, Eleanor E. and Carol Jacklin. 1974. *The Psychology of Sex Differences.* Stanford, CA: Stanford University Press.

Macy, Michael. 1993. "Backward-Looking Social Control." *American Sociological Review* 58:819-36.

Major, Brenda. 1987. "Gender, Justice, and the Psychology of Entitlement." Pp. 124-148 in *Sex and Gender,* Vol. 7, edited by P. Shaver and C. Hendrick. Newbury Park, CA: Sage.

———. 1989. "Gender Differences in Comparisons and Entitlement: Implications for Comparable Worth." *Journal of Social Issues* 45:99-115.

———. 1993. "Gender, Entitlement, and the Distribution of Family Labor." *Journal of Social Issues* 49:141-59.

Major, Brenda and Jeffrey B. Adams. 1983. "Role of Gender, Interpersonal Orientation and Self-Presentation in Distributive-Justice Behavior." *Journal of Personality and Social Psychology* 45:598-608.

Major, Brenda and Kay Deaux. 1982. "Individual Differences in Justice Behavior." Pp. 43-76 in *Equity and Justice in Social Behavior,* edited by J. Greenberg and R. L. Cohen. New York: Plenum.

Mamet, David. 1992. *Oleanna.* New York: Vintage.

Manegold, Catherine. 1993. "Women Say Wood Is Victim of Double Standard; Clinton Under Fire." *Seattle Times* (Seattle, WA), February 7, p. A6.

Margolin, L. 1992. "Beyond Maternal Blame: Physical Child Abuse as a Phenomenon of Gender." *Journal of Family Issues* 13:410-23.

Markus, Hazel, Marie Crane, Stan Bernstein, and Michael Siladi. 1982. "Self-Schemas and Gender." *Journal of Personality and Social Psychology* 42:38-50.

Martin, Patricia Yancey and Robert A. Hummer. 1993. "Fraternities and Rape on Campus." Pp. 114-131 in *Violence against Women: The Bloody Footprints,* edited by P. Bart and E. G. Moran. Newbury Park, CA: Sage.

Marx, Karl and Friedrich Engels. 1974. *The German Ideology.* New York: International Publishers.

Massey, Douglas S. and Nancy A. Denton. 1993. *American Apartheid: Segregation and the Making of the Underclass.* Cambridge, MA: Harvard University Press.

McArthur, Leslie Zebrowitz and Linda K. Solomon. 1978. "Perceptions of an Aggressive Encounter as a Function of the Victim's Salience and the Perceiver's Arousal." *Journal of Personality and Social Psychology* 36:1278-90.

McCall, George J. and J. L. Simmons. 1978. *Identities and Interactions: An Examination of Human Associations in Everyday Life.* New York: Free Press.

McGuire, William J., Claire V. McGuire, Pamela Child, and Terry Fujioka. 1978. "Salience of Ethnicity in the Spontaneous Self-Concept as a Function of One's Ethnic Distinctiveness in the Social Environment." *Journal of Personality and Social Psychology* 36:511-20.

Mead, George Herbert. 1934. *Mind, Self, and Society.* Chicago: University of Chicago Press.

Meeker, B. F. and P. A. Weitzel-O'Neill. 1977. "Sex Roles and Interpersonal Behavior in Task-Oriented Groups." *American Sociological Review* 42:91-105.

Mehan, Hugh M. and Houston W. Wood. 1975. *The Reality of Ethnomethodology.* New York: John Wiley.

Messerschmidt, James W. 1993. *Masculinities and Crime: Critique and Reconceptualization of Theory.* Lanham, MD: Rowman & Littlefield.

Messner, Michael A. and Donald E. Sabo. 1994. *Sex, Violence, and Power in Sports: Rethinking Masculinity.* Freedom, CA: Crossing Press.

Mikula, Gerold, ed. 1980. *Justice and Social Interaction.* New York: Springer-Verlag.

Miller, Joan G. 1984. "Culture and the Development of Everyday Social Explanation." *Journal of Personality and Social Psychology* 46:961-78.

Miller, Joan G., D. G. Bersoff, and R. L. Harwood. 1990. "Perceptions of Social Responsibilities in India and in the United States: Moral Imperatives or Personal Decisions?" *Journal of Personality and Social Psychology* 58:33-47.

Mischel, Walter. 1966. "A Social Learning View of Sex Differences in Behavior." Pp. 56-81 in *The Development of Sex Differences,* edited by E. Maccoby. Stanford, CA: Stanford University Press.

Moghaddam, Fathali M., Donald M. Taylor, and Stephen C. Wright. 1993. *Social Psychology in Cross-Cultural Perspective.* New York: W. H. Freeman.

Molm, Linda D. 1981. "The Legitimacy of Behavioral Theory as a Sociological Perspective." *American Sociologist* 16:153-65.

————. 1987. "Power-Dependence Theory: Power Processes and Negative Outcomes." Pp. 171-98 in *Advances in Group Processes*, Vol. 4, edited by E. J. Lawler and B. Markovsky. Greenwich, CT: JAI.

————. 1988. "The Structure and Use of Power: A Comparison of Reward and Punishment Power." *Social Psychology Quarterly* 51:108-22.

————. 1989a. "An Experimental Analysis of Imbalance in Punishment Power." *Social Forces* 68:178-203.

————. 1989b. "Punishment Power: A Balancing Process in Power-Dependence Relations." *American Journal of Sociology* 94:1392-1428.

————. 1990. "Structure, Action, and Outcomes: The Dynamics of Power in Social Exchange." *American Sociological Review* 55:427-47.

Molm, Linda D. and Karen S. Cook. 1995. "Social Exchange and Exchange Networks." Pp. 209-35 in *Sociological Perspectives on Social Psychology*, edited by K. S. Cook, G. A. Fine, and J. S. House. Boston: Allyn & Bacon.

Money, J. and Anke Ehrhardt. 1972. *Man and Woman, Boy and Girl.* Baltimore: Johns Hopkins University Press.

Monmaney, Terence. 1995. "The Essence of Maleness May Also Provide Birth Control." *Seattle Times* (Seattle, WA), July 31, p. A1.

Morgan, Carolyn S. and Alexis J. Walker. 1983. "Predicting Sex Role Attitudes." *Social Psychology Quarterly* 46:148-51.

Morris, Jan. 1974. *Conundrum.* New York: Harcourt Brace Jovanovich.

Morrow-Howell, Nancy, Leanne Lott, and Martha Ozawa. 1990. "The Impact of Race on Volunteer Helping Relationships among the Elderly." *Social Work* 35:395-402.

Moss, M. K. and R. A. Page. 1972. "Reinforcement and Helping Behavior." *Journal of Applied Social Psychology* 2:360-71.

Muehlenhard, Charlene L. 1988. "Misinterpreted Dating Behaviors and the Risk of Date Rape." *Journal of Social and Clinical Psychology* 6:20-37.

Murphy-Berman, Virginia, John J. Berman, Purnima Singh, Anju Pachauri, and Pramod Kumar. 1984. "Factors Affecting Allocation to Needy and Meritorious Recipients: A Cross-Cultural Comparison." *Journal of Personality and Social Psychology* 46:1267-72.

Nicholson, Linda. 1994. "Interpreting Gender." *Signs: Journal of Women in Culture and Society* 20:79-105.

Nirenberg, Theodore D. and Jacquelyn W. Gaebelein. 1979. "Third Party Instigated Aggression: Traditional versus Liberal Sex Role Attitudes." *Personality and Social Psychology Bulletin* 5:348-51.

Olson, Toska. Forthcoming. "The Price of Parenting: What Happens When Workers Parent and Parents Work?" Ph.D. dissertation, Department of Sociology, University of Washington, Seattle.

Omi, Michael and Howard Winant. 1986. *Racial Formation in the United States: From the 1960s to the 1980s.* New York: Routledge & Kegan Paul.

Parsons, Talcott. 1955. "Family Structure and the Socialization of the Child." In *Family Socialization and Interaction Process,* edited by T. Parsons and R. F. Bales. Glencoe, IL: Free Press.

Pate, Carl Edward. 1995. "Acknowledgment Rituals: Greeting Phenomena between Strangers." Paper presented to the Annual Meeting of The Pacific Sociological Association, San Francisco, CA, April.

Phillips, David P. 1983. "The Impact of Mass Media Violence on U.S. Homicides." *American Sociological Review* 48:560-68.

———. 1986. "Natural Experiments on the Effects of Mass Media Violence on Fatal Aggression: Strengths and Weaknesses of a New Approach." Pp. 207-250 in *Advances in Experimental Social Psychology,* Vol. 19, edited by L. Berkowitz. Orlando, FL: Academic Press.

Phinney, Jean S. 1990. "Ethnic Identity in Adolescents and Adults: Review of Research." *Psychological Bulletin* 108:499-514.

Piliavin, Jane Allyn and Hong-Wen Charng. 1990. "Altruism: A Review of Recent Theory and Research." *Annual Review of Sociology* 16:27-65.

Piliavin, Jane Allyn and Rhoda Kesler Unger. 1985. "The Helpful but Helpless Female: Myth or Reality?" Pp. 149-89 in *Women, Gender, and Social Psychology,* edited by Virginia E. O'Leary, Rhoda Kesler Unger, and Barbara Strudler Wallston. Hillsdale, NJ: Lawrence Erlbaum.

Pitchford, Susan. 1992. "Race." Pp. 1615-19 in *The Encyclopedia of Sociology,* Vol. 3, edited by E. F. Borgatta and M. L. Borgatta. New York: Macmillan Publishing Co.

Pleck, Joseph H., Freya Lund Sonenstein, and Leighton C. Ku. 1993. "Masculinity Ideology and Its Correlates." Pp. 85-110 in *Gender Issues in Contemporary Society,* edited by S. Oskamp and M. Constanzo. Newbury Park, CA: Sage.

Pugh, Meredith D. and Ralph Wahrman. 1983. "Neutralizing Sexism in Mixed-Sex Groups: Do Women Have to be Better Than Men?" *American Journal of Sociology* 88:746-62.

Ramos, Reyes. 1979. "Movidas: The Methodological and Theoretical Relevance of Interactional Strategies." *Studies in Symbolic Interaction* 2:141-65.

Reid, Pamela Trotman. 1993. "Poor Women in Psychological Research: Shut Up and Shut Out." *Psychology of Women Quarterly* 17:133-50.

Reiman, Jeffrey. 1995. *The Rich Get Richer and the Poor Get Prison,* 4th ed. Boston: Allyn & Bacon.

Renzetti, Clare. 1988. "Violence in Lesbian Relationships: A Preliminary Analysis of Causal Factors." *Journal of Interpersonal Violence* 3:381-99.

———. 1992. *Violent Betrayal: Partner Abuse in Lesbian Relationships.* Newbury Park, CA: Sage.

Rich, Adrienne. 1980. "Compulsory Heterosexuality and Lesbian Existence." *Signs: Journal of Women in Culture and Society* 5:631-60.

Ridgeway, Cecilia L. 1982. "Status in Groups: The Importance of Motivation." *American Sociological Review* 47:76-88.

———. 1993. "Gender, Status, and the Social Psychology of Expectations." Pp. 175-97 in *Theory on Gender/Feminism on Theory*, edited by P. England. New York: Aldine de Gruyter.

Ridgeway, Cecilia L. and Henry A. Walker. 1995. "Status Structures." Pp. 281-310 in *Sociological Perspectives on Social Psychology*, edited by K. S. Cook, G. A. Fine, and J. S. House. Boston: Allyn & Bacon.

Rime, Bernard and Jacques-Phillipe Leyens. 1988. "Violence dans les Stades: La Réponse des Psychologues [Violence in the Stadiums: The Response of Psychologists]." *La Recherche* 19:528-31.

Risman, Barbara. Forthcoming. *Toward a Post-Gender Family*. New Haven, CT: Yale University Press.

Robinson, Robert V. and Wendell Bell. 1978. "Equality, Success, and Social Justice in England and the United States." *American Sociological Review* 43:125-43.

Rodriquez, S. Fernando and Veronica A. Henderson. 1995. "Intimate Homicide: Victim-Offender Relationship in Female-Perpetrated Homicide." *Deviant Behavior* 16:45-57.

Roff, James D. 1992. "Childhood Aggression, Peer Status, and Social Class as Predictors of Delinquency." *Psychological Reports* 70:31-34.

Romer, Nancy and Debra Cherry. 1980. "Ethnic and Social Class Differences in Children's Sex-Role Concepts." *Sex Roles* 6:245-63.

Rose, Robert M., Irwin S. Bernstein, and Thomas P. Gordon. 1975. "Consequences of Social Conflict on Plasma Testosterone Levels in Rhesus Monkeys." *Psychosomatic Medicine* 37:50-61.

Rosenblum, Karen E. and Toni-Michelle C. Travis. 1996. *The Meaning of Difference: American Constructions of Race, Sex and Gender, Social Class, and Sexual Orientation.* New York: McGraw-Hill.

Rosenhan, David L. 1973. "On Being Sane in Insane Places." *Science* 179:250-58.

Rosenkrantz, Paul S., Susan R. Vogel, H. Bee, Inge K. Broverman, and Donald M. Broverman. 1968. "Sex-Role Stereotypes and Self Concepts among College Students." *Journal of Consulting and Clinical Psychology* 32:287-95.

Rosenthal, Robert and Lenore Jacobson. 1968. *Pygmalion in the Classroom: Teacher Expectations and Pupils Intellectual Development.* New York: Holt, Rinehart & Winston.

Rothman, Robert A. 1993. *Inequality and Stratification: Class, Color, and Gender.* Englewood Cliffs, NJ: Prentice Hall.

Routman, Peter. 1995. "Bonded by Adversity—Pair Save a Man and Gain a Friend." *Seattle Times* (Seattle, WA), November 23, p. A1.

Rubin, Jeffrey Z., F. J. Provenzano, and Zella Luria. 1974. "The Eye of the Beholder: Parents' Views on Sex of Newborns." *American Journal of Orthopsychiatry* 44:512-19.

Rubin, Lillian. 1976. *Worlds of Pain: Life in the Working Class Family.* New York: Basic Books.

Sampson, Edward E. 1975. "On Justice as Equality." *Journal of Social Issues* 31(3):45-64.

Sanchez, Laura. 1993. "Women's Power and the Gendered Division of Domestic Labor in the Third World." *Gender & Society* 7:434-59.

Schwalbe, Michael L. 1991. "Social Structure and the Moral Self." Pp. 281-303 in *The Self-Society Dynamic: Cognition, Emotion and Action,* edited by J. A. Howard and P. L. Callero. New York: Cambridge University Press.

Schwartz, Gary S., Thomas R. Kane, Joanne M. Joseph, and James T. Tedeschi. 1978. "The Effects of Post-Transgression Remorse on Perceived Aggression, Attribution of Intent, and Level of Punishment." *Journal of Social and Clinical Psychology* 17:293-97.

Schwartz, Pepper. 1994. *Peer Marriage: How Love between Equals Really Works.* New York: Free Press.

Schwartz, Pepper and Virginia Rutter. Forthcoming. *Gender, Sex, and Society.* Thousand Oaks, CA: Sage.

Schwartz, Shalom H. and Avi Gottlieb. 1980. "Bystander Anonymity and Reactions to Emergencies." *Social Psychology Quarterly* 39:418-30.

Schwartz, Shalom H. and Judith A. Howard. 1984. "Internalized Values as Motivators of Altruism." Pp. 229-45 in *Development and Maintenance of Prosocial Behavior: International Perspectives on Positive Morality,* edited by Ervin Staub, Daniel Bar-Tal, J. Karylowsk, and Janusz Reykowski. New York: Plenum.

Scott, Joan. 1988. *Gender and the Politics of History.* New York: Columbia University Press.

Scott, John P. 1992. "Aggression: Functions and Control in Social Systems." *Aggressive Behavior* 18:1-20.

Scott, Marvin B. and Stanford M. Lyman. 1968. "Accounts." *American Sociological Review* 33:46-62.

Sears, David O. 1988. "Symbolic Racism." Pp. 64-84 in *Eliminating Racism: Profiles in Controversy,* edited by P. A Katz and D. A. Taylor. New York: Plenum.

Segal, Lynne. 1993. "Does Pornography Cause Violence? Pp. 5-21 in *Dirty Looks: Women, Pornography, Power,* edited by P. C. Gibson and R. Gibson. London: BFI.

Shaw, Jerry I., Hans W. Borough, and Matthew I. Fink. 1994. "Perceived Sexual Orientation and Helping Behavior by Males and Females: The Wrong Number Technique." *Journal of Psychology and Human Sexuality* 6:73-81.

Shelton, Beth A. and Daphne John. 1993. "Does Marital Status Make a Difference? Housework among Married and Cohabiting Men and Women." *Journal of Family Issues* 14:401-20.

Shotland, R. Lance and Jane M. Craig. 1988. "Can Men and Women Differentiate between Friendly and Sexually Interested Behavior?" *Social Psychology Quarterly* 51:66-73.

Shotland, R. Lance and Margaret K. Straw. 1976. "Bystander Response to an Assault: When a Man Attacks a Woman." *Journal of Personality and Social Psychology* 34:990-99.

Simon, Rita J. and J. Landis. 1991. *The Crimes Women Commit, the Punishments They Receive.* Lexington, MA: D. C. Heath.

Simon, Stephanie S. and Bill B. Boyarsky. 1995. "Gloves 'Too Tight,' Simpson Says." *Seattle Times* (Seattle, WA), June 16, p. A2.

Skinner, B. F. 1938. *The Behavior of Organisms.* New York: Appleton-Century-Crofts.

———. 1974. *About Behaviorism.* New York: Knopf.

Skrypnek, Berna J. and Mark Snyder. 1982. "On the Self-Perpetuating Nature of Stereotypes about Men and Women." *Journal of Experimental Social Psychology* 18:277-91.

Smedley, Audrey. 1993. *Race in North America: Origin and Evolution of a Worldview.* Boulder, CO: Westview.

Smedley, Joseph W. and James A. Bayton. 1978. "Evaluative Race-Class Stereotypes by Race and Perceived Class of Subjects." *Journal of Personality and Social Psychology* 36:530-35.

Smith, Patricia A. and Elizabeth Midlarsky. 1985. "Empirically Derived Conceptions of Femaleness and Maleness: A Current View." *Sex Roles* 12:313-28.

Snow, David A. and Leon Anderson. 1987. "Identity Work among the Homeless: The Verbal Construction and Avowal of Personal Identities." *American Journal of Sociology* 92:1336-71.

———. 1993. *Down on Their Luck: A Study of Homeless Street People.* Berkeley: University of California Press.

Snyder, Mark. 1984. "When Belief Creates Reality." Pp. 248-305 in *Advances in Experimental Social Psychology*, Vol. 18, edited by L. Berkowitz. Orlando, FL: Academic Press.

Snyder, Mark and Berna J. Skrypnek. 1981. "Testing Hypotheses about the Self: Assessment of Job Suitability." *Journal of Personality* 49:193-211.

Snyder, Mark, Elizabeth Decker Tanke, and Ellen Berscheid. 1977. "Social Perception and Interpersonal Behavior: On the Self-Fulfilling Nature of Social Stereotypes." *Journal of Personality and Social Psychology* 35:656-66.

Snyder, Mark and Seymour W. Uranowitz. 1978. "Reconstructing the Past: Some Cognitive Consequences of Person Perception." *Journal of Personality and Social Psychology* 36:941-50.

South, Scott J. and Glenna Spitze. 1994. "Housework in Marital and Nonmarital Households." *American Sociological Review* 59:327-47.

Spence, Janet T., Kay Deaux, and Robert L. Helmreich. 1985. "Sex Roles in Contemporary American Society." Pp. 149-78 in *The Handbook of Social Psychology*, 3d ed., edited by G. Lindzey and E. Aronson. New York: Random House.

Spence, Janet T. and Robert L. Helmreich. 1972. "The Attitudes Toward Women Scale: An Objective Instrument to Measure Attitudes Toward the Rights and Role of Women in Contemporary Society." *JSAS Catalog of Selected Documents in Psychology* 2:66.

Spence, Janet T., Robert L. Helmreich, and Joy Stapp. 1974. "The Personal Attributes Questionnaire: A Measure of Sex-Role Stereotypes and Masculinity-Femininity." *JSAS Catalog of Selected Documents in Psychology* 4:43-44.

Spence, Janet T., and Linda L. Savin. 1985. "Images of Masculinity and Femininity." Pp. 35-66 in *Women, Gender, and Social Psychology*, edited by V. E. O'Leary, R. K. Unger, and B. S. Wallston. Hillsdale, NJ: Lawrence Erlbaum.

Spitze, Glenna. 1988. "Women's Employment and Family Relations: A Review." *Journal of Marriage and the Family* 50:595-618.

Spitze, Glenna and John R. Logan 1990. "Sons, Daughters and Intergenerational Social Support." *Journal of Marriage and the Family* 52:420-30.

Sprafkin, J. N., R. M. Liebert, and R. W. Poulos. 1975. "Effects of Prosocial Televised Examples on Children's Helping." *Journal of Experimental Child Psychology* 20:119-26.

Sprague, Joey. 1995. "Self-Determination and Empowerment: Making the Connection." Unpublished paper, University of Kansas.

Stacey, Judith and Barrie Thorne. 1985. "The Missing Feminist Revolution in Sociology." *Social Problems* 32:301-16.

Stack, Carol 1974. *All Our Kin: Strategies for Survival in the Black Community.* New York: Harper & Row.

Stangor, Charles, Laure Lynch, Changming Duan, and Beth Glass. 1992. "Categorization of Individuals on the Basis of Multiple Social Features." *Journal of Personality and Social Psychology* 62:207-18.

Stanko, Elizabeth. 1990. *Everyday Violence.* London: Pandora.

Staples, Brent. 1994. "Black Men and Public Space." Pp. 156-58 in *The Production of Reality: Essays and Readings in Social Psychology*, edited by P. Kollock and J. O'Brien. Thousand Oaks, CA: Pine Forge Press.

Steele, Claude M. and Joshua Aronson. 1995. "Stereotype Threat and the Intellectual Performance of African Americans." *Journal of Personality and Social Psychology* 69:797-811.

Steinmetz, Suzanne K. 1977/78. "The Battered Husband Syndrome." *Victimology* 2:499-509.

Stephan, Walter G. and David Rosenfield. 1982. "Racial and Ethnic Stereotypes." Pp. 92-136 in *In the Eye of the Beholder: Contemporary Issues in Stereotyping*, edited by A. G. Miller. New York: Praeger.

Stolte, John F. 1987. "The Formation of Justice Norms." *American Sociological Review* 52:774-84.

Straus, Murray A. 1990. *Physical Violence in American Families.* New Brunswick, NJ: Transaction Books.

———. 1991. "Discipline and Deviance: Physical Punishment of Children and Violence and Other Crime in Adulthood." *Social Problems* 38:133-54.

Straus, Murray A. and Richard J. Gelles. 1986. "Societal Change and Change in Family Violence from 1975 to 1985 as Revealed by Two National Surveys." *Journal of Marriage and the Family* 48:465-79.

Stryker, Sheldon. 1980. *Symbolic Interactionism: A Social Structural Version.* Menlo Park, CA: Benjamin-Cummings.

Stryker, Sheldon, and Anne Statham. 1985. "Symbolic Interaction and Role Theory." Pp. 311-78 in *The Handbook of Social Psychology*, Vol. 1, edited by G. Lindzey and E. Aronson. 3rd ed. New York: Random House.

Sullivan, Christopher. 1995. "Judge Refuses to Declare Mistrial; Sentencing Begins: Jury Must Decide if Smith Deserves Death Penalty." *Seattle Times* (Seattle, WA), July 24, p. A2.

Tajfel, Henri. 1981. *Human Groups and Social Categories: Studies in Social Psychology.* Cambridge, UK: Cambridge University Press.

———. 1982. *Social Identity and Intergroup Relations.* London: Cambridge University Press.

Tavris, Carol. 1989. *Anger: The Misunderstood Emotion.* New York: Touchstone.

Taylor, Donald M. and Vaishna Jaggi. 1974. "Ethnocentrism and Causal Attribution in a South Indian Context." *Journal of Cross-Cultural Psychology* 5:162-71.

Taylor, Shelley E., Susan T. Fiske, Nancy L. Etcoff, and Audrey J. Ruderman. 1978. "Categorical Bases of Person Memory and Stereotyping." *Journal of Personality and Social Psychology* 36:778-93.

Taylor, Shelley E., Anne Peplau, and David O. Sears. 1994. *Social Psychology*, 8th ed. Englewood Cliffs, NJ: Prentice Hall.

Taylor, Stuart P. and James D. Sears. 1988. "The Effects of Alcohol and Persuasive Social Pressure on Human Physical Aggression." *Aggressive Behavior* 14:237-43.

Terman, Lewis M. and Catherine Cox Miles. 1936. *Sex and Personality: Studies in Masculinity and Femininity.* New York: McGraw-Hill.

Thibaut, John W. and Harold H. Kelley. 1959. *The Social Psychology of Groups.* New York: John Wiley.

Thompson, Linda. 1991. "Family Work: Women's Sense of Fairness." *Journal of Family Issues* 12:181-96.

Thompson, Linda and Alexis J. Walker. 1989. "Gender in Families: Women and Men in Marriage, Work, and Parenthood." *Journal of Marriage and the Family* 51:845-71.

Thorne, Barrie. 1993. *Gender Play: Girls and Boys in School.* New Brunswick, NJ: Rutgers University Press.

Thorne, Barrie, Cheris Kramarae, and Nancy Henley. 1983. *Language, Gender, and Society.* Rowley, MA: Newbury House.

Timmer, Susan G., Jacquelynne Eccles, and Keith O'Brien. 1985. "How Children Use Time." Pp. 353-82 in *Time, Goods, and Well-Being,* edited by F. T. Juster and F. P. Stafford. Ann Arbor: University of Michigan Institute for Social Research.

Towson, Shelagh M. and Mark P. Zanna. 1982. "Toward a Situational Analysis of Gender Differences in Aggression." *Sex Roles* 8:903-14.

Triandis, Harry C. 1976. "The Future of Pluralism." *Journal of Social Issues,* 32(4):179-207.

Tsang, Ellen. 1994. "Investigating the Effects of Race and Apparent Lesbianism upon Helping Behaviour." *Feminism & Psychology* 4:469-71.

Turk, James L. and Norman W. Bell. 1972. "Measuring Power in Families." *Journal of Marriage and the Family* 34:215-23.

Turner, Jonathan H. 1982. *The Structure of Sociological Theory.* Homewood, IL: Dorsey.

Unger, Rhoda K. 1976. "Male Is Greater Than Female: The Socialization of Status Inequality." *The Counseling Psychologist* 6:2-9.

———. 1978. "The Politics of Gender: A Review of Relevant Literature." In *Psychology of Women: Future Directions of Research,* edited by J. Sherman and F. Denmark. New York: Psychological Dimensions.

Unger, Rhoda and Mary Crawford. 1992. *Women and Gender: A Feminist Psychology.* New York: McGraw-Hill.

Vander Zanden, James W. 1990. *The Social Experience: An Introduction to Sociology.* New York: McGraw-Hill.

Visher, Christy A. 1983. "Gender, Police Arrest Decisions, and Notions of Chivalry." *Criminology* 21(1):5-28.

von Baeyer, Carl L., Debbie L. Sherk, and Mark P. Zanna. 1981. "Impression Management in the Job Interview: When the Female Applicant Meets the Male (Chauvinist) Interviewer." *Personality and Social Psychology Bulletin* 7:45-51.

Wagner, David G., Rebecca S. Ford, and Thomas W. Ford. 1986. "Can Gender Inequalities Be Reduced?" *American Sociological Review* 51:47-61.

Watson, John B. 1924. *Behaviorism.* Chicago: University of Chicago Press.

Watts, Barbara L., Lawrence A. Messe, and Robin R. Vallacher. 1982. "Toward Understanding Sex Differences in Pay Allocation: Agency, Communion, and Reward Distribution Behavior." *Sex Roles* 8:1175-81.

Wegner, Daniel. 1986. "Transactive Memory: A Contemporary Analysis of the Group Mind." Pp. 185-208 in *Theories of Group Behavior,* edited by B. Mullen and G. R. Goethals. New York: Springer-Verlag.

Wegner, Daniel M. and William D. Crano. 1975. "Racial Factors in Helping Behavior: An Unobtrusive Field Experiment." *Journal of Personality and Social Psychology* 32:901-5.

Weisstein, Naomi. 1970. " 'Kinder, Kuche, Kirche' as Scientific Law: Psychology Constructs the Female." Pp. 205-20 in *Sisterhood Is Powerful,* edited by R. Morgan. New York: Vintage.

Weitz, Rose and Leonard Gordon. 1993. "Images of Black Women among Anglo College Students." *Sex Roles* 28:19-34.

West, Candace and Sarah Fenstermaker. 1995. "Doing Difference." *Gender & Society* 9:8-37.

West, Candace and Don H. Zimmerman. 1987. "Doing Gender." *Gender & Society* 1:125-51.

West, Stephen G., Glayde Whitney, and Robert Schnedler. 1975. "Helping a Motorist in Distress: The Effects of Sex, Race and Neighborhood." *Journal of Personality & Social Psychology* 31:691-98.

Wexler, Phil. 1983. *Critical Social Psychology.* Boston MA: Routledge & Kegan Paul.

White, Jacquelyn W. and Robin M. Kowalski. 1994. "Deconstructing the Myth of the Nonaggressive Woman." *Psychology of Women Quarterly* 18:487-508.

White, Jacquelyn W. and Susan B. Sorenson. 1992. "A Sociocultural View of Sexual Assault: From Discrepancy to Diversity." *Journal of Social Issues* 48(1):187-95.

Whiting, Beatrice B. and C. P. Edwards. 1988. *Children of Different Worlds: The Foundation of Social Behavior.* Cambridge: Harvard University Press.

Whiting, Beatrice B. and John W. M. Whiting. 1975. *Children of Six Cultures: A Psychocultural Analysis.* Cambridge, MA: Harvard University Press.

Wicker, Alan W. 1969. "Attitudes Versus Actions: The Relationship of Verbal and Overt Behavioral Responses to Attitude Objects." *Journal of Social Issues* 25(4):41-78.

Wispe, L. G. and H. B. Freshley. 1971. "Race, Sex, and Sympathetic Helping Behavior: The Broken Bag Caper." *Journal of Personality and Social Psychology* 17:59-65.

Wittig, Michelle A., Gary Marks, and Gary A. Jones. 1981. "Luck Versus Effort Attributions: Effect on Reward Allocations to Self and Other." *Personality and Social Psychology* 7:71-78.

Wood, Wendy and Steven J. Karten. 1986. "Sex Differences in Interaction Style as a Product of Perceived Sex Differences in Competence." *Journal of Personality and Social Psychology* 50:341-47.

Wooley, Helen Thompson. 1910. "Psychological Literature: A Review of the Most Recent Literature on the Psychology of Sex." *Psychological Bulletin* 7:335-42.

Word, Carl O., Mark P. Zanna, and Joel Cooper. 1974. "The Nonverbal Mediation of Self-Fulfilling Prophecies in Interracial Interaction." *Journal of Experimental Social Psychology* 10:109-20.

Wright, Erik O., Karen Shire, Shu-ling Hwang, Maureen Dolan, and Janeen Baxter. 1992. "The Non-Effects of Class on the Gender Division of Labor in the Home: A Comparative Study of Sweden and the United States." *Gender & Society* 6:252-82.

Wunderlich, Elizabeth and Frank N. Willis. 1977. "The Youth of Victims as a Factor Affecting the Probability of Receiving Aid." *Journal of Psychology* 97:93-94.

Yamagishi, Toshio, Mary R. Gillmore, and Karen S. Cook. 1988. "Network Connections and the Distribution of Power in Exchange Networks." *American Journal of Sociology* 93:833.

Yarrow, Marian R., Phyllis M. Scott, and Carolyn Z. Waxler. 1973. "Learning Concern for Others." *Developmental Psychology* 8:240-60.

About the Authors

Judith A. Howard (Ph.D., 1982, University of Wisconsin—Madison) is Professor of Sociology at the University of Washington in Seattle. She studies gender dynamics and interactions, emphasizing microlevel cognitions—stereotypes, attitudes, expectations about gendered situations—and how they shape and are shaped by social interactions and macrolevel social institutions. Currently, she coedits *Signs: Journal of Women in Culture and Society,* a position that never fails to make her acutely aware of gendered situations and gendered selves. She is also immersed in her department's teacher training programs, another context that enlivens her understanding of the complexities of social interactions. As one of the four editors of the *Gender Lens* series, she is deeply grateful for the ongoing stimulation, hard work, and fun associated with working so closely with such a committed group of feminist sociologists.

Jocelyn A. Hollander is about to receive her Ph.D. in sociology from the University of Washington in Seattle. Her research focuses on gender, power, and culture, and especially on violence against women. In her dissertation, she examines the fear of violence and how it is constructed in everyday conversation—a process intimately tied to both gendered selves and gendered situations. She teaches classes on gender and the social structure, the sociology of families, and gender and violence. She gains particular satisfaction from teaching self-defense for women, which she sees as a way of using sociology to promote social change.